# The Korean American Dream

*A volume in the series*

**Anthropology of Contemporary Issues**

Edited by Roger Sanjek

A full list of titles in the series appears at the end of the book.

# The Korean American Dream

IMMIGRANTS AND SMALL

BUSINESS IN NEW YORK CITY

## *Kyeyoung Park*

*Cornell University Press*

Ithaca and London

First published 1997 by Cornell University Press
First printing, Cornell Paperbacks, 1997

*Library of Congress Cataloging-in-Publication Data*

Park, Kyeyoung, 1956–
    The Korean American dream : immigrants and small business in New York City / Kyeyoung Park.
        p.   cm. — (Anthropology of contemporary issues)
    Includes bibliographical references and index.
        ISBN 0-8014-3343-6 (cloth : alk. paper). — ISBN 0-8014-8391-3 (pbk. : alk. paper)
        1. Korean American business enterprises—New York (State)—New York.  2. Korean American businesspeople—New York (State)—New York.  3. Small business—New York (State)—New York.  4. Queens (New York, N.Y.)—Economic conditions.  5. Queens (New York, N.Y.) —Social conditions.  6. Korea (South)—Emigration and immigration. 7. United States—Emigration and immigration.  I. Title. II. Series.
    HD2346.U52N547    1997
    338.6'422'08995707471—dc21                                    97-3083

Printed in the United States of America

Cornell University Press strives to use environmentally responsible suppliers and materials to the fullest extent possible in the publishing of its books. Such materials include vegetable-based, low-VOC inks and acid-free papers that are recycled, totally chlorine-free, or partly composed of nonwood fibers.

Cloth printing    10  9  8  7  6  5  4  3  2  1

Paperback printing    10  9  8  7  6  5  4  3

*To my parents*

# Contents

# Illustrations

## Figures

## Plates

# Tables

# Preface

In 1984, I joined the New Immigrants and Old Americans Project directed by Roger Sanjek at Queens College CUNY. Our team members conducted research on African American, Latin American, Chinese, Indian, Korean, and white populations in Queens (See Gregory 1992, 1993; Danta 1989; Chen 1992; and Khandelwal 1991). To conduct my research, I moved from Manhattan to a three-generation Korean immigrant household in Queens, where I lived for eighteen months observing the community and conducting open-ended and loosely structured interviews. I listened to my interviewees' sometimes lengthy stories which resembled *Sinse T'aryŏng* or traditional Korean narrative. *T'aryŏng* is a kind of storytelling performed to the rhythmic beat of a drum. *Sinse* is an account of one's lot, fate, or circumstance; the term connotes self-pity or a sense of sadness. Thus, Sinse T'aryŏng is the telling of one's experience to obtain sympathy from listeners. For immigrants such storytelling becomes a strategy for coping with class distinctions in American society and status inconsistency between new and old homes. Sinse T'aryŏng narratives often sound bitter and negative, and they contrast with immigrants' overall evaluations of life in America.

Most of my interviews were conducted at the stores of Korean immigrants, and I often had to stop every few minutes so that my interviewees could attend to their customers. Some subjects, however, could not be interviewed in the workplace. In such cases, unless they invited me to their houses, I met them after work, sometimes after ten o'clock at night, at a nearby pizza parlor, coffee shop, or bar. Often I felt guilty because I was disturbing their work or making them even more tired after a long day. But ultimately I became one of them—a hardworking Korean immigrant keeping long hours.

During my fieldwork, I often was treated as a "no name woman" (see Kingston 1975). I was seen by my interviewees as a young female student, *yǒja yuhaksaeng*. Because in Korea only middle- and upper-class families are able to send their children to America for graduate education, I became an object of envy and some resentment. That I was a graduate of the most prestigious university in Korea, Seoul National University, added to these perceptions. But because Koreans respect learning, I also came to be treated as an authority on certain issues. On the other hand, my status as an unmarried female student seemed to make my interviewees feel less intimidated. Most female interviewees treated me as a younger female who needed to be informed about women's life experiences. Some even stated that my goal of a Ph.D. was useless unless I married. These experiences reinforced my interest in exploring the nuances of gender roles in the United States.

One strategy that I employed in my interviews with both female and male immigrants was to use my ethnographic knowledge in order to participate fully in everyday discourse about small business ownership. Then they seemed quickly to forget gender differences and concentrate on discussions. When I began to present my research findings in talks and articles, many Korean immigrants became intensely interested in my work, especially my findings on the status of women in the workplace and the household. My interpretations provoked strong reactions from some immigrant men, who did not want them presented to the larger public.

Along with fieldwork, I found myself doing advocacy when interviewees requested help in translating or preparing paperwork for the Immigration and Naturalization Service, the Social Security Administration, the New York Asian Women's Center, or lawyers. After my fieldwork was finished, I took on leadership roles in various community organizations—for instance, as vice president of the Korean American Association of Flushing and coordinator of Korean American Women for Action.

Several people had particular influence on my work. One of the most important was my landlady, Mrs. Lee, an immigrant in her sixties. When I moved into a room in her apartment, she probably saw me as a typical Korean student. At first she suggested that I think of marriage before it became too late. She often mentioned that my mother was worried about me and my future, which made me feel guilty. Later, however, she assumed a different attitude. Without any prompting from me, she began to talk about why she had stopped going to school:

> I truly regret it. During Japanese colonial rule, I grew up in a remote village. Although my Mom wanted me to go to school, I failed in it. My teacher, who was the only teacher at the elementary school, used to hit the students. Once I was beaten so severely that I happened to urinate in the classroom. After that I was afraid and did not want to go to school. However, once my father found out that I was cutting class, he hit me, too. So I often hid myself in the rice paddy. Now I blame it on my Mom. She should have forced me to continue in school. If I were educated like you, I would not have had to stay in this horrible marriage for the past forty years.

I was horrified at her account, which tells us how male teachers and fathers treated women in colonial Korea. At the same time, I felt relieved that I did not live during that period.

Mrs. Lee was clearly unhappy in her marriage. Her husband, who used to do construction work in Korea, spent his earnings on drinking and socializing with his friends. He used to come home late or not at all. She alone managed the household and raised the children. Not only did her husband ignore the household; he was not at all affectionate toward his children. Unlike other Korean fathers, he did not bring them snacks or fruit after work. I thought of my own father, who used to come home with such treats for my family.

My relationship with Mrs. Lee seemed to affect her thinking deeply. She began to reflect on her past more and more and to express to me new ideas about gender roles and marital relations. She realized that she was unhappy with her marriage and that she did not want to stay with her husband. When her husband moved into senior citizen housing, she insisted that she would not join him but would live with her adult sons. She excused herself by saying that her sons needed her to cook and do other domestic work. I wondered, however, how she would manage to remain independent after her daughters-in-law arrived from Korea to join her sons.

Learning from Mrs. Lee and other interviews, I came to view each one as a philosopher (see Gramsci 1971: 47). To protect their privacy, however, I use pseudonyms in this book, although I identify community leaders by name when discussing public events that are part of Korean American history in New York City.

Most Korean words in the *Han'gŭl* script have been Romanized except for a few standard words (for example, Seoul not Sŏul), according to the McCune-Reischauer Romanization System (see "Romanization of the Korean Language," *Transactions of the Korea Branch of the Royal Asiatic Society* (Seoul) 29 (1939); 1–55). Informants' names, however, are written as Korean immigrants spell them.

I am indebted to many people who helped me with this book in all its stages.

First and foremost, I am grateful to the Korean immigrant community of Queens. Those willing to be interviewed include greengrocery workers talking in pizza parlors near their jobs, garment factory workers opening their homes at nine or ten o'clock at night, and a nurse who spoke with me after work at one o'clock in the morning at a diner near her hospital. I even had to wait for six months so that one informant could take time off from two day and night jobs.

I am particularly thankful to the following people: Mr. Kim Sung Soo, president of the Korean American Small Business Service Center of New York; Mr. Pyun Chun Soo, president of the Korean American Association of Flushing; Mr. Hong Chong Hak, founder of the Queens Korean Culture Society; Mrs. Lee Han Young, chair of the National Korean Parents Council; Mr. Chun Sung Jin, founder, and Mr. Hong Seung Ha, chair of the board of the Korean American Association of Mid-Queens; and Ms. Kim Nanwon, founder of the Young Korean American Service and Education Center.

In Queens, Mrs. Lee and her family welcomed me into their home as a young Korean female student, yuhaksaeng, to be guided with kindness and patience. Other Korean immigrants also generously shared their time, memories, and friendship. I hope that in presenting their stories and daily experiences I convey a sense of their lives. Their struggle is, I think, also a dimension of my own struggle.

This research has been supported by a grant from the National Science Foundation and the Ford Foundation. A Korean American Scholarship from the Korean American Scientists and Engineers Association also provided help. In addition, I wish to express my appreciation to the Asian/American Center at Queens College, where from 1987 to 1990 I worked as a research anthropologist and received support and help from my colleagues there. A Faculty Career Development Award and an award from the Institute of American Cultures at the University of California at Los Angeles facilitated the progress of this manuscript.

My training in the Department of Anthropology at City University of New York as well as in the Department of Anthropology at Seoul National University (Korea) brought me back to the hub of the Korean immigrant community. My academic sensibility has been guided by my graduate colleagues and thesis advisors, especially Roger Sanjek, Eric Wolf, Jane Schneider, and Burton Pasternak.

Roger Sanjek took an early interest in my work. Without him, it would not have been possible for me to complete this project. His tremendous efforts and detailed advice guided my research. I am also grateful for the limitless time and energy he shared in discussing, editing, and polishing my drafts. Laurel Kendall, Gary Okihiro, and anonymous reviewers provided thoughtful suggestions and expertise as I began the task of revision for publication. I also thank Sook Ryul Ryu for allowing me to use her poem, "Yellow Woman," and Chase Langford for preparing a map for inclusion in this book. Thanks are also due to the colleagues, students, and friends who generously contributed to this project in a myriad of ways: Thomas Burgess, Glenn Omatsu, Russell Leong, Don Nakanishi, Shirley Hune, and Helen Na as well as anthropologists and other scholars studying Korea and Asian American communities. I am grateful to Peter Agree at Cornell University Press for his interest and help with the book. I thank Robert Hong as well as my parents, brother, and sisters for their loving support throughout this endeavor. Finally, the Department of Anthropology and the Asian American Studies Center at the University of California at Los Angeles provided important support.

KYEYOUNG PARK

*Los Angeles, California*

# The Korean American Dream

# [1]

# Introduction

Korean immigrants today are constructing a new American identity in the complex ethnic and racial mosaic of New York City. Two-thirds of the city's Koreans live in the borough of Queens, where they interact daily with persons of other races and ethnic groups. In the neighborhoods of northwestern Queens one encounters mixed populations of Asian Americans (Koreans, Chinese, Indians, and Filipinos), Latin Americans, African Americans, and white Americans. Here, Koreans' most meaningful interactions with other ethnic groups occur in the context of operating small businesses.

During the 1980s, conflict between Koreans and blacks arose in predominantly African American neighborhoods in New York City, such as Harlem in Manhattan and Bedford-Stuyvesant and Flatbush in Brooklyn. A typical case exploded early in 1990. According to the *New York Times*, 8 May 1990: "A minor scuffle in January in a Korean-American grocery in Brooklyn has turned into an ugly boycott aimed at driving all Korean merchants out of a largely black neighborhood in Flatbush. There are several versions of the original incident. A Haitian customer says she was pummeled by store employees without provocation when she tried to buy some plantains and peppers. The Korean store owner says the woman refused to pay for the goods, started an argument, and was restrained. Despite charges of a brutal beating, hospital records indicate only a facial scratch."

Most previous sociological studies of new Korean immigrants have focused on entrepreneurship and black-Korean tensions in inner-city neighborhoods. These studies have largely ignored new immigrant ideologies or

[1]

the way that people make sense of their new lives in America. In contrast, I focus on the construction of new immigrant culture in a multiethnic part of New York City where such racial conflicts have been rare. I examine how immigrants' gravitation toward small business activities transforms Korean culture in domains such as family/kinship, gender, ethnicity, politics, and religion. I present the human voices of small business proprietors and, more important, the often unheard laments of workers, women, youth, and other sectors of the community. As an anthropologist and a new Korean immigrant myself, I attempt to provide insight into the process of crafting identities, cultures, and ideologies.

My main theoretical interest is analyzing the ideologies of Korean immigrants as they relate to small business activities. Therborn defines ideology as "the medium through which . . . consciousness and meaningfulness is formed. . . . Thus the conception of ideology employed here deliberately includes both everyday notions and 'experience' and elaborates intellectual doctrines, both the 'consciousness' of social actors and the institutionalized thought-systems and discourses of a given society. But to study these as ideology means to look at them from a particular perspective . . . as manifestations of a particular being-in-the-world of conscious actors, human subjects" (1980: 2, quoted in Wright 1985). I focus on how Korean immigrants feel and think about their lives in America and place special emphasis on the meaning of small business enterprise for Korean immigrants. Not only has this economic activity been of great importance to their lives; it has also influenced their social, political, and cultural orientations.

I follow the proposition that ideologies arise from a given set of material interests (see Gramsci 1971; Larrain 1979, 1983; Lenin 1960; Mannheim 1936; McLellan 1986; Marx 1845–46, 1859; Williams 1977; Wolf 1982). I stress that people formulate their ideologies in many ways—by generating new ideologies or employing old ideologies in new ways. Individuals are also influenced by variations in the cognitive universes of others despite the overriding processes of ideological formation that affect everyone and make a dominant social system appear legitimate and natural to its members. In studying international migrants, we have to bear in mind that, while they bring cultural baggage with them, they are also influenced by American culture, including its various subcultures. Koreans in New York City adopt American culture selectively, according to their own experiences. They try to make sense of their new lives in America and at the same time, refocus their understanding of Korean culture.

[2]

It is in this context that I examine the Korean immigrant concept of *anjŏng*. This is the key to understanding the Korean American dream, and provides a way to interpret particular social practices in the immigrant community. *Anjŏng* (establishment, stability, or security) and *chagigage katki* (establishing one's own small business) are concepts that epitomize Korean immigrants' adaptation to the American ideology of individual success. This adaptation occurs as middle-class Koreans from a semi-peripheral part of the world system take on a new status as minority immigrant shopkeepers in the United States. Within their ideology of anjŏng, Korean immigrants analyze the causes and consequences of their experience and social relations and formulate particular methods to take advantage of the opportunities available to them. They see establishment of their own small businesses as a route to the American dream. In striving toward this ideal, they play upon deeply rooted Korean concepts of worthiness (*poram*) and reciprocity (*hohye*) (see Mauss 1967 and Chun 1984). They frequently invoke the saying that in the United States "all trades are equal," thus justifying their downward mobility from professional status. In their pursuit of anjŏng, they also alter Korean gender and kinship relations and find their places within a new women-centered and sister-initiated kinship structure. Finally, as a result of their commitment to anjŏng, immigrants elaborate new understandings of class, ethnicity, and race and develop new religious ideas and practices. Thus, anjŏng plays the lead role in the drama of ideological change among Korean immigrants in Queens.

In my discussion of the Korean American dream, I distinguish, first, concepts that come directly from my informants and, second, those that I develop to analyze immigrant ideology. In the first category are *chagigage katki* (establishing one's own business); *ilchŏmose* (the one-and-a-half, 1.5, or "knee-high" generation, referring to teenage immigrants who arrive with their parents); *migukpyŏng* (American fever); *kŏdŭp nam* (born again); *pangŏn* (speaking in tongues); *han* (unresolved longing); *chŏng* (deep affection); *tut'ŏun kwangye* (deep or thick relationship); and *ppaek* (social connections).

The cultural framework that I develop for analyzing anjŏng requires some explanation. I distinguish several stages of establishment, a framework that my informants may not necessarily articulate. According to my analysis, for a single man anjŏng means primarily marriage and beginning a family. For a young couple, anjŏng means establishing their own business. For a couple operating a business successfully, anjŏng means having

[3]

children and inviting parents in Korea to join them in America. At a later stage, anjŏng means buying a house in a "good" suburban neighborhood. At a more advanced stage, anjŏng means sending children to good universities, getting them trained as professionals, and marrying them to fellow Korean Americans.

In order to complete the steps, Korean immigrants must reorganize the elements of anjŏng from their natal culture and apply them to their experience in the United States. My use of anjŏng synthesizes these various meanings and depends on cultural analysis rather than culturally sensitive translation. First, gender roles are redefined. For example, my interviewees often said that, unless a family had a working wife (hardly universal in Korea), they could not realize the Korean American dream. Second, immigrants reorganize their domestic lives to accommodate the needs of small business activities. As a result, their kinship structure turns completely upside down in terms of gender and seniority. Third, class relations are reorganized around small business activities: Small business proprietors, workers, and professionals, as we shall see, are each influenced by the immigrant community's focus on entrepreneurship. The next chapter discusses how and why Koreans immigrated to the United States.

# PART I

# From Korea to Queens

# [2]

# Korean Migration to America: Dependent Development and "American Fever"

Korean immigration to America can be interpreted as one outcome of American political, economic, missionary, and military involvement in Korea since the late nineteenth century. Taking this viewpoint, Illsoo Kim (1981) has focused on such immigration as an interplay between the political and economic problems, social structure, and foreign policy of Korea on the one hand and the international trade, economic structure, and immigration policies of the United States on the other. More bluntly, Light and Bonacich (1988) attribute Korea's rising number of emigrants to its role as supplier of cheap labor in the world economic system.

The historical phases of Korean immigration to the United States are summarized in table 1. Korean immigration before 1965 resulted from the need for cheap labor in Hawaii and U.S. political and military involvement in the Korean peninsula. Since 1965, five main factors have influenced Korean emigration to the United States: Korea's partition; the continuing involvement of the U.S. government in the Korean peninsula in political, military, and economic issues; the rise of the new middle class in Korea; the development of a new international division of labor and the changing status of Korea in this new situation; and the migration policies created by both the U.S. and Korean governments.

## Immigration to the United States before 1965

By 1888, a small number of Korean students, political exiles, *insam* (ginseng) merchants, and migrant laborers began to arrive on American shores (Hurh and Kim 1980: 25); but the total number of Koreans in the

[7]

*Table 1.* Korean immigration to the United States, 1903–1994

| Year admitted | Number of immigrants | Category |
| --- | --- | --- |
| 1903–5 | 7,226 | Labor migration to Hawaii |
| 1910–24 | 1,100 | Picture brides |
| 1951–64 | 14,027 | Post–Korean War immigration |
| 1965 | 2,139 | Early wave of new immigrants |
| 1966 | 2,492 | |
| 1967 | 3,956 | |
| 1968 | 3,811 | |
| 1969 | 6,045 | |
| 1970 | 9,314 | |
| 1971 | 14,297 | |
| 1972 | 18,876 | |
| 1973 | 22,930 | |
| 1974 | 28,028 | |
| 1975 | 28,362 | |
| 1976 | 30,803 | Later wave of new immigrants |
| 1977 | 30,917 | |
| 1978 | 29,288 | |
| 1979 | 29,248 | |
| 1980 | 32,320 | |
| 1981 | 32,633 | |
| 1982 | 31,724 | |
| 1983 | 33,339 | |
| 1984 | 33,042 | |
| 1985 | 35,000 | |
| 1986 | 35,776 | |
| 1987 | 35,849 | |
| 1988 | 34,703 | |
| 1989 | 34,222 | |
| 1990 | 32,301 | |
| 1991 | 26,518 | |
| 1992 | 19,359 | |
| 1993 | 18,026 | |
| 1994 | 10,799 | |

Note: No data are shown for 1906–9 and 1925–50 because no official immigration occurred in those years.

*Source:* U.S. Immigration and Naturalization Service, *Annual Report* (Washington, D.C.: U.S. Government Printing Office, 1995).

United States before the twentieth century was estimated at fewer than fifty. The first major wave of immigrants reached Hawaii during 1903–5. This phase of immigration brought a total of 7,226 Koreans as contract laborers for sugar plantations (W. Kim 1971: 1–4; Choy 1979: 69–72; Patterson 1988). Most were brought as strike breakers to replace Japanese workers, who demanded wage increases after they had served their time as contract laborers and initiated strikes in the sugarcane fields.

About two thousand of these Korean laborers later came to the U.S. mainland, although most remained on the West Coast. The class origin of these early immigrants is unclear, but most seem to have been peasants or urban workers. The majority were young bachelors between the ages of twenty and thirty. Coming from port cities throughout Korea, they were largely uneducated and engaged in semiskilled or unskilled occupations; some also had contact with Christian missionaries (Hurh and Kim 1980: 31).

In 1905 the Korean government, at that time a de facto Japanese protectorate, suddenly forbade further emigration. The Japanese government wanted to stop "anti-Japanese colonial resistance" activities among the overseas Koreans and protect Japanese immigrants in the Hawaiian islands from Korean competition. But after the conclusion of the Gentlemen's Agreement between the United States and Japan in 1908, Koreans in Hawaii were granted permission to bring their wives and families. Subsequently, more than eight hundred "picture brides" came to join their husbands between 1910 and 1924 (see Chai 1981).

Following passage of the Immigration Act of 1924, only a few Koreans entered the United States until the end of the 1950–53 Korean War. Between the war and 1965, a new cohort of Koreans arrived as war orphans or wives and relatives of American servicemen who had been stationed in Korea. By 1980 approximately fifty thousand Korean women who had married Americans were living in the United States (Barringer and Cho 1989). Although it is not clear how many Koreans came to New York City in this period, those who did were the first to settle in Queens, one of the five boroughs of New York City. Bok-Lim Kim summarizes the demographic profile of the typical Korean war bride in America: "A relatively young to early-middle-aged woman, with a median education level of eighth grade. Her husband has an even chance of being either a few years older, or much older or younger than she. He is likely to be employed in military service or engaged in skilled or semiskilled work. The couple has two or fewer children and have practically no organizational affiliations, with extremely limited participation in social activities" (1977: 103).

## Korea's Dependent Development and Class Process

Korea's partition into north and south, *pundan*, was an outcome of the Korean War, and continuing fears about the possibility of another war have influenced Koreans' decisions about migration. Since the 1950s, the United States has accelerated its political, military, and economic presence in Korea. (Hereafter "Korea" indicates South Korea.) From an agrarian society, Korea has been transformed into an industrial country (see Ki-baik Lee 1961 and Eckert et al. 1990). One of the poorest countries in the world in 1950, it achieved the status of an "upper-middle income level" country by the late 1980s. As a result of this rapid economic development, new middle and working classes have emerged.

Since the end of World War II, a major objective of U.S. foreign policy has been to keep friendly Third World nations within its sphere of influence. As the cold war intensified, the Korean peninsula became the focus of East-West political and military rivalry that culminated in the Korean War. Korea then became an American client state: The United States has not only given massive economic and military aid but also intervened in Korea's domestic political affairs. Indeed, U.S. economic and military aid to Korea amounted to $12.5 billion between 1946 and 1976 (Mason et al. 1980: 182). Since the mid-sixties, a reduction in U.S. aid has been compensated for by a large increase in foreign investment.

Few Third World countries can match Korea in terms of the central role that the state plays in promoting development. According to Lim (1982: 28), the state has played an unusually strong role in mobilizing resources and manpower and managing social and political tensions. Continuous threats from the Communists in the north have imposed a heavy defense burden, thereby limiting the allocation of available resources for the promotion of industrialization. These threats have also been used as an excuse for the suspension of democracy in the name of security, stability, and growth.

Korea's experience has been labeled "dependent development" (see Amsden 1989; Deyo 1987; Evans 1979): dependent because it is indelibly characterized by continued dependence on foreign capital, technology, and trade; development because of the capital accumulation and differen-

*Table 2.* Changes in class structure in Korea, 1960–1975

| Classes | 1960 | 1966 | 1970 | 1975 |
|---|---|---|---|---|
| Upper class[a] | 0.7 | 0.9 | 1.0 | 0.8 |
| New middle class[b] | 8.6 | 8.6 | 9.5 | 10.5 |
| Old middle class[c] | 5.6 | 10.3 | 6.3 | 6.8 |
| Working class[d] | 8.7 | 12.4 | 19.2 | 21.1 |
| Marginal sector[e] | 10.2 | 11.0 | 12.8 | 11.5 |
| Farmers[f] | 66.2 | 56.8 | 51.2 | 59.2 |
| Total | 100.0 | 100.0 | 100.0 | 100.0 |

[a]Capitalist class and state managers.
[b]White-collar workers and rank-and-file civil servants.
[c]Small-scale unorganized urban shopkeepers.
[d]Blue-collar workers.
[e]Propertyless laborers in urban areas.
[f]Independent farmers, landless tenant farmers, and farm laborers.
*Source:* Hagen Koo, "A Preliminary Approach to Contemporary Korean Class Structure," in *Society in Transition*, ed. Yunshik Chang (Seoul: Seoul National University Press, 1982), p. 53. Reproduced by courtesy of the author.

tiation in its productive structure (Lim 1982: 4). Korea's dependent development started with Japanese colonial rule (1910 to 1945). It was developed economically as a complement to the Japanese empire and thus became dependent as an export market with a single product, rice. An industrial bourgeoisie took form after independence from Japan. Even more than postliberation social reforms, the Korean War contributed to the dissolution of agrarian classes and status hierarchies. By the late 1950s, a group of entrepreneurs who had successfully exploited their political connections had become the big bourgeoisie, *chaebŏl*. According to Jones and Sakong (1980: 166–209), these modern entrepreneurs came from various class backgrounds: large to medium landowners (47 percent), merchants (19 percent), factory owners (16 percent), civil servants (6 percent), teachers (4 percent), and professionals (7 percent).

The most conspicuous change in the Korean class structure during dependent development was the rapid growth of the working class (see table 2). While limiting the economic penetration of multinationals, the state and the big bourgeoisie took for themselves a large share of the fruits of growth, to the relative exclusion of workers. The working class was disappointed by increasing income differentials, and labor disputes occurred almost daily during the late 1980s (see S. K. Kim 1990). In addition, the late 1980s and early 1990s saw burgeoning white-collar labor unions, such as those composed of teachers and bank employees, which represented a polarization in the middle classes and a proletarianization of the lower echelons of white-collar labor.

## Immigration to the United States: 1965 to Today

The process of Korea's development provides a context for understanding the background of recent Korean immigrants, who were largely middle-class professionals in their homeland. Korea's rapid development led to the rise of both a new middle class and a new working class. The new middle class is a contradictory one characterized by conservative sectors aspiring to move upward within the status quo and liberal or radical sectors—primarily the intelligentsia—who side with labor and work to promote a more democratic, egalitarian society (see Koo 1987).

The most important reason cited for emigration of middle-class Koreans has been an economic one (I. Kim 1981; Light and Bonacich 1988). They heard about only the good sides of American economic life. The dollar was very strong against the Korean *wŏn*, and the annual income of Americans was at least ten times that of Koreans until the early 1980s. (As of 1993, average income in the United States is only about three times larger than Korea's). Economic factors, however, were not the only reasons for emigration. The strong economic, political, and cultural influence of the United States—what I call American fever—has influenced Koreans since the nation came under U.S. military rule after the defeat of Japan in 1945.

Because of oppressive regimes in Korea during the 1970s and the early 1980s and severe tension between North and South Korea during the late 1970s, many Koreans who feared political instability sought to go to the United States (I. Kim 1981; J. Yi 1993). For North Korean Christians who fled from Communist North Korea during the Korean War, America seemed an especially safe and attractive place. It was easy for them to leave South Korea because they did not have strong kinship ties and feared being the first victims in the event that North Korea invaded South Korea. The authoritarian regime in South Korea also caused some intellectuals to emigrate.

According to their time of arrival in the United States, the new Korean immigrants can be classified into two cohorts: One group arrived after the 1965 Immigration Act, the other after the 1976 amendment. These groups differ in both background characteristics and the circumstances under which they came.

The Immigration Act of 3 October 1965 (PL 89–236) set an annual limit of 170,000 immigrants from the eastern hemisphere, with a maximum of 20,000 for any individual country, exclusive of immediate relatives of American citizens. The 1965 law, which took effect in 1968, ended the national origins quota system in favor of a system of graded preferences, including preferences for family members of persons already in the United States and workers with needed skills. Although work skills were emphasized, there was a major shift in policy to family reunification. The first, second, fourth, and fifth preferences allotted up to 74 percent of a country's quota to close family members of U.S. citizens and permanent resident aliens (Bouvier and Gardner 1986: 14). Also admitted beyond the numerical quotas were spouses, parents, and unmarried children under age eighteen of U.S. citizens and designated refugees (Gardner, Robey, and Smith 1985: 9).

Labor qualifications were the criterion only for the third preference (members of the professions, scientists, and nonperforming artists of exceptional ability) and the sixth preference (skilled and unskilled workers "in occupations for which labor is in short supply"), with 10 percent apiece. No worker under these preferences could enter the United States unless the secretary of labor certified that the alien would have no adverse effect on wages and working conditions: "[The policy] places the burden of proving no adverse effect upon the applying alien" (Keely 1980: 16). With this new legislation, the Asian share of total immigration to the United States increased from 7.6 percent (1961–65) to 27.4 percent (1969–73), exceeding the European share for the first time in American immigration history. In the 1970s, Asian immigration rose to 34 percent. Between 1980 and 1988, Asians made up 40 to 47 percent of all U.S. immigrants (Min 1995: 12).

The 1960s and 1970s were a period in Korea of rapid urbanization and industrial development, leading to the rise of a new middle class of professionals, managers, and entrepreneurs. In 1988, professionals and white-collar employees of large business and government bureaucracies formed about 20 percent of the total labor force, compared with only 7 percent in the 1960s (EPB 1989). Koreans themselves are very conscious of the rapid growth of the middle class—what the mass media has called *chung-sanch'ŭng* (literally, a "middle propertied stratum"). This sector symbolizes economic prosperity and changing cultural values in contemporary

Korean society. The critical role of this middle class in the 1987 democratization movement is widely recognized.

Many in this new stratum eventually emigrated to America, causing a brain drain of educated professionals. Portes considers this drain to be part of world system theory: "Professional emigration is basically a consequence of the reproduction of the technical apparatus of advanced nations in underdeveloped ones. Implanted [educational] institutions come to function more in accordance with needs requirements of the advanced societies than those of the country that receives them" (Portes and Walton 1981: 37). According to Ong, Bonacich, and Cheng (1994), new Asian immigrants have been profoundly influenced by the restructuring of the global economy, particularly in Pacific Rim industries. Asian countries are producing more highly trained professionals, managers, and entrepreneurs than they can absorb. This imbalance "is a product of the contradictions of capitalism, the resulting class struggle, and the efforts to restructure the global economy" (1994: 26–27).

Although Light and Bonacich (1988) argue that social and economic dislocation induced the Korean middle class to emigrate, I contend that developments in the world system, particularly the American labor market, prompted emigration. On the one hand, U.S. government policies allowed the Korean middle class, not the poor, to emigrate; on the other hand, the Korean government was not able to absorb its mass-produced professional managerial class.

Many emigrants left Korea in pursuit of mobility and modernity and felt that these aspirations could be better achieved in the American labor market. Some middle-class people were frustrated with the rigid Korean social structure. For instance, if a person leaves a job as a high-level executive, he or she will have difficulty finding a similar post in Korea. Many doctors aspired to go to America after working with high-level technology imported from the United States. Other professionals found it difficult to obtain jobs in the Korean labor market due to its skewed development. For example, some doctors did not want to serve at public health centers in the countryside, preferring private practice in Seoul. The situation confronting nurses was worse: They were mass-trained under government policy with the expectation that they could go to nations such as West Germany. In Korea nurses were not paid well, and many began to consider emigration to the United States as prospects for working in West Germany declined.

In the late 1960s emigration to the United States began in earnest (see table 1).[1] By 1973 some 20,000 Koreans annually obtained immigration clearance under occupational and family reunification preferences. The Korean share of total U.S. immigration quickly mounted. In 1965 the top three countries sending immigrants the United States were the United Kingdom, Germany, and Italy. In 1975, they were the Philippines, Korea, and China (Hurh and Kim 1980: 49). From 1965 to 1985, Koreans immigrating to America on the basis of their labor skills and under family reunification numbered 463,481. The earlier wave of immigrants, those arriving up to 1976, consisted mostly of medical professionals—doctors, dentists, pharmacists, nurses, medical technicians—and scientists, engineers, and other skilled professionals. It is estimated that at least 13,000 Korean medical professionals immigrated to the United States by 1977 (I. Kim 1981: 148).

An important category was nurses. Korean exchange nurses in the United States during the late 1960s formed the second-largest nationality group in the profession (Ishi 1988: 36). By 1974, one-third of Korean immigrant professionals admitted to the United States were nurses. They made a major contribution to the establishment of the Korean community in New York City, first by working in their profession and later by starting small businesses with their husbands. Many husbands, in fact, were sponsored for immigration visas by their nurse wives.

Other Koreans came here as remigrants after working as miners, construction and transportation workers, sailors, and nurses in West Germany, Vietnam, and the Middle East. Still more remigrated to America after first settling in South American countries, Canada, or Japan. There were also many students who became immigrants.

The second wave of new Korean immigrants came after President Gerald Ford signed the Immigration and Nationality Act amendments of 1976, which limited the entry of professionals. One amendment downgraded professionals such as nurses, physicians, and dentists from third to sixth preference. This meant that before entry they, too, would have to

1. In 1962 the South Korean government passed an overseas emigration law to encourage emigration as a means of controlling population, alleviating unemployment, earning foreign exchange, and acquiring knowledge of advanced technology (I. Kim 1981: 52–53; Light and Bonacich 1988: 103). The first seven families, encompassing ninety-two individuals, emigrated to Brazil, while others went to Paraguay and Argentina. The total number of South American emigrants amounted to 40,000 as of 1990. For further information on the Korean government's overseas contract program to West Germany, Vietnam, Thailand, Malaysia, Uganda, and the Middle East, see I. Kim 1981: 53–57.

find an American employer willing to hire them (I. Kim 1981: 30). Although Asians made up a large percentage of the health professionals admitted before 1977, this amendment limited their chances of getting an immigrant visa on the basis of their skills. Therefore, an increasing number of Asian doctors, nurses, and pharmacists now attempted to enter under family reunification criteria instead. As a consequence, the proportion of Koreans admitted under the employment-related third and sixth preferences dropped. The percentage of entries under the occupational preferences reached a peak of 45.1 percent in 1972; it then began to fall, reaching 22 percent in 1975 (I. Kim 1981: 31). Since 1980, that share has been just 3.9 percent for all immigrants (Bouvier and Gardner 1986: 17).

This shift, however, does not mean that fewer Korean professionals are entering the United States. While the proportion who enter through the occupational categories has decreased during the last fifteen years, the absolute number of professionals has not. In 1969, 1,164 immigrants indicated that they were professionals or managers before entry. This figure rose to 3,955 in 1972, 2,782 in 1985, and 3,109 in 1989 (quoted in Hing 1993: 99). In short, as a result of the 1976 legislation, the principal channel by which Koreans could enter America was family reunification.[2] While the pre-1976 wave of immigrants included mainly middle-class professionals, the later wave included Koreans from a variety of class backgrounds and educational and skill levels.

Another change occurred in 1978 when the Korean government lifted the limit of $1,000 that emigrants could convert to dollars and bring with them. In 1979, the limit was raised to $3,000 for each emigrant to the United States. Later in the 1980s, the government became more flexible and allowed each family to take up to $100,000, and in 1990 the figure was raised to $200,000 (Paek Su Yong of the Bank of Korea, personal communication, July 1990). These capital flows should be understood in relation to the changing position of Korea in the world economic system, including closer trading ties with the United States. Some immigrants took advantage of this relationship by directly involving themselves in trade or dis-

2. Another major revision of the 1965 immigration law took place in 1986. The Immigration Reform and Control Act imposed civil and criminal penalties on employers who knowingly hire illegal aliens, granted temporary resident status to aliens who had resided in the United States before 1 January 1982, and promised permanent resident status to those same aliens after eighteen months. Because there are fewer undocumented Asian immigrants than Mexicans in the United States, the 1986 law has affected Asians less than it has Mexicans (Chan 1991: 148).

tributing and retailing Korean goods in the United States. (See I. Kim 1981 for a detailed discussion of the impact of the trade in women's wigs exported from Korea on Korean immigrants in New York City.)

Some post-1978 immigrants are from the richer classes, but others are now also from lower income groups. These latter immigrants have kin or family in the United States who invite them to America through family reunification preferences. Still others attempt to enter illegally, sometimes across the Mexican border or through other Latin American countries. This newest wave of immigrants has increased stratification by wealth and education in the New York Korean American community.

## The Korean Community in America

The United States census counted Koreans as a distinct ethnic group for the first time in 1970. Earlier, Koreans were included in the "other Asian" category. According to the 1970 count, there were 70,598 Koreans in the United States. In 1980, 357,393 were counted, making up 10.3 percent of all Asian Americans (Gardner, Robey, and Smith 1985: 5). The 1990 census counted 798,849 Koreans.

Some 43 percent of Koreans live on the West Coast (Gardner, Robey, and Smith 1985: 11). The Korean communities in Los Angeles and New York are, respectively, the first- and second-largest aggregations of Koreans in America. The 1980 census showed that there were 103,000 in California and 33,000 in New York; 1990 census data counted 259,941 in California and 95,648 in New York, but this undoubtedly is an undercount. Several factors make it difficult for Koreans to be accounted for fully in the census. In addition to their language and cultural barriers, Koreans work from early in the morning till late at night and are thus away from residential areas when census takers visit. According to estimates from community leaders, in 1989 there were some 200,000 Koreans in greater New York and 300,000 in greater Los Angeles (*Korea Times*, 31 December 1989).

### Koreans in Queens

Even if the 1980 census underestimated the total number, it did show that in New York City more than 62 percent of Koreans live in the borough of Queens. We find them in several neighborhoods (see figure 1).

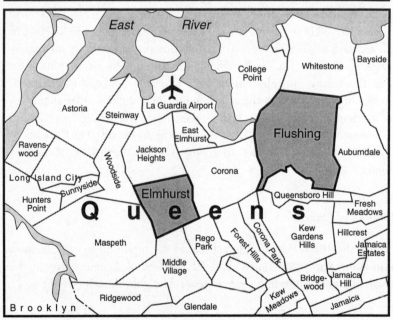

Many live along the number 7 subway route, extending from Sunnyside and Woodside through Elmhurst, Jackson Heights, and Corona to Flushing. Forest Hills, Bayside, and Little Neck contain other concentrations. The largest concentration is said to be in Flushing, the second largest in Elmhurst (see plate 1). According to a 1983 Chemical Bank report, there were 40,000 Koreans in Flushing, and they formed the largest Asian group.[3] By 1989 the Korean American Association of Flushing claimed 65,000 Koreans. Korean language newspapers frequently report that there are at least 115,000 Koreans in Queens. But nobody knows the exact number; and like all ethnic estimates, they seem to be inflated for political reasons. Estimates in Queens, in particular, seem to grow in competition with those for the Chinese community (*Korea Times*, 31 December 1989).

Even before the 1960s, some Korean students had settled in Sunnyside, enjoying the efficient public transportation system to Manhattan. Several pioneer Korean Flushing residents were businessmen who participated in the 1964 World's Fair in Flushing Meadow-Corona Park and then decided to stay in America. In Elmhurst, two large apartment buildings in front of Elmhurst City Hospital were initially occupied by a few Korean nurses and their families in 1971.[4] Today they house three hundred Korean households that have moved into Elmhurst since that time.

During the 1980s, Broadway, a major Elmhurst commercial strip, was revitalized by immigrant businesses, many of them Korean-owned. According to the Korean American Association of Mid-Queens, which represents many of these businesses, in 1985 there were 250 Korean-owned stores and professional businesses in Elmhurst and nearby Jackson Heights, Woodside, and Sunnyside. According to a 1986 survey, out of 912 Elmhurst businesses, Koreans ran 105, the largest number of businesses

3. Flushing (Community District 7), originally part of the Colony of New Netherlands, was founded in 1645 with the granting of lands to English colonists from Massachusetts (Kupka 1949). The first occupation of the settlers was farming, followed by the establishment of nurseries in 1737. In 1898 Flushing became part of New York City, and the IRT subway line opened in 1928.

4. In 1652, farmers from England first settled in the center of what is today Elmhurst and named it Newtown; the name Elmhurst was bestowed by a real estate agent in 1890 (Tauber and Kaplan 1966). Like Flushing, Elmhurst became part of New York City in 1898. Many ethnic groups have resided in Elmhurst. German, Irish, and Swedish immigrants were the first wave of nineteenth-century residents here. In 1970 the community had 23 percent Latin American residents, 70 percent whites, 3 percent blacks, and 4 percent others (including Asians). In 1980, 15 percent of Community District 4's population was Asian, and 83 percent of them lived in Elmhurst.

*Plate 1.* A view from 74th Street in Elmhurst of the various ethnic businesses. Photo author

for any of Elmhurst's forty nationalities, with the exception of "Americans," who operated two hundred (Yuan 1986). Since that time, the number and variety of Korean small businesses in Elmhurst have increased.[5] By 1989, stores included supermarkets, groceries (carrying either Western or Asian foods), fruit and vegetable stands, fish stores, delicatessens, bakeries, restaurants, stationeries, gift shops, candy stores, general merchandise stores, fashion stores, jewelry stores, video rental stores, shoe stores, dry cleaners, shoe repair shops, beauty salons, real estate offices, driving schools, language schools, insurance agencies, travel agencies, a chess parlor, moving agencies, car repair shops, sign companies, construction

5. The distribution pattern of businesses differs in communities where Koreans do business with other Koreans and communities where there are non-Korean customers. For example, vegetable stands and fish stores often proliferate in neighborhoods with mostly non-Korean customers.

firms, security companies, refrigeration companies, craft stores, doctors' offices, dentists, accountants, lawyers, a Korean-owned medical center, pharmacies, Korean herb doctors and acupuncturists, a fortune teller, garment factories, a bowling alley, massage parlors, and bars.

Even while I was doing my fieldwork in Elmhurst, I noticed more Korean businesses opening. I also observed many non-Korean businesses, including real estate agencies, beauty salons, and law firms, hiring Korean employees. At the same time, Korean stores were hiring Latin American, Chinese, and white American employees. In general, most business owners in Elmhurst tried to hire a range of bilingual staff members to cater to the multiethnic local population.

The greater Elmhurst area has also seen the development of Korean social and political organizations, such as the Korean American Association of Mid-Queens, the Elmhurst Korean Senior Center (*Sarangbang*), the Korean-American Senior Center (in Woodside), the Young Korean American Service and Education Center (in Jackson Heights), Young Koreans United of New York (in Jackson Heights), Korean Americans for Peace and Justice (in Corona), Asian American Mental Health Services Korean Unit, the Korean Blind Foundation in the United States of America, Professional United States of America Photographer Club, forty-four Korean churches (fourteen in Elmhurst, six in Jackson Heights, twenty-four in Woodside) (see chapter 9), and a Buddhist temple. In 1986 and 1987, two Korean women and one man were appointed to Community Board 4 (Elmhurst-Corona) to advise on land use issues, oversee municipal services, and make formal budget recommendations.

Most Korean residents of Elmhurst live in rented one-bedroom apartments and single-family houses in nuclear families with fairly young husbands and wives, many with children, a few without. This picture is also true of the Korean community in Flushing. In Sunnyside, however, according to a minister whose church is located there, many Koreans are single men or women who are attracted by the neighborhood's fairly small apartment complexes.

In the first phase of my fieldwork I interviewed eighteen Korean immigrants, focusing on their life stories. I then conducted systematic household and thematic interviews with ninety-one immigrants. My research methodology was different from traditional anthropological studies in that I did not focus on a bounded locality. The 109 interviews do not constitute a random sample, nor can they be considered representative in a statistical sense. Rather, they are an attempt to examine the diversity of experiences within the Korean immigrant community. I also conducted interviews with sixteen activists and leaders in community organizations. Equally important, I observed more than fifty events, such as monthly meetings of the Korean American Association of Flushing, the Korean Parade, the Korean Mid-Autumn Festival, the Queens Festival, and other events in which Koreans from Queens participate.

The statistical presentations that follow concern the 91 households I interviewed, plus data from my 18 other interviews. (For this reason, some tables include a total of more than 91 cases.) In recent writings on migration, several researchers have recommended the use of the household as a basic unit of analysis because it contributes to and mediates both macro- and microlevel processes (Grasmuck and Pessar 1991: 133). Out of the 91 households, 83 are composed of first-generation adults. All my informants either live, work, or attend church in Queens.[6] Among 109 households, 69 were located in Elmhurst, 13 in Jackson Heights, 17 in the rest of Queens, 3 elsewhere in New York City, and 7 in New Jersey. The workplaces of my informants (one from each household) were mainly in Queens: 55 in Elmhurst, 9 in Jackson Heights, and 10 elsewhere. Of the remaining 23, 11 were in Manhattan and 12 on Long Island or in New Jersey.

## The Migration Process

Although Koreans who have arrived since 1965 are often called new immigrants, I refer to those who arrived between 1965 and 1976 as "the early wave." While the early wave came mostly through occupational preference, those after 1976 came mainly by family reunification. Overall, only 20 percent of my informants came to the United States through occupational preference. Among these, the majority were medical professionals. Another 54 percent migrated through family reunification, either invited by immediate family members (parents and children) with green cards or by a brother or a sister who was an American citizen. Some 4 percent came as students and later decided to stay permanently. A larger group, about 15 percent, came with tourist, visitor, business, or nonimmigrant employment visas. According to the Immigration and Naturalization Service, in 1981–82 close to 100,000 Koreans came to the United

6. For my interviewees, the definition of community goes beyond the boundary of a geographical locality. For instance, residents of Elmhurst also considered Flushing and nearby neighborhoods as part of their community.

States on nonimmigrant visas, including 8,000 students; we do not know how many of these 100,000 eventually remained in America (*Korea Times*, 6 September 1985). Finally, 7 percent of my informants entered the United States illegally.

Among my 91 informants, 18 came here by occupational preference, including 4 medical doctors, 1 nurse, 2 medical technicians, 4 pharmacists, 1 beautician, 2 automobile mechanics, 1 welder, and 1 cook. As I. Kim (1981) and Light and Bonanich (1988) have pointed out, most people emigrating under this preference were from Korea's highly educated middle or upper class; but as one can gather, not all of my informants fit this profile. Some went through special training in automobile and television repair, metalworking, computer programming, or hairdressing expressly for the sake of immigration. Most of the medical professionals applied for immigration visas directly, but the automobile mechanics and other skilled workers paid fees to Korean agencies (see I. Kim 1981: 60–64), which obtained work permits for them. A common early-wave pattern was for men to come first and, after establishing themselves in America, bring their families. Many female nurses, however, came by themselves and met husbands here. Some men came legally on business visas but overstayed their visas and remained illegally.

Among my informants who came to the United States by occupational preference, two automobile mechanics are now retired. The cook and his wife, a waitress, have worked for the same employer since they emigrated from Korea twenty years ago. The nurse is now a real estate saleswoman, and the pharmacists now run their own drugstores. All four medical doctors have remained in their profession; they now live on Long Island, although some continue to keep offices for Korean patients in Elmhurst or Flushing.

Among the early-wave immigrants, I met several men who came as students and decided to stay. One of my informants quit his studies, married a nurse, and went into business with her. He now runs a successful Korean supermarket. Three men came to work in a branch office of a Korean company. After living for a few years in America, they decided to stay and applied for immigrant visas under the sponsorship of their company. One now runs a Korean restaurant, which he began as a coffee shop.

Mr. Kim, an early-wave immigrant and a pharmacist, came to America in 1973. In Korea he had worked for a pharmaceutical company for a year; and since 1987, he has run his own drugstore. His story reveals that he prepared to obtain training in skilled work, knowing that it would take time for a Korea-trained pharmacist to practice in the United States.

> In Korea I had been informed that in America it is hard to get a job as a pharmacist immediately, so I studied camera repair for a few months. I was supposed to repair five cameras a day. In six months I took stock of what I had done in my life. After another six months, I started to work as an intern at a hospital in the Bronx. While in Korea it takes four years to finish pharmacology, it takes five years in America. Therefore, I was supposed to add 1,000 hours more, which is equivalent to one year and two months work. Although it was not difficult to do, it was not easy to do the work without pay. At that time there were many pharmacists from such countries as Korea, India, Pakistan, the Philippines, and Taiwan. Thanks to their better English, many of those from India and Pakistan took internships and got jobs fairly easily compared with those from Korea and Taiwan. To make matters worse, the job market was oversupplied, making it very difficult to get employment. Now it is impossible for pharmacists from foreign countries to immigrate here. But it is less difficult to be hired now. Then, due to the city fiscal crisis, it was hard to be hired as a pharmacist, I remember.

Some early-wave Korean immigrants also came to America by way of South America, Germany, or Canada. Mr. Lee, a garment factory owner, was born in Pyongyang, North Korea, and later moved to South Korea, where he ran a knitting factory.

> I was informed by my uncle who had studied in Brazil that the living conditions in any South American country are good. He told me there was no racism. So I immigrated to Paraguay first as an agricultural immigrant, and later to Argentina in 1965. At that time the minimum wage was better in Argentina than in the United States. I remember that it was only fifty cents for a good meal, and one could earn three dollars for one day's work in Argentina. In Buenos Aires, I ran a knitting mill. There were few Koreans. For ten years my business went well, employing ten workers. However, after I came to the United States to buy a machine, I decided to stay here. Immediately after I left, there was economic chaos in Buenos Aires.

In Germany and Canada, Koreans worked as miners, nurses, and ministers. One of my informants, Mrs. Yang, was a nurse in Germany; another, Reverend Chung, was a minister in Canada. A few early-wave immigrants were sponsored by female relatives—a mother's sister, for example, who had married an American serviceman stationed in Korea.

Among the post-1976 wave are two groups—those who brought in large amounts of capital and those who arrived with empty hands. The latter group migrated through the family reunification provisions. The former group brought in large sums of money after the Korean government lifted the $1,000 limit on capital outflow in 1978. Mrs. Park is a typical later-wave immigrant. She and her family immigrated to America in 1984 and immediately bought a craft store with money they had brought from Korea. The store cost $20,000 for "key money" to the former owner, $3,000 for rental deposit, and $900 for monthly rent. In Korea, her husband ran a transportation company.

In general, immigrants of both waves came here to seek political stability and pursue social mobility. The later wave had additional motives: Those who were rich came to invest; those who were poor came to survive. As economic conditions changed in Korea and people heard stories of success in America, more Koreans thought about emigration as an alternative.

Thus far I have only mentioned persons who immigrated through legal channels. Now I turn to those who came without proper documents, both the so-called "visa abusers" and undocumented border crossers. Among my informants, ten came on tourist or other nonimmigrant visas, and seven came without documents. Seven of the tourists have since regularized their status in the United States, but three still do not have green cards. Those who are middle and upper class in Korea find it easier to manipulate the immigration procedures, usually through sponsorship by relatives already here. But lower-class Koreans who have no kin to sponsor them are more desperate. For many, this entails being smuggled into the United States by way of South America, Mexico, or the Caribbean.

Among my informants, two entered via the Bahamas, one through Paraguay, and four by crossing the Mexican border. Before they left Korea, they were briefed on their migratory arrangements and paid large fees to Korean brokers, which included a share for local Latin American brokers. If they are caught crossing the U.S. border, their kin, friends, or brokers must pay a bond of delivery for aliens. They are not released until a final decision on their case is made. In most cases, deportation to Korea follows. Despite such experiences, a few are ready to try again.

The increasing numbers of people who enter the United States without proper documents are called *pigongsik imin* (informal immigrants) in Korean. As of now, their stories have not been documented by researchers. A 1985 National Research Council study defined such a newcomer as "a noncitizen physically present in the United States who entered the country illegally and has not regularized his or her situation, or who has violated his or her terms of entry" (Levine, Hill, and Warren 1985: 225). About half the illegal immigrants in the United States are border crossers, and half are visa abusers—people who enter the country legally on temporary nonimmigrant visas but remain illegally.

Mrs. Chung was one of my informants who lacked proper documents. She traveled from Korea to Mexico, where she searched for other Koreans but encountered only Japanese. Eventually she met Mr. Park, who treated her to a Korean dinner. He couldn't believe that a woman would want to be smuggled into the United States. With his help, however, she traveled to Tijuana, within four hours of the U.S. border. There she took a bus from the airport, which dropped her at a Chinese motel. The motel was full of professional brokers, including three Koreans. She was so glad that she started to cry. She made contact by telephone with a Korean broker in Los Angeles, who told her what to do, step by step. In all, she needed $1,500.

She paid $10 for bus fare to the airport and $20 for a Mexican translator. Her group was taken on a ten-minute bus ride to the border. She saw fields on one side and a stony open area on the other. Group members were instructed to say "O.K." to whatever questions they were asked. They began walking. Mrs. Chung was wearing high heels, which hurt her feet. After some time, they came to an artificial tunnel under an electric fence. The group of four Koreans and one other person crawled into the tunnel and waited there from 6 A.M. to 6 P.M. Then they boarded a farm truck carrying vegetables and fruit and crawled behind the seat to a space under the produce. After an hour they arrived in San Diego and were moved to a van. In the next hour they were transferred to seven different trucks. Finally, Mrs. Chung was dropped near Koreatown in Los Angeles. There she had to pay the rest of the fee. Her husband was shocked to learn of her arrival, believing she was still in Pusan. Later I heard more chilling stories about young female border crossers, who were often raped as well as deported.

Mr. Kang feels that he was deceived by brokers. He met a migration broker through his father's brother in Korea. He gave the broker 6 million wŏn (in 1984, about $10,000). The broker told him that there was a way to enter America directly and legally. Later, it turned out that everything in the process was illegal except for Mr. Kang's documents for training in agricultural technology. Seven people were in his group, which went to

Mexico City by plane. Then Mr. Kang flew to Tijuana, where he met the original broker. The broker reassured the group, telling them not to worry, and introduced a Mexican agent. The group was taken by bus to the nearby border, thirty minutes away. There they were told to walk, which meant climbing out of a steep valley. During the day they had to hide, and at night they could only crawl. There were twenty-seven people in the group, including a five-year-old child, and they had no food. They would crawl for five hundred meters and then stop. In this manner, they progressed for two days. Although it was hard to see anything at night, they finally crossed the border. Then they rode in a van for two hours. For three more days they had no food and slept on the ground. On the next morning they boarded another car, but fourteen miles later they were caught by an inspector.

Although they were so hungry that they cried, for three days they were held without food. They were kept for fifteen days in a detention camp. Then, after his father's brother paid a $3,500 bond of delivery for an alien, Mr. Kang took a plane to La Guardia Airport in New York City. It took him seven months to clear his debt, paying back $500 per month. During this time and afterward, he worked "off the books" in a Korean greengrocery. Now that he has lived through such hardships, he feels that nothing can frighten him.

In the future there will be more working-class immigrants from Korea, and perhaps some will enter the United States illegally. Although living conditions for both the working class and the middle class have improved greatly in Korea, dissatisfaction about wages has intensified since 1987, when it became legal to organize labor unions.

## Downward Mobility

While current trends are producing greater diversity among Korean immigrants, the immigrant population is now relatively alike: Most are young, married, and highly educated; many were white-collar workers in Korea, and most are products of urban culture. Of my informants, 58 percent (N=91) are between the ages of twenty-one and forty (see table 3). About 67 percent (N=91) are married. Single persons account for 21 percent; divorced, separated, or widowed are 12 percent. (My data are consistent with the 1980 census data for New York and statistics from Los Angeles.)

[27]

*Table 3.* Age distribution and sex of informants (N = 91)

| Age | Male | Female | Total |
|-----|------|--------|-------|
| Up to 20 | 0 | 1 | 1 |
| 21 to 25 | 5 | 0 | 5 |
| 26 to 30 | 15 | 4 | 19 |
| 31 to 35 | 8 | 3 | 11 |
| 36 to 40 | 10 | 7 | 17 |
| 41 to 45 | 6 | 0 | 6 |
| 46 to 50 | 4 | 3 | 7 |
| 51 to 55 | 7 | 2 | 9 |
| 56 to 60 | 0 | 3 | 3 |
| 61 to 65 | 2 | 1 | 3 |
| 66 to 70 | 2 | 3 | 5 |
| Age unknown | 5 | | 5 |
| Total | 64 | 27 | 91 |

Among my informants, 25 percent are college graduates, and another 28 percent attended college. In all, 75 percent were employed in Korea, and the remaining 25 percent were housewives. Some 56 percent had held white-collar jobs as professionals, proprietors, managers, civil servants, or skilled workers. In New York, however, only 17 percent (N=109) hold white-collar jobs. The majority (73 percent) are involved in small business, either as employers (36 percent) or employees (37 percent). The rest (10 percent) are unemployed, students, or retired. It is evident that many immigrants experience downward mobility from white-collar positions in Korea to small business status or manual work in America. Because of difficulties with licensure and language, many professionals do not find jobs comparable to those in their home country (see Chapter 2). For instance, a former engineer found it almost impossible to work as an engineer in New York unless he went through training again.

Some immigrants are able to regain their occupational status. Yu reports that the percentage of professionals rises and the percentage of manual laborers falls as the length of residence for immigrants increases, indicating a general upward occupational mobility (1990: 14). The typical pattern of occupational mobility, nonetheless, is first the transition from white-collar work in Korea to manual work in America and later, to small business proprietor.

Many new immigrants work in low-paying, dead-end jobs—for example, Mrs. Lee, a teacher in Korea and now a garment factory worker.

At first it hurt my pride. But I came to think that I would make the desperate effort, however. I envied those who did well. The first day I earned only six dollars for ten hours work. On the second day I earned twelve dollars. It was difficult to do a manual job, and it was not easy to work under someone, compared with what I had done in Korea. In my class, as a teacher I was in charge of the students. As I worked with many workers here, sometimes it led to friction. However, I tried to consider garment work as only the first step. And I could maintain close friendships with fellow church members, regardless of our different levels of education.

She added that she has tried to lead a frugal life since her arrival in America. The only thing that she has purchased here is a pair of jeans for her children.

## American Fever and Migration

So far I have examined the broad framework of Korean immigration to America. But the question of why any specific individual immigrates remains. Koreans do not emigrate because they cannot survive in their home country but because they dream about America (compare I. Kim 1981). This dream is especially true of the early wave of immigrants, those arriving between 1965 and 1976. The later wave, from 1976 till the present, has additional reasons. But all immigrants are fed by cultural colonialism from America. In Korea, this is described as American fever.

Several informants told me stories similar to this one: "Without any deep thought, I was just eager to go to America. I was told again and again that America is a wonderful and beautiful country, full of gold, indeed a paradise in this world. In a word, I had the American fever [migukpyŏng]." American fever in Korea is like a sickness. It is contagious, and it spreads. People call those gripped by this fever ghosts, beings eaten or possessed by the Western spirit. American fever is more than interest in American culture. It is a cultural complex of longing for political, economic, social, and cultural well-being, all identified with U.S. society. The only cure lies in leaving for the United States.

This fever has developed in the context of postcolonial Korea. Neither cultural colonialism—rooted in American political, economic, and military involvement in the Korean peninsula—nor the fever it has produced have been seriously studied. Yet migukpyŏng *is* a cultural reality discussed by Korean immigrants. For instance, more than half of medical school

[29]

graduates from Yonsei University, a prestigious private university in Seoul, are said to be in America through immigration; and at many nursing schools in Korea, most students say they plan to immigrate. Imagining the journey to America becomes a way of life—a rite de passage, in anthropological terminology. As I. Kim explains, "One of the psychological consequences of the booming economy is that consciousness of social mobility has been much intensified even among those unsuccessful in achieving a higher status. This mobility consciousness stimulates the inclinations of mobility-oriented Koreans to emigrate to the United States, where better economic opportunities are expected" (1981: 96).

As we have seen, however, American fever includes aspirations for more than just economic well-being. Some immigrants now in New York mentioned fascination with America and curiosity about this new world as reasons for leaving Korea. I predict that in the future this sociocultural inducement will play a more significant role in emigration once the Korean political and economic situation improves. Mr. Choi, who runs a chess parlor in Elmhurst and sells Korean herbs, is an example of a recent Korean cultural refugee: "In Korea I had an American foster-father whom I knew since I was twelve years old. Because of my foster father's influence, I did not care for Korean food, which is very hot and spicy.[7] I was very close to my American foster-father, learning English and much about American culture from him. My foster-father was an American colonel in Korea, and later died in Texas."

Mr. and Mrs. Park are both pharmacists. Mrs. Park said that it was her husband who wanted to immigrate: "We had been in Korea around thirty years, and he said, "Why don't we try to go to a new world, with great ambition and with a frontier spirit?" We both thought that Korea is small, and we are not very crazy about Korean food. We would suffer less than others from going abroad since my husband has been in *Katusa* [Koreans Attached to the United States Army], and he is familiar with Western food to some extent. However, I opposed his desire for immigration as I heard that life in America is tough and bitter. But I *was* curious about America, to be honest with you. After we petitioned, we hesitated for six months." Others, especially professionals such as doctors and ministers, expressed

7. For most people, Korean food is very important for sustaining Korean identity. Some of my interviewees told me that they were worried about American food: "How can a Korean survive by living on bread only?" But their fears turned out to be groundless: Korean immigrants have access to plenty of Korean food wherever there is a sizable Korean community.

the desire both to further their education and to learn more about America.

What about the later wave of new immigrants? What is the content of their American fever? By the late 1970s and 1980s, poorer Koreans faced greater economic problems than early-wave immigrants had. Their prospects as workers in Korean companies offered little opportunity for advancement. One later-wave informant told me, "If we had remained in Korea, it would be impossible for us to educate our children. However, here we can even afford to give our kids piano or violin lessons. So for that, we are very grateful, all due to immigration to the United States." In addition, there are few Korean families today without at least one emigrant relative in America. This makes information about American life widely available through networks of kin or friends. These contacts bring not only news but also judgments and perceptions about life in America. These evaluations help shape understandings about what is possible in the United States.

Notions about American fever and migration in general differ for immigrant women and men. As they are exposed to the American notion of "ladies first," women see America as a place where they will be treated much better than in Korea (see Chapter 6). Some women such as Mrs. Park, who now works at a nail salon, perceived America as a place of economic independence for women. This was her major reason for agreeing with the family decision to immigrate.

Thus, the reasons for immigration are complex. Sometimes I heard statements that emphasized certain reasons over others. For example, when my respondents were asked to talk about why they had migrated, quite often those with children mentioned better educational opportunities for their offspring. But one informant, who works for a Korean driving school in Elmhurst, pointed out : "Many Korean immigrants say that they decided to immigrate to America in order to offer their children a better education. They tell a lie by saying so. They want to justify their emigration and to save their face in front of others. In fact, I think that they run away from the home country in order to enjoy better economic well-being. Otherwise, why do they work twenty-four hours, not even taking care of their children properly? In my opinion, if they think of their children's education as the most important reason for migration, they could send their children abroad later."

In Korea, the culturally articulated Confucian tradition values everything related to education, although in the past formal education was available only for the elite. Government policies in the 1950s and 1960s emphasized the importance of schooling. But "my children's education" as a motive for migration is more easily justified than "my material success," which cannot be justified by appeals to the Confucian tradition. Thus, education for their children is indeed part of the complex of factors motivating many Koreans to immigrate. Immigrants firmly believe that their children's education is a route to social mobility for the family. Statements about migration for the sake of children's education thus involve at least four considerations: education as a marker of class status, the ability of children to provide care for their elderly parents, a concern for generational continuity stemming from the tradition of ancestor worship, and the denial of more selfish motivations in leaving Korea for America. The first consideration is closely related to Bourdieu's interpretation of class reproduction (Bourdieu and Passeron 1970). He proposes that there is "a very close relationship linking cultural practices . . . to education capital (measured by qualifications) and secondarily, to social origins (measured by father's occupation)" (1984: 13).

The relationship between migration and the desire for political stability is very close. In this regard migratory considerations are related to class background and the macropolitical situation. If a person is from a middle- or upper-class background, political impediments to mobility may be cited as influencing migration. If a person is poor or from a lower-class background, economic upward mobility is usually paramount. But for all persons, economic limitations are tied to Korea's level of political turmoil. One of my informants, for instance, said that he decided to leave Korea because his business did not go well: "I used to run a factory in Seoul. Student demonstrations were serious and greatly influenced my employees. How could I run my factory peacefully?" So he declared bankruptcy and emigrated to America. For him, political and economic motives influenced one another.

Few of my informants specify only political reasons for immigration; however, their comparison between life in Korea and America includes such considerations, intermixed with others we have examined. While they often criticized dictatorship and political instability in Korea, few mentioned it as their primary reason for immigration. Many Koreans strongly believe that a person should stay in Korea if he or she considers the country's political future important. Only when a person is targeted for his or her political activity are political reasons a valid excuse for migration. If a person is dissatisfied with Korea's political instability but has not been mistreated for political beliefs, he or she should not use that justification. Thus, Korean immigrants seldom articulate their reasons for migration in political terms alone. Nevertheless, it is apparent that, as a result of turmoil in Korea, political factors have influenced emigration. For example, in the 1976 ax-murder incident at the DMZ (demilitarized zone) in Korea, two American officers were killed, reportedly by North Korean soldiers, following a dispute over trimming tree branches. Immediately after that incident, deep anxiety about another Korean war swept through some elite segments of Seoul's population (I. Kim 1981: 34). The incident had little effect on emigration in 1976, but in subsequent years the number of people seeking to leave increased.

## Reasons for Migration: Immigrant Voices

In sum, less than 3 percent of my informants mentioned political factors as prime motives for their emigration. Some 48 percent mentioned economic reasons, including securing resources for their children's education; 38 percent mentioned familial or kinship considerations (see Chapters 4 and 5); and 11 percent mentioned sociocultural reasons, with some overtly referring to American fever. These explanations should be analyzed as part of an ideological discourse in which my interviewees are consciously and unconsciously appealing to me, citing the reasons they think they should mention. Generally, my respondents mentioned more than one reason as our dialogues continued. Economic reasons for migration were most readily offered. They include three subcategories: For people of lower-class origin, migration was for survival; for most middle- and upper-class immigrants, migration was for better political and economic well-being and capital investment; for others (such as those who were bankrupt or fired in midcareer), migration to America offered a new beginning.

An early-wave immigrant named Mr. Kye came to study new medical technology. He ran a drugstore before he left Korea. As a pharmacist, he immigrated to America in 1974 under the occupational preference: "I had made up my mind to learn new technological developments in America and return to Korea. However, now I feel hopeless about medical technology. That's because, in my opinion, it is monopolized by America and there is a rigid division of labor internationally. . . . Perhaps we can

[33]

achieve our own momentum in the newly developing disciplines, like computer science." In the mid-1980s, Mr. Kye returned to Korea.

Typically, Korean immigrants express a combination of reasons—opportunity for children's education, self-improvement, and a desire for a higher living standard. Mrs. Park, for example, came to America in 1984. Her daughter, who immigrated as a nurse but no longer works as one, invited Mrs. Park and her family to join her. Mrs. Park told me, "I thought of educating my youngest son here and of making a fortune in America. That's because I heard that in America it is easy to make a fortune, and that all legitimate trades are equally honorable." This last statement deserves attention. It illustrates how Koreans perceive American society: that there is equality in terms of mental and manual labor and even among different occupations.

Many people immigrate due to familial ties, the second set of prime reasons most often cited by my interviewers. In order to understand the role of family ties in the immigrant community, it is necessary to understand Korean kinship, a topic we will study in later chapters. Thus, my remarks here are introductory. Korean culture puts much emphasis on family bonds. For example, if a household head decides to migrate, each family member is supposed to follow, no matter how old he or she is, especially if the person is unmarried. Some in their twenties or thirties immediately follow the decision of the household, not wanting to be left by themselves. Others, including older parents and young children, join adult relatives later through family reunification. A few also migrate because of a family dispute in Korea. Mr. Sung runs a sewing machine store in Jackson Heights, assisted by his wife. In Korea his wife was in favor of emigration, but he did not want to leave. He said that the reason his wife wanted to leave was that she had problems with his family, in particular with his mother.

Despite the particularities of each individual's decision to emigrate, it is likely that the changing political and economic situation in Korea will continue to spur migration for some time to come. No one, however, can predict whether emigrants will continue to come to America if the U.S. economy enters a new recession or an even worse economic phase. In the past, Korean emigrants have followed the flow of capital and labor to the Middle East, South America, and Vietnam as well as to Germany, Canada, and the United States. Events within Korea will also influence emigration. For example, after the political reforms of 1987 and the 1988 Olympics in Seoul, many overseas Koreans noticed new economic growth and political liberalization in Korea and thought about returning home.[8] This was particularly true for middle- and upper-class Korean immigrants. In addition, the 1986 Immigration Reform and Control Act in the United States forced some Koreans who could not secure immigration status to return to Korea. They could not find employment in the United States under the employer-sanctions provision of this legislation.

In this chapter, I placed the questions of how and why Koreans immigrate to the United States in a historical and structural framework. I also presented the voices of some individual immigrants discussing why they came to America. Koreans come here with their own version of an American dream, a dream shaped by their experiences in Korea as well as their subjective perceptions of America. In the following chapters, I explore how new immigrants seek to realize this dream through their daily experience in New York City.

8. According to the Korean Ministry of Foreign Affairs, in 1989 there were 6,176 overseas Koreans who had returned permanently to Korea, a 44.5 percent increase over the previous year (*Korea Times*, 4 January 1990). For some of these returnees this represents a "reverse brain drain," where South Korea's surging economy and liberalized political environment have attracted expatriates, many of them academic scientists (*Chronicle of Higher Education*, 15 November 1989).

# [3]

# The Gravitation to Small Business

Sook Ryul Ryu's "Poem by a Yellow Woman" (Ryu 1996) shows us the choices that many Korean immigrants must make:

> My brother who has Master's degree in English literature
> thinks about Norman Mailer's American Dream
> while selling fishes and vegetables to his white neighbors
> 24 hours a day.
> My sister, who liked the paintings of Picasso's Blue
> Period, is working on a sewing machine, with dyed blond
> hair.

Korean immigrants are distributed in the U.S. labor force differently from other Americans. Relatively few are wage-earning or salaried employees in large corporations. To a greater degree even than other recent immigrants, Koreans have gravitated to small businesses. This chapter explores the importance of immigrant small business activities. First, I explain the Korean American dream and discuss how and why Korean immigrants involve themselves in small business activities. Second, I explore the position of Korean enterpreneurship in the American capitalist economy in terms of the segmented labor market. Third, I provide an ethnographic description of several representative small businesses to aid in understanding the nature of immigrants' business practices. Fourth, I examine the process by which Korean entrepreneurs obtain capital, labor, and business information. Finally, I discuss the implications of this small business focus on the lives of professionals and the working class.

[36]

*Table 4.* Occupations of Informants (N = 109)

## Occupational categories

|  | Number of immigrants |
|---|---|
| Workers | 40 |
| Business proprietors | 39 |
| Professionals | 19 |
| Others | 11 |

## Workers (N = 40)

| Korean workplaces | Number of workers |
|---|---|
| Greengrocery | 13 |
| Garment factory | 8 |
| Office worker | 5 |
| Grocery and supermarket | 4 |
| Coffee shop | 1 |
| Construction firm | 2 |
| General merchandise store | 1 |
| Wholesaler | 1 |
| Gift shop | 1 |
| Baby-sitter | 1 |
| Cab driver | 1 |
| Non-Korean workplaces | 2 |

## Business proprietors (N = 39)

| Business type | Number of proprietors |
|---|---|
| Grocery and supermarket | 6 |
| Greengrocery | 5 |
| Fish market | 4 |
| Dry cleaner | 3 |
| Garment factory | 3 |
| Restaurant | 3 |
| Wholesaler | 2 |
| Beauty salon | 2 |
| Craft and Korean dress salon | 2 |
| Meat market | 1 |
| Fashion store | 1 |
| Stationery | 1 |
| Hardware store | 1 |
| Sewing machine store | 1 |
| Chess parlor | 1 |
| Travel service | 1 |
| Real estate office | 1 |
| Automobile body shop | 1 |

(*continued*)

Table 4. (Continued)

Professionals (N = 19)

| Professional category | Number of professionals |
|---|---|
| Medical doctor (including Korean medicine) | 4 |
| Pharmacist | 4 |
| Accountant and certified public accountant | 3 |
| Medical and dental technician | 2 |
| Minister | 2 |
| Real estate broker | 2 |
| Nurse | 1 |
| Engineer | 1 |

Korean immigrants are highly concentrated in retail and service businesses. The 1980 census reported that 13.5 percent of employed Koreans in the United States were self-employed or unpaid family workers.[1] In marked contrast, only 7 percent of the general U.S. working population is self-employed (U.S. Bureau of the Census 1983). A 1973 Los Angeles survey found 25 percent of Korean families in small business (Bonacich, Light, and Wong 1976). Later surveys in metropolitan New York and Atlanta found 34 percent of Korean families engaged in small business (I. Kim 1981; Min 1988a).

There is widespread recognition of this concentration in small business. Much media attention has been devoted to the phenomenon—from television documentaries to newspaper feature stories to the 1989 film *Do the Right Thing*. In one Queens neighborhood newspaper, a local resident's letter to the editor invited Koreans to take over a family-owned Italian delicatessen. Korean immigrants were portrayed as the only people who could now operate such businesses. "For some reason it closed, reportedly and understandably because the children did not want to put in the long hours their parents did. I have a message for the Korean community—Please, please open an *Italian deli in Woodside*! *I won't put in the long hours to do it. But you will*" (*Woodsider*, June 1987).

In my research in Queens, I studied not only business proprietors but also workers and professionals (see table 4). The professionals were 17

1. The disparity in accounts of small business ownership between census figures and results of studies stems from the difference in unit of measurement: household or individual.

[38]

percent of my 109 informants, the workers 37 percent. The small business proprietors amounted to 36 percent. My panel of informants is perhaps more heavily weighted to small business proprietors than the overall New York City Korean population. It is no exaggeration to say that "at least 70 percent of Koreans in New York City are involved in small business, either as employers or employees, and their family members, if we figure the total number who depend upon the 9,500 Korean businesses in New York City" (S. S. Kim 1986: 66). Moreover, even some Korean professionals are independent practitioners serving the Korean immigrant community and are considered to be similar to small business proprietors. Relatively few of these professionals work for American firms. Finally, many ministers in the four hundred New York area Korean Protestant churches also depend on small business owners and workers, as we shall see in Chapter 8.

## The Korean American Dream

Before emigrating, Koreans have preconceived ideas about America. They come with dreams and ideas about how American society works. Until recently, Koreans had a rosy picture of America as a free and equal society with a clean, safe environment where everybody is kind to each other. These notions were expressed by many of my informants.

The Korean American dream includes several themes. The most powerful is that one will be rewarded in proportion to how hard one works, *norŏkŭi taekka*. This phrase echoed throughout my interviews. The theme, of course, is not particular to Korean immigrant culture. According to America's Horatio Alger myth, "a poor boy of low status, but with total faith in the American system, works very hard and ultimately becomes rich and powerful. The myth formulates both the American conception of success—wealth and power—and suggests that there is a simple (but not easy) way of achieving them—single-minded hard work" (Ortner 1979: 95). Koreans, however, understand the American dream from a purely Korean perspective. For them, success following hard work is more in the order of things than the result of competition, as it is for other Americans.[2] Koreans interpret reward according to the expression "If you do good to others, someday they do good to you" and according to cultural notions of

2. The denial of competition jars with an occasional mention of competitive conspicuous consumption and complaints about there being too many Korean grocery stores on the same street.

*ingwa ŭngbo* (cause and effect) and *poram* (worthiness). This conception of American society is closely related to Koreans' position in the American labor market: as petite bourgeoisie. Because many work as self-employed small business proprietors, they feel that their earnings correspond to how hard they work. For instance, they can make more money if they work sixteen hours instead of eight hours. Their perspective is also related to the ideology of individualism in American society.

Korean immigrants' view of success is revealed in their comparisons between America and Korea. According to Mr. Chung, a fish market owner, "I made a good decision to come to America, at just the right time. In Korea, when I went broke all of a sudden, it hurt my pride. It was due to the unstable economy in Korea: with a little wind, a small twig cannot stand. In Korea, as one knows, political connections, *ppaek*, or other good connections influence every aspect of a person's life. Without such a background, if you are broke, it is hard to recover. Here there is little difference between rich and poor. What is most important is that if you work hard, you will be rewarded to some extent." His reference to "connections" should be understood in relationship to the particularly unstable social and political climate in Korea after the Korean War (See H. Lim 1982: 105 for further discussion.)

This belief that success can come more easily in America than in Korea might have much to do with the large gap in wages between the two nations. In addition, immigrants' image of the United States has been cultivated by the involvement of the U.S. government in Korea. We should also note that, until recently, Koreans were insulated and therefore held a naive view about the outside world, including the United States. But most important in shaping beliefs is Korean immigrants' engagement in small business activities in America.

The second important theme in the Korean American dream is the focus on freedom and equality. Koreans think of America as a free society, one offering both personal and political freedom. Their conception of freedom contains interpretations found in liberal political and Marxian theories. According to standard liberal views, freedom is the absence of interference or (more narrowly) coercion. Marxism invokes "wider notions of restrictions and options, and places more emphasis on human agency" (Bottomore 1983: 146).

Mr. Choi works at a greengrocery in Jackson Heights and has been in America for three years. He still sees America as an equal society. "Unlike Korea, here we do not have to care about the boss's social position, *nunch'iboda* [studying one's face]. Moreover, here people can easily lead a Bohemian life, especially in New York. But I feel nervous about so much violence." These thoughts about America are not identical among all Koreans. Class background, gender, and experience in the United States all produce variations. Women and people from low-income backgrounds in Korea attach more importance to the ideology of opportunity and equality, whereas middle- and upper-class men stress freedom and individualism.

## Why Koreans Enter Small Business

There is nothing surprising about the kinds of businesses that Koreans operate in American cities. They are the businesses that immigrants in America have operated for hundreds of years—labor-intensive produce stands, convenience stores, and garment factories (Light and Bonacich 1988: 8).

Koreans are among several new immigrant groups who have entered the United States in large numbers since the late 1960s. Some groups—especially Indians, Filipinos, and those from the Caribbean—arrived in America with English language skills and found jobs in public and private organizations and firms. Some also opened labor-intensive small businesses. But in contrast to Korean immigrant entrepreneurs, most new immigrant proprietors operate businesses *within* their own ethnic communities. In New York City, "large immigrant concentrations have spawned small businesses that serve the needs of new arrivals, ranging from Soviet-style restaurants and pastry shops along Brighton Beach Avenue and Haitian and Jamaican bakeries and groceries in East Flatbush, to Korean beauty and barber shops in Flushing" (Foner 1987: 7). In contrast, Korean entrepreneurs do not serve Koreans exclusively. They have opened businesses in white and black neighborhoods as well as in multiethnic neighborhoods such as northwestern Queens. Koreans who do business in low-income African American neighborhoods such as Harlem are usually at the beginning stage of a business development cycle. As they accumulate capital, some of them move into more economically diverse neighborhoods.

Scholars have developed a number of explanations regarding the propensity of Asians to pursue self-employment. According to I. Kim (1987: 220), existing theoretical approaches (e.g., Light 1972; Bonacich and

[41]

Modell 1980) treat immigrant enterprises as "self-contained," "traditional" subsystems somewhat independent of external, "modernized" forces.

Other scholars focus on social processes in capitalist economies, such as supply and demand, and assert that ethnic entrepreneurship is the product of opportunity structures and group characteristics. For example, Min and Jaret (1985) have linked Korean immigrant small business success in Atlanta, a predominantly African American city, to hard work and frugality, and to the cooperative efforts of family members. They did not find Korean business success dependent upon contacts with large American corporations or based on particular Korean ethnic characteristics or ethnic solidarity.

In contrast, Light and Bonacich (1988: 18–19), in a synthesis of previous studies, attribute Korean success in small business to "class resources" and "ethnic resources." It should be noted that class and ethnic variables are not independent of one another. In terms of class resources, Light and Bonacich point out that Koreans were highly educated in their country of origin, often arrived in the United States with large sums of money, and are of middle- or upper-middle-class origins. In terms of ethnic resources, the authors stress that Koreans pass on business information among themselves; work long hours; mobilize unpaid family labor; maintain patterns of nepotism and employer paternalism; worship a Calvinist deity; use alumni, family, and congregational solidarities; think of themselves as sojourners; express satisfaction with what others see as poorly remunerated work; and use rotating credit associations to finance their businesses. Several of these ethnic resources also characterize other Asian, Latin American, and Caribbean entrepreneurs in New York City but are certainly pervasive among Koreans.

Other scholars have viewed the movement of new immigrant groups into small businesses from the theory of ethnic succession: "If the supply of native owners is leaking out of a small business industry, then immigrants may take up ownership activities in response to a replacement demand" (Waldinger 1986: 30). As I. Kim (1981: 111) explains, "Korean immigrants [in New York City] are able to buy shops from white minority shopkeepers, especially Jews, because the second- or third-generation children of these older immigrants have already entered the mainstream of the American occupational structure, and so they are reluctant to take over their parents' business."

Although the ethnic succession model explains certain aspects of ethnic entrepreneurship, it doesn't explain why certain groups enter a particular business sector. The weakness of explanations based on ethnic succession or ethnic and class resources is their narrow conception of ethnic entrepreneurship. What is missing is an analysis of the larger system in which ethnic entrepreneurship is embedded (Bonacich 1993: 4). Moreover, little attention is paid to providing a structural analysis of the ethnic economy in relationship to the overall restructuring of the U.S. economy.

The most important structural factor in understanding the concentration of Korean immigrants in small business is the segmented labor market in the United States. This model argues that workers are separated into two or more labor markets with different job characteristics and outcomes.[3] Primary and secondary labor market segments are characterized by differences in human capital returns, job tenure, working conditions, wages, and promotional opportunities. There are two main sources of exclusion from the primary market, which tend to operate even if all other qualifications are equal. One is a gender disqualification strongly influencing the conditions of female employment; the other is a racial/ethnic disqualification. Therefore, in the segmented labor market model, immigrants, particularly ethnic groups, are relegated to the secondary labor market (Sanders and Nee 1987; Mar 1991: 7). Jobs in the secondary labor markets are shunned by native-born workers. Mar defines the ethnic labor market as a particular segment of the market characterized by the employment of ethnic immigrants by ethnic capitalists (1991: 7). The segmented labor market model explains the position of Korean immigrants in the U.S. economy.

Korean immigrants' language/culture barrier as well as problems with untransferable skills and education also contribute to their disadvantaged status in the American labor market. Although many immigrants previously held white-collar jobs in Korea, their education is of little use in New York. Their professional certificates are not recognized, and their unfamiliarity with English makes it difficult for them to obtain good jobs. Koreans resent the low wages and racial discrimination they encounter working for other Americans. They also dislike the formal and superficial work relationships with American colleagues. They contrast these conditions to those in Korea or at Korean-run workplaces in America.

Large numbers of Korean immigrants arrived in America at a time when the economy was rapidly changing. In the New York region, many

3. Radical theorists argue that labor market segmentation is a control device to keep labor divided (Mar 1991: 6).

factory jobs were disappearing, leading to other changes: "a 30 percent overall decline in manufacturing jobs (1969–77), with a significant expansion in certain manufacturing branches; increased poverty, unemployment, and deterioration of several areas of the city, along with a boom in gentrification and an associated high consumption capacity for real estate and the services sector" (Sassen-Koob 1981: 16–17).

Most jobs in the expanding service sector are, in fact, low-paid, short-tenure jobs, including jobs in household work and food service. Many have been filled by women and youths from minority groups. For New York, the service, or tertiary sector, was the major employer of both native and immigrant labor in 1980. Immigrant workers from Latin America, Asia, and the non-Hispanic Caribbean were overrepresented in several economic activities in the service sector: In the case of men, in eating and drinking establishments (Latin Americans and Asians), wholesale trade (Asians), personal and household services (Latin American and non-Hispanic Caribbeans); in the case of women, in eating and drinking establishments (Asians), personal and household services (Latin American and non-Hispanic Caribbeans, the latter particularly in private households), and professional services, including a wide range of nonprofessional jobs in hospitals (non-Hispanic Caribbeans) (unpublished data from the Census of Population 1980 quoted in Marshall 1987: 88). Nonetheless, according to Sanjek (n.d.)

would-be immigrant entrepreneurs arriving in Queens during the 1960s found a borough that was losing its traditional retail stores as white proprietors retired or moved away. This loss accelerated considerably during the 1970s. But at the same time, the total population of potential customers was increasing, and especially in Community District 4 [Elmhurst-Corona]. While Queens gained some 177,000 residents during the 1960s, its total number of retail businesses dropped by 1,200 between 1958 and 1967, an average loss of 90 stores in each community district. Closures occurred in businesses that immigrants would enter in great numbers: meat and fish stores fell by 321; groceries by 315; furniture and appliance stores by 132; general merchandise stores by 81; and drugstores by 46. Nonetheless, the combined annual sales of Queens' retail businesses increased even as their number declined—from $1.7 billion in 1958 to $2.4 billion in 1967. Clearly there was a profitable small-business frontier for immigrants willing to pioneer.

Korean immigrants would become the pioneers.

## A Non-Ethnic Enclave Economy

In establishing their place in the labor market, immigrants form what Portes and Bach (1985) call *ethnic enclaves*. Enclaves are places where a group's culture, identity, and internal solidarity are preserved. For such an enclave to emerge, there must be substantial numbers of immigrants, sufficient sources of capital, and an available supply of ethnic labor. Portes and Bach cite the Koreans of Los Angeles and the Cubans of Miami as examples of established ethnic enclaves. In such enclaves, newly arrived immigrants can survive with little knowledge of the host culture and language.

Sanders and Nee (1987) have challenged the Portes and Bach view of the enclave economy as a vehicle for immigrant upward mobility. Similarly, Mar (1991) suggests that it is unlikely that the ethnic labor market can serve as a crucible for the development of ethnic entrepreneurs. In his scenario, the enclave economy is wrought with class conflict: "Ethnic entrepreneurs must subordinate workers in the ethnic labor market in order to raise their entrepreneurial earnings above wages from alternative jobs in the secondary labor market" (Mar 1991: 19).

Correlatively, Light and Bonacich document that, for both the United States overall and Los Angeles in particular, mean receipts of Korean-owned firms fell short of mean receipts for all firms (1988: 165). They also found that employees of Korean firms earned 48 percent of what employees of other firms earned. The smallest wage discrepancy, however, occurred in retail and service industries. Here employees of Korean firms earned 81 percent of the general wage rate for their industry (1988: 170).

Korean small businesses are independently owned but, as we shall see, they are dependent on non-Korean as well as Korean suppliers, workers, and customers. Except for a few Korean grocery stores and restaurants, most Korean proprietors have customers who are not Korean. And since the 1986 passage of the Immigration Reform and Control Act, Korean proprietors rely now on non-Korean workers.

Bonacich (1979; 1988) has advanced a vastly different thesis from the ethnic enclave one. She argues that immigrant small businesses operate in the context of corporate capitalism. Either the profit-motivated marketing strategies of large corporations leave gaps in the economy, which Korean immigrants conveniently and efficiently fill, or monopoly capitalism uses Korean immigrants as middlemen to distribute products cheaply to less

[45]

affluent customers. In Bonacich's view, Korean small business is not even business per se but "a form of utilization of cheap immigrant labor by American capitalism." For these reasons, Light and Bonacich suggest the term *immigrant entrepreneurs*, meaning "self-employment within the immigrant group at a rate in excess of the general" (1988: 18) instead of the older concept of *middleman minorities.*

It may not be necessary to go this far. A few kinds of Korean businesses, such as import-export trades with Korea or even nail salons, do show more or less autonomous development. Some Korean retailers depend on Korean suppliers for imported goods. What is more, some Korean immigrant capitalists build factories near the Mexican border and in Central and South American countries, reflecting the new international division of labor. In other cases, Korean retailers rely on non-Korean suppliers, just like other small businesses in the United States. In sum, Korean immigrant entrepreneurship encompasses a variety of forms in relation to the American capitalist economy. The main distinction is that Korean immigrants operate within the segmented labor market.

## Characteristics of Korean Business

Most Korean businesses are quite small. In 1972, the U.S. Census Bureau found that only 21 percent had any paid employees, and for these the average number of employees was six. In Elmhurst, most Korean small businesses, except garment factories, have fewer than ten employees. Most are leased establishments. In Elmhurst in 1986 only 9 percent of the 105 Korean stores were owned, and in neighboring Corona only 5 percent were owned. In contrast, for the longer-established Italian American businesses in Elmhurst, ownership of location was 25 percent and in Corona 47 percent (Yuan 1986: 9, 25). Korean businesses are also young. As of 1986, the oldest Korean business in Elmhurst was only ten years old. In contrast, the oldest business in Elmhurst was sixty-five years old (Yuan 1986: 7).

In New York City, Koreans now dominate several retail business lines. As of 1989, there were 1,400 Korean vegetable stands out of 1,500 in New York City (Korean Produce Retailers Association's calculation; see *New York Daily News*, 22 January 1989). In the dry-cleaning business, Koreans ran 2,000 out of a total of 3,000 stores. Korean fish stores and sewing factories in 1987 both numbered between 500 and 600.

By 1986 there were so many nail salons run by Koreans in New York City that competition became fierce (*New York Times*, 21 February 1986). In 1989, Mr. and Mrs. Kwak, who run a nail salon in Westchester County, told me that there were an estimated 1,500 nail salons run by Koreans in the tri-state area. There are several reasons for this boom. Unlike barbers or hairdressers, manicurists do not need licenses in New York State. Anyone who knows how to give a manicure can open a nail salon. The startup capital for this type of business is relatively low, about $20,000. It takes six months for Korean women to become skilled, after which many open their own businesses.

Korean men and women involved in small business often work more than twelve hours daily and six or seven days a week. According to an August 1987 survey by the Korean American Small Business Service Center of New York, 85 percent of Korean proprietors kept their stores open more than ten hours per day. Some 70 percent used family labor, 73 percent suffered from insufficient operating funds, 55 percent had competition problems with other nearby Korean stores, and 57 percent acknowledged problems with their employees. For 94 percent, efforts to increase profits were made through improving services, because they could not afford either capital investment or additional staff (*Korean American Small Business Service Center of New York Newsletter* 15 August 1987). Finally, 20 to 25 percent of Korean immigrant entrepreneurs fail in small businesses every year (K. K. Lee 1991).

Even so, elements of the Korean entrepreneurial story vindicate the Horatio Alger-like route to their American dream. During the late 1980s it was well known among Koreans that the income from small businesses could range from $50,000 to $100,000. Starting a business in Los Angeles permitted the immigrant to increase his or her income by an average of 82 percent (Light and Bonacich 1988: 176). Obviously, such favorable returns encouraged entrepreneurship elsewhere, including New York City (Light 1984; Min 1984: 344; Young 1983).

Figures 2, 3, and 4 show the basic business structure of three main types of Korean small businesses: garment factories, greengroceries, and dry cleaners. Each of the industries is a highly competitive market where Koreans and many other ethnic groups encounter each other. Korean entrepreneurs have been slowly moving to higher levels within each industry.

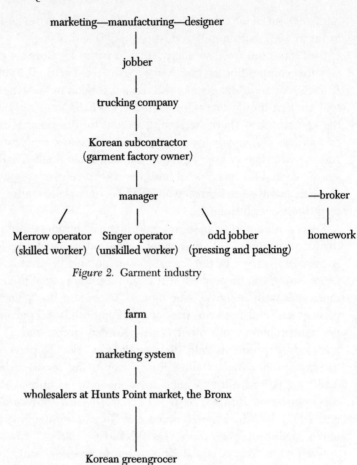

marketing—manufacturing—designer
|
jobber
|
trucking company
|
Korean subcontractor
(garment factory owner)
|
manager                                              —broker
/            |            \                              |
Merrow operator  Singer operator    odd jobber        homework
(skilled worker)  (unskilled worker)  (pressing and packing)

*Figure 2.* Garment industry

farm
|
marketing system
|
wholesalers at Hunts Point market, the Bronx

|

Korean greengrocer
(with help of Korean buyer, deliverer, or driver)

|

manager
/        /     |     \        \
worker   worker cashier worker worker
/        /     |     \        \
in charge of fruits  in charge of vegetables  |  for salad bar  for flowers

|

customer

*Figure 3.* Fruit and vegetable business and the Korean greengrocery

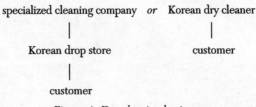

Figure 4. Dry-cleaning business

## Greengrocers

According to the *New York Times*, "The Korean fruit stands started popping up about fifteen years ago [in the mid-1970s]. They arrived just in time. Earlier groups of immigrants were abandoning the trade, and it was an open question as to whether New Yorkers would be condemned to wandering in all-night supermarkets in neighborhoods of dubious virtue. Single people trembled. Then, like the Seventh Cavalry, like a cool breeze, like a check in the mail, the Koreans arrived, opening their impeccable emporia all over town. It was the greatest event in the lives of single people since the invention of the VCR" (October [date missing] 1989). Koreans in New York are perhaps best known as greengrocers (see plate 2 for a typical establishment). Immigrants began to enter the fruit and vegetable business in the city in 1971 (I. Kim 1981: 112). Those who entered the United States via Latin American nations, particularly Argentina, were the first to open greengroceries. These immigrants had run various businesses in Latin America "after having encountered severe difficulties in progressing from the designated agricultural colonies of their original settlements to the metropolitan areas of Latin America" (I. Kim 1981: 113). Young (1983: 60) described the daily schedule of a Korean greengrocer:

| | |
|---|---|
| 4:00 A.M. to 6:00 A.M. | shop for produce at Hunts Point market in the Bronx |
| 6:30 A.M. to 8:30 A.M. | prepare for day's sales (clean, trim, stack, and arrange produce) |
| 8:30 A.M. to 8:00 P.M. | open for business, clean up, store unsold produce |

In Queens, I found that there are in fact two kinds of daily schedules, depending on when one goes to the Hunts Point produce market. Some go to shop at midnight, while those who are better established go early in the morning, like Young's "typical" proprietor.

[49]

*Plate 2.* Korean greengrocery in Elmhurst. Photo author

*Plate 3.* Korean grocery store where people can purchase food and rent videos. Photo author

[50]

Mr. Suh has a vegetable stand on Grand Avenue in Elmhurst. Around 1 or 2 A.M. he goes to the market to shop. He opens his store around 8 A.M. and starts arranging his fruits and vegetables as attractively as he can. He works making sales until his wife takes her turn, after preparing his lunch. He then goes home to eat and sleeps for five or six hours. Because his job is tiring, I asked him whether he could hire somebody to purchase produce or help at the store. He answered, "If I hire anybody to deliver goods or work as a cashier instead of myself, I will have little profit, and the business cannot run well." He feels that the proper selection of inexpensive but good quality produce is a complicated task that he cannot assign to anyone else.

Many greengrocers began by working for other greengrocers and then opened their own stores. Young (1983) found that owners generally agreed that a person needed to work in a greengrocery for at least six months in order to learn the business before opening a store. For Mr. Ryu, who lives in Elmhurst and operates a vegetable stand in Jackson Heights, the apprenticeship took six years. During that time, his wife also worked at the greengrocery as a cashier, and they eventually bought out the business.

Korean small business owners develop different strategies to cater to customers in different neighborhoods. In Manhattan, an owner often employs a manager to take care of the store, which is open for up to twenty-four hours. Manhattan greengrocers hire more workers, including managers, than those in Queens. In twenty-four-hour stores there are typically a manager and several workers employed during the daytime and a manager who doubles as cashier and one worker to take care of fruit and vegetables at night. In Queens, a greengrocer often goes to the market and manages the store by himself. Because of smaller space and higher rents, Manhattan businesses require more intensive labor than those in Queens. Wages are also higher in Manhattan. In both places, preparation includes cutting, wrapping, and packing. A Manhattan store often offers a self-service salad bar and hot dishes to satisfy health-conscious New Yorkers looking for quick, convenient meals. Greengrocers also try to provide different food items to suit the tastes of various neighborhoods.

In the 1980s, a new greengrocer business strategy emerged. This was a response to Korean-Korean competition, increasing commercial rents, reduced consumer purchasing power resulting from federal cutbacks in food stamps, and economic recession. Greengrocers began to sell flowers and additional grocery items, establish salad bars, and even rent video-

[51]

tapes (see plate 3). There was also a growing number of partnerships and new business corporations in the retail produce trade (Young 1983: 70). Two organizations reportedly owned chains of stores. A few Koreans even penetrated upward into the wholesale produce business. This level of business is more complex and required, as of 1983, at least $1.5 million in startup capital. Koreans still do not have direct access to the produce marketing system and farms, which they say continue to be dominated by Jewish Americans.

While greengrocers may enjoy a quick cash return on their work, they must contend with the frustration of substantial downward mobility. Some lament, "All that we do is deal with rotten tomatoes." Also, unlike professionals working in mainstream society, they are reminded daily of their marginal status.

## Dry Cleaners

In the early years of Korean immigration, the dry-cleaning business was not popular. It required more capital than greengroceries or seafood stores. But in the late 1970s, Koreans who had accumulated savings from more labor-intensive operations began to purchase dry-cleaning businesses from owners belonging to other ethnic groups. Korean immigrants after 1978 who were able to bring capital from Korea also entered the industry. In some cases, women joined their husbands, using sewing skills that they learned.

This business is called a "clean" (*kkakkŭthan*) business.[4] It is seen as easy to run and profitable. Moreover, families do not have to work long hours or on Sundays. Today Koreans also often run shoe-repair shops, which are more labor-intensive than dry cleaning; and some of these repair businesses are actually operated as part of a dry-cleaning establishment. The Korean Dry Cleaners' Association estimates that there are as many as four hundred Korean shoe-repair shops in New York City.

My informant, Mr. Yi, stated that the dry-cleaner business creates something from nothing—by getting the customers' clothing and making them clean. Mr. Yi sends out all clothing to a specialized Latin American-

4. In Korean culture, the binary opposition of clean and dirty is often used to comment on personal character, money, business, and people.

owned dry-cleaning factory. In order to save wages, he does shirt washing and pressing himself. He also accepts fur coats for storage.

Although Mr. Yi works alone, dry cleaners with more capital operate on a larger scale. Mr. Jo employs six workers at his Joel Dry Cleaner store in Jackson Heights; he lives nearby in Elmhurst. His father actually owns the business. After a failure in the wig business, Mr. Jo's father and a cousin who runs a laundry in Forest Hills became dealers in gems and curios from South America. With 50 percent of the capital from savings in this business and the rest borrowed from the cousin, Mr. Jo's father bought the dry-cleaning shop. Mr. Jo's mother, who used to work at a garment factory as a pattern maker, quit to join this family business.

According to Mr. Jo, the laundry business is very slow in July and August but is better in the fall. Except for fur coats and white shirts, all cleaning is done at his store. Fur coats are brought to a company specializing in them, and white shirts are sent to a Jewish-owned business in Jamaica. These specialized items are picked up and delivered to the Joel Dry Cleaner.

There are four full-time and two part-time workers, including a Turkish tailor and a South American presser. The tailor came to the job through an advertisement in a Korean newspaper, and he works very diligently. Mr. Jo mans the counter and does spot cleaning by himself. He complains about the heat and the long working hours, from seven in the morning to seven in the evening. He finds the work tedious and repetitious. Sometimes, he says, it is also hard to deal with customers' complaints, particularly when they lie—such as a customer who brings back clothes with complaints about the cleaning job when, in fact, he or she has already worn them.

## Fish Stores

There are about five hundred Korean fish markets in New York City. Although Koreans entered this business soon after the rise of greengroceries, this activity is less well known to the public as a predominantly Korean enterprise. Fish markets hire fewer workers than greengroceries do, only one or two at each market. But as they did with greengroceries, many Koreans bought out fish markets from aging Italian owners. In the 1980s, fish markets, like greengroceries, also went through a process of diversification. Many in Manhattan now sell fried shrimp, clams, and fish and chips or even sushi and sashimi. This creates a need for more workers—usually women who are hired to fry fish. Besides the owner, who is also the cashier, two or more workers clean, cut, and wrap fish selected by customers. With experience gained here, these workers can later work at sushi bars in Korean-Japanese or Korean restaurants.

The owners of seafood stores go to buy fish early in the morning at the Fulton fish market in lower Manhattan. There, most wholesalers are Italian; only one is Korean. Fish market owners do not spend as much time there as greengrocers do at the Hunts Point produce market. But at the Fulton market, they do gather at one café to exchange market information and socialize among themselves. In this business, the owner needs to be familiar with his neighborhood in order to know which kinds of fish his customers like most. Korean fish market owners call themselves "fish doctors" who practice "surgery" on fish, at the request of their customers.

Through a friend from his Pyongyang hometown, Mr. Chin got his first job in America thirteen years ago at a fish store, then considered the largest in New York City. The Jewish owner treated him very well, and he learned a lot. After working there for six years, he bought his own seafood store. He begins his day at the Fulton fish market, arriving between 2 and 4 A.M. According to Mr. Chin, 90 percent of the wholesalers are Italians and Mafia-controlled. The other 10 percent are Jewish.

His employee opens his store at 7 A.M. every day except Sunday. Now in his fifties, Mr. Chin has become a fish expert. "How wonderful a food fish is! If I drink, and accompany it with fish, I have no hangover. If I drink with meat, I usually develop a serious headache. I like this business; it is very neat in its own way. Expenses are minimal. There is very little inventory, and the profits are very immediate. I pay $1,100 a month for rent. That is the cheapest rent in this good neighborhood. About 90 percent of my customers are whites, such as Italians and Jews. They are very particular about quality, regardless of price. I offer really good fish. In my experience, Latin Americans do not seem to like fish. The other 10 percent of my customers are Korean."

## The Garment Industry

So far, I have examined Korean immigrant participation in the retail and service sector. I now shift to their involvement in the manufacturing sector, first discussing the garment industry. Mr. Pi, a garment factory owner, estimated that in 1984 there were more than 2,000 garment factories in New York City. He guessed that 99 percent of the clothing manufacturers who supply work to these shops were Jewish or Italian, most located in the "7th Avenue" Manhattan garment district between 29th and 40th streets. In Chinatown there were six hundred garment shops. Overall, there were two hundred or three hundred Korean ones, with 80 percent in Manhattan and 20 percent in Flushing. By 1989, however, according to a Korean organizer for the International Ladies Garment Workers Union, there were 1,500 garment factories run by Koreans in the New York City area, including some in New Jersey. In recent years, many have relocated from Manhattan to Queens, looking for lower rents.

A few Korean women had worked in Chinatown garment factories as early as the late 1960s. Gradually Koreans who amassed enough savings bought garment factories, using their wives' work experience for business guidance. Now Latin Americans and Chinese work alongside Koreans in the Korean-owned garment factories in Elmhurst and Corona. These factories receive subcontracts from jobbers who get their contracts from the primarily Jewish Manhattan manufacturers.

Mr. Pi observes: "Koreans are very skillful with their fingers, but they are quick-tempered. As is often said, they lack esprit de corps, too easily speaking ill of others. Compared with Korean workers, Latin Americans and Chinese are patient, viewing their jobs as near to their mission in life. Within a month, most Korean workers learn all that is needed, and try to get jobs in another shop where they can get better pay." For this reason that Mr. Pi is reluctant to hire Koreans. He knows, however, that garment shops make a great contribution to Korean survival in New York City, with some 7,000 or 8,000 Koreans working in the industry in the mid-1980s. Until recently, most Korean workers could not begin at basic pay rates because they had never worked in the industry in Korea. But now some make it a point to learn sewing industry skills before coming to the United States.

To some extent, Mr. Pi is critical of the Korean garment industry, saying that it is "eating the chicken it has raised" by violating labor laws. "But what can I do about that? If it was otherwise, Koreans could hardly compete with other contractors. Workers seem to be in too much hurry to succeed. They think, if a husband and wife work hard for two years and set up a small shop, why cannot I? Also, they are quite encouraged by the ideology of America as the country of freedom. These days, they seem to

[55]

acquire egoism even before coming to America." Compared to the days when he first migrated, he thinks jobs are now more easily available to new immigrants. But he says that today there are no workers with whom he can have an easy conversation.

Analyzing the position of proprietors such as Mr. Pi, Bonacich describes the sandwich position of garment subcontractors—"as embedded in a much larger, hierarchically organized structure and, like most others in it, they are both victimizers and victimized. Since they are fairly near the bottom of the hierarchy, they are more hurt than those higher up, though not as hurt as the workers they employ" (Bonacich 1994: 139).

In Korean garment factories, there are one or two managers (one often a wife or a relative of the owner), several skilled Merrow machine workers, many more Singer machine seamstresses, and a few unskilled assistants. The Merrow machine is used to finish jobs, making a clothing item from parts by sewing them together. Merrow operators must be skilled and are better paid than Singer operators. For both categories, most Korean factories choose the piece-rate wage system over the time-rate system in order to obtain the fullest advantage from their workers.

Some employees work overtime or take work home. Those working overtime are not paid overtime. Those who do homework earn less than they would during regular hours. To avoid conflict with union organizers, Korean employers attempt to treat their workers better by improving working conditions but at the same time often find it necessary to run factories with poor working conditions to meet the prices of jobbers. If workers joined a union, owners say, the increase in wages might threaten the survival of the garment industry by seriously eroding their marginal operating capital. In a few cases, Korean owners have been forced to open union shops and let their workers become union members.

## Capital Formation

There has been an evolution of Korean small business in the past two decades, from the labor-intensive greengrocery, fish store, and garment factory to the more capital-intensive dry cleaner, gift shop, and delicatessen. This, however, has not meant replacing old businesses with new businesses but expanding the kinds of businesses. One can still say that the greengrocery is a stepping stone for Korean proprietors. New entrepreneurs continue to enter at the labor-intensive end, save, and hope to reinvest in a more capital-intensive business later. With such an evolution clearly understood *within* the Korean community, Koreans in New York smart over their portrayal by other New Yorkers as "Moonies" who buy businesses with money from the Reverend Sun Myung Moon.

Today, the method of capital formation has changed. Until the mid-1970s, it was common for new immigrants to get a start in business and free room and board from their kin. Thus, a husband and wife could save and establish their own store in two or three years. From the mid-1970s, with the increase in Korean immigration, it became more common for new immigrants to receive loans from kin or friends and to combine this with personal savings to acquire a business. Since the beginning of the 1980s, with more cash in circulation in the Korean community and more arriving from Korea, it has become easier to organize a rotating credit association, or *kye*.

Before 1978, when the limit on the amount of money immigrants could bring out of Korea was lifted, few persons could think of joining rotating credit clubs and none of opening a business immediately on arrival. I cannot emphasize too much the importance of savings as the main means of business startups through the 1960s and 1970s. In a way, Korean immigrants were well prepared for saving because at first they could find little here to buy. When coming to America, they would bring almost everything they needed, including clothing. In addition, they had little time to spend money because of long work schedules. Or, as Koreans say, when spouses work together, they usually spend the wages of one person for living expenses and save the wages of the other.

As better-established Koreans accumulated savings and business earnings, loans to kin and friends became possible. One did not have to worry about when to return such loans, and some were even made without interest. Often a Korean employer was a financial supporter when his former employee wanted to establish his own business. When these loans bore interest, they became another way to invest capital, but some were extended out of pure friendship.

Not all would-be business owners follow the same path. An unmarried man takes more time to establish his own business because he will first save money for a wedding and other marriage expenses. Since the late 1970s, as more single men have migrated, such waiting periods are more common. Moreover, if one has to adjust visa status here, legal expenses will delay opening a business for several years. Since 1978, there has been an increase in not only single-male labor migration but also capital migra-

[57]

tion. Some people are able to bring large amounts of money from Korea, and this is now the common way to open a dry-cleaning store or supermarket, even without prior experience in the business. The following story shows how this can be done: "Mr. and Mrs. Lee, both teachers in Korea, immigrated in 1982 to the United States, sponsored by Mrs. Lee's sister, a nurse. Mrs. Lee worked in a garment factory for two years. During that time her husband attended English classes at Queens College and worked at various sportswear, grocery, and greengrocery stores. In 1984, they spent three months looking for a business to buy. Eventually they bought a dry-cleaning store near their home in Elmhurst. They purchased it from a Korean owner, locating it through a Korean newspaper advertisement. They invested all of the $56,000 that they brought from Korea."

During the 1980s, Koreans raised business acquisition capital through their own financial institution, the kye (pronounced "keh") rotating credit clubs. A kye consists of a group that pools its funds on a regular basis, and each member in turn takes the pool until all group members have received it. In this manner, all but the last receive some advance use from pooled savings. The organizer receives the first draw, which gives him or her the maximum amount of credit among Kye members.

Rotating credit associations are a worldwide phenomenon (Ardener 1964; Bascom 1952; Bonnett 1981; Geertz 1962). With origins in southern China, Japan, West Africa, and elsewhere, these associations may differ in size, criteria of membership, amount of funds, and sanctions imposed on members (Bonnett 1981: 4). Among West Indians in New York City in the 1920s, money from these associations was used to bury the dead; membership in such "benevolent societies" also gave a sense of pride (Bonnett 1981: 58). Prewar Chinese and Japanese immigrants to the United States made extensive use of rotating credit associations for the purpose of capitalizing small and medium-sized business enterprises as well as for other purposes (Light 1972). But today "Hui, the Chinese rotating club, is not as important as described for earlier immigrants" among Taiwanese immigrants in Queens (Chen 1992: 102).

Between 1903 and 1918, Koreans on the Pacific coast and in Hawaii also used rotating credit associations for business capitalization (Moon 1976: 192). Among contemporary Korean immigrants, however, the kye is much larger and more central to business success. Furthermore, Koreans may join several rotating credit clubs, and kye pools can be as great as several hundred thousand dollars—or even a few million. Many Korean community organizations in New York City start off as rotating credit societies, and Korean restaurants are booming because they cater to meetings of such clubs. In Korea, kye are organized more often by women than men, but here it is common for both husband and wife to attend monthly meetings, with membership by family (see Chun 1984: 127; Janelli and Janelli 1988–89).

I concur with Light and Bonacich (1988: 255) that survey research fails to uncover the extent to which kye is used for business capitalization as opposed to its use for real estate investment or consumption. My experience is like that of Light and Bonacich's assistants, whose ethnographic studies uniformly reported more kye use than did the Los Angeles surveys. Some Los Angeles Koreans believed kye was illegal in the United States, a misconception that explains in part their reluctance to admit participation to survey researchers (Light and Bonacich 1988). Another reason for such reluctance, I suggest, is the Korean government's policy that discourages people from joining kye and fosters bank deposits that the government can use. In addition, when asked to identify the source of business capital, most people mention personal savings, loans, or gifts from others and do not add that rotating credit clubs are where their funds originated.

Among my interviewees (N=91), 40 percent were kye participants. One-fourth of my survey subjects belonged to more than one kye. Another survey (1989) by the Korean American Small Business Service Center of New York found that 63 percent of Korean proprietors (N=64) were involved in kye activities. These kye operated on a minimum of $10,000. As Koreans in Queens see it, rotating credit clubs play the double role of friendship and mutual aid. I suspect that, among those financially secure Koreans who use rotating credit clubs for business investment, their use will persist even when they have greater familiarity with the American banking system. It is, however, already apparent that the second-generation Korean Americans are more likely to invest in securities, bonds, stocks, and real estate than kye.

Some immigrants join a kye purely for friendship and mutual aid, *ch'in-mok kye*, while others join for business investment purposes. In the former case, participants may contribute different amounts of money according to the order in which each takes his or her turn. Such social kye, organized by a *kyechu* (kye organizer), involve standard numbers of participants, either twelve, twenty-four, or thirty-six or several hundred. They participate for consumption purposes—for a large household purchase such as jewelry, household items, educational expenses, or the high costs of social events. Kye members get together monthly, either at a home or a restaurant, with plenty of food.

In business investment-oriented *nakch'al kye*, precisely calculated amounts of interest are paid. For example, "eight people each contribute $250 a month, creating a $2,000 pool. . . . members bid for the cash by offering various rates of interest. . . . the $2,000 loan goes to the highest bidder, who immediately distributes the entire interest payment to the members" (*Time*, July 1988). Bidding is not possible in the more socially oriented ch'inmok kye.

Another combined form is *pŏnho kye*, a popular kye in the Korean immigrant community. Its organization follows a standard format: "Each month one member receives a lump sum of cash comprised of the contribution of all the others; and though the lump sum received by each member remains constant, the amounts contributed by each of the members varies according to the rank order of her turn" (Janelli and Janelli 1988–89: 172–73).

Despite the popularity of kye activity, it is not unusual to hear about cases of kye fraud. In the summer of 1985, for instance, a deaconess in a Korean church in Flushing ran away to South Korea with a large amount of money she had borrowed from some church members and the pooled kye fund she had been holding for a group in the church (I. Kim 1987: 234).

In Queens, Koreans acquire business capital through savings, kye, loans from kin or a friend, capital brought from Korea, and bank loans. They rely most heavily on savings and loans from kin or friends. Some 48 percent relied on savings alone, 35 percent had loans or gifts, 16 percent brought capital from Korea, and only 2 percent used bank loans. In several cases, they combined different capital sources. Moreover, the source of savings is often capital brought earlier from Korea, one or more kye, and loans. While immigrants who came to America in the 1980s brought substantial capital from Korea, those with longer residence in the United States have appealed more frequently to Korean immigrant communal resources for business capital.

## Securing Labor and Business Information

When scholars depict immigrant businesses within an ethnic enclave economy (such as Chinese businesses in Chinatowns), they focus on the ethnic clientele and the labor of the family or kin. In his 1981 survey of Korean greengrocers in New York City, Young discovered that, "of the forty stores, only three did not employ any family members. . . . Of the thirty-seven owners who employed at least one family member, thirty-five did not pay them regular wages. Of the thirty-eight owners who were married, thirty-four were assisted in the store by their wives. As expected, none of the wives were paid a regular wage." Thus, he calculated, "if an owner can cut his fixed expenses in half by using two unpaid family members (his wife, son, or brother), and by working eighteen hours instead of ten hours per day, fixed expenses would be reduced by $750, or profits increased by the same amount" (1983: 62).

My most intensive research was in the mid-1980s, some five years after Young's. Overall, I found less use of family labor and, most often, a combination of family and wage labor. In all, 38 percent of the Korean firms relied on family labor. Of these business operators, 73 percent used family and wage labor, but only 27 percent of them relied solely on family labor. In businesses such as stationeries, fashion stores, fish markets, dry cleaners, and craft stores, owners relied less on family labor but also had few workers overall.

The use of family labor has an interesting relationship to wage labor. When family labor is available, non-kin employees tend to be fired. Business owners sometimes exploit kin labor, taking advantage of relatives' hopes that they will be helped later to start their own business. When family or kin employees establish their own businesses, they are replaced by wage laborers.

In Los Angeles, Light and Bonacich (1988: 178–79) found that the percentage of firms employing nuclear or extended kin was 56.8 percent. I found that 49 percent of family labor consisted of husbands and wives; 29 percent were parents and children; 11 percent were siblings of family members; another 11 percent were other relatives. Clearly, there is greater reliance on immediate family members than on extended kin. (Chapters 4 and 5 discuss the mobilization of family/kin labor in more detail.) According to the U.S. Immigration and Naturalization Service (1985), immediate kin constituted 87.9 percent of Korean immigrants admitted to the United States between 1966 and 1981.

This use of family labor is particularly important in the earliest years of immigrant life. When Korean immigrant husbands begin stores, in most cases wives join them, which is very different from the pattern of Latin American grocery owners (Young 1983). It is almost required that successful Korean immigrant men have wives to work with them. Men are advised within the community to get married first, achieve marital stability, and then establish their own business. Whether one calls it a "family profit" (Young 1983) or a "family sacrifice" as I see it, the wife's labor is certainly beneficial for men (although problematic for Korean women).

It is also the case that "unpaid" family labor, as Young puts it, may be compensated in many indirect ways—in residential accommodations; long-term capital, labor, and business information; and support for weddings and other expenses. The following case illustrates the Korean use of family labor:

> Mr. Yi, now in his seventies, has three sons and four daughters. He lives with his wife, third son, and second daughter and her husband. Mr. Yi's second daughter's husband works for an insurance company. His third son runs a fried fish store near the central Manhattan post office at 34th Street and 8th Avenue. Half the capital for this business was brought from Korea by Mr. Yi and his son. In addition, his third and fourth daughters, who attend college, stay at his home during summer vacations and assist on occasion in the third son's store. At first, this son hired a skilled worker, but he has since replaced him with his mother, Mrs. Yi. Mr. Yi goes to this son's fish store by subway, working there from 8 A.M. to 3 P.M. selling Lotto.

In securing their current business or job, 53 percent of my informants (N=79) did so through personal connections; 21 percent through newspaper advertisements, mostly in Korean newspapers; 3 percent through an agency; and 21 percent by beginning their own business or in other ways. Even though they rely heavily on personal connections, particularly for their first job, Koreans use non-kin schoolmates, former co-workers, and church members as well as family or kin. With more years of residence in America, however, Koreans rely less on personal connections and more on formal channels or self-employment. In the garment industry, Waldinger (1986: 157) found that nonimmigrant firms recruit workers more through market mechanisms, while immigrant firms rely heavily on kinship and ethnic ties. Mobilization of social networks in running small business is not limited to obtaining business information. As I will discuss in the following chapters, immigrants also rely on church connections and political ties.

## Small Business Establishment and Class Relations

A Korean fisher cleaner said: "I have no time to do anything except work and sleep. I work and sleep, work and sleep. On Sundays? I sleep all day long or sometimes I watch Korean video tapes. I don't know what happens in New York City or in the world. I can't do anything because I am tired. I just want to open my business soon. I don't think of anything else" (J. Yi 1993: 13). Korean immigrants turn to small business as the means to realize their American dream. As a result, their small business careers become the main way they talk about and evaluate their lives. Here, I explore how Korean immigrants' focus on small business ownership affects all sectors of the community, especially professionals and workers. As we will see, some professionals become small business proprietors. So did many workers before the 1980s, when it was easier to set up a business than it is today.

According to the 1990 U.S. census, the median income of a Korean family was similar to that of white Americans. But more than 15 percent of Korean families had incomes below the poverty level, a proportion nearly twice that of white Americans, which was 9 percent (Ong 1994: 36). This indicates that in the 1980s, in addition to successful and well-educated Korean immigrants, there were less well-off compatriots.

In the mid-1980s, the Korean community in Queens experienced polarization and tension among different social strata. Distinct classes of workers and petty bourgeoisie emerged. (Refer to Chapter 8 to see why I consider small business proprietors a class.) Here, I use the concept of class in its most general sense to refer to the "shared position in the social relations of production" (Wright 1980: 326). According to my interviewees' perception of class, the Korean immigrant community consists of three distinct segments: professionals, small business proprietors, and the working class (see figure 5). They are different in not only their access to means of production but also standards of living. For instance, while established professionals and business proprietors live in spacious suburban areas in their own homes, workers rent crowded apartments. Although on some occasions immigrants think of themselves as "we Koreans," at other times the factors of small business ownership, individual occupation, and social status lead people to frown upon others seen as inferior or superior.

Korean small businesses have confronted problems in labor relations. For example, the decision in 1983 by the Korean Produce Retailers Association to raise wages for greengrocery workers was not put into effect by many store owners. Workers at several Korean sewing factories went on strike, demanding union representation.

As I have mentioned, 17 percent of my informants in Queens were professionals and 37 percent workers. Here I will examine their experiences, highlighting factors that propel some to turn to small business ownership as the route to establishment.

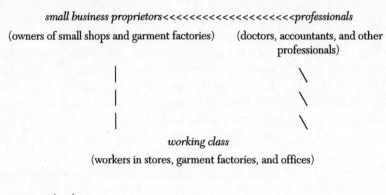

*small business proprietors* <<<<<<<<<<<<<<<<<<<<<<<*professionals*
(owners of small shops and garment factories)    (doctors, accountants, and other professionals)

*working class*
(workers in stores, garment factories, and offices)

<<<    ambivalence
\\\    domination
| | |    exploitation and domination

*Figure 5.* Class categories of new Korean immigrants

## Professionals

In Elmhurst and Corona, I found Korean immigrant medical doctors, dentists, medical and dental technicians, nurses, lawyers, accountants, certified public accountants, insurance brokers, real estate salespersons, teachers, professors, designers, artists, civil servants, and acupuncturists. Most were highly educated in Korea or America, or both. Many had worked previously for U.S. companies but later opened their own professional firms serving mainly Korean clients. Others ran small businesses while working as professionals at an American workplace. Still others quit professional jobs and devoted themselves to running small businesses.

The most important professional category is the medical doctor. Some fifteen thousand Korean doctors immigrated during 1965–75, and many have set up private practice (I. Kim 1981: chap. 6). The New York metropolitan area has the largest concentration of Korean medical personnel. In the United States, Korean immigrant medical technicians and nurses who work for large hospitals often feel limited in realizing their work potential or feel that they are not really accepted by their employers. Korean nurses often work in third-class hospitals in remote areas or in low-level jobs. Generally, Korean medical professionals do not have good command of English in contrast to many Filipino and Indian immigrants. Because they cannot achieve independent professional status, some are ready to turn to a completely different arena, such as small business proprietorship, in their search for advancement.

Many Korean immigrant professionals have class interests different from those of working-class people. Nonetheless, being immigrants locates them structurally in the marginal sector of the professional job market. What is unique about Korean immigrant professionals is that they are also influenced by Korean immigrants' quest for small business establishment.

## Workers

Many Korean workers are employed in the ethnic labor market (that is, for Korean employers), often in garment factories and offices. As I will discuss, workers employed in the ethnic labor market earn lower wages, experience higher turnover, and have less promotional opportunities than workers in other labor market segments. Mar (1991), in his study of Chinese immigrant workers, demonstrated that workers in the ethnic labor market are generally paid wages lower than those of workers in the secondary labor market. These results suggest that the ethnic labor market is a lower tier of the secondary labor market rather than a distinct labor market that possesses more desirable employment characteristics than the secondary labor market (Mar 1991: 17). This structural analysis can be applied to Korean immigrant workers as well. I also argue that there are additional sociocultural reasons (for example, seeing jobs in the ethnic workplace as part of an adjustment to immigrant life or as a way to learn how to set up small businesses) that influence immigrant workers' employment in the ethnic labor market.

How different is it for Koreans to work for Korean employers than for non-Koreans? Some characteristics of the Korean workplace in America are typical of any small business. Thus, when we observe a patron-client relationship between Korean employer and employees, how are we to interpret it? We do see Korean employers sharing activities and concerning themselves with the lives of their workers. Some even give assistance in terms of loans, labor, or business information to help employees establish their own businesses. It is a mistake to treat this relationship as a carryover from the home country, where paternalistic relationships are tied to exploitation. But there is little of the same type of sharing between Korean shopkeepers and their African American or Latin American work-

[65]

ers. We also see Korean employers exploit employees by paying less, demanding more work, and caring little about working conditions.

When work tasks are completed at the typical Korean workplace, employees are not supposed to rest, sit down, or read a newspaper. Therefore, in greengroceries, spinach may be washed and trimmed several times and thus deteriorates faster. Mr. Kang describes a worker's job on the night shift of a grocery:

> I have been paid $280 for the past five months. Although I can get up to $320 elsewhere, I stay here because of an easygoing boss. If one works at night, one doesn't even have to pay attention to the boss. As I moisten these fruit and vegetables through the night, my hands become numb with cold. During the day there are the boss, a female cashier, and four other workers—one for the salad bar, one for the vegetables, a manager, and a watchman. At night I am the manager and work with a male cashier. I arrive at work around nine and I am then expected to eat dinner. As I awake just before work, I usually have no appetite. I attend to the carrot, scallion, and spinach boxes until eleven by cutting, trimming, and displaying these items for sale. Then I smoke one cigarette. Around midnight, the cashier and I eat rice and kimch'i, each by turn. It is 3:30 A.M. when I finish the vegetables. Then I have a half-hour break to smoke. After that, I begin to set up the fruit outside. I preserve the orange juice and salad at the salad bar by icing it. Around 8:45 A.M. I finish, passing on my job to the daytime worker.

Mr. Park, another greengrocer, has a more critical opinion of his employer. Mr. Park works at a greengrocery on Broadway in Elmhurst. He laments, "I want to be treated as an equal human being. I do not care as much as about the pay. The employers treat us like slaves. It is worse if one doesn't speak good English. It is clear in their language and behavior—they seem to look down upon us, not to mention giving us less pay."

In sweatshops, skilled Merrow workers who finish garments are paid better than the majority of Singer seamstresses, who earn piece-rate wages as low as $180 for a six-day work week. There is a Korean saying, *Palbara samchŏlli* (sew three thousand li, with a *li* being nearly four hundred meters), referring to the tedious nature of sewing.[5] The working environment of sweatshops is often horrible: Many are located in basements, which are not well ventilated. Because of work-produced dust, workers often have problems with their lungs or throats. Piecework leads

5. This expression comes from a reference to the entire land area of Korea. It is often used to mean a long distance.

workers to postpone trips to the rest room, resulting in problems with digestion or constipation. Ms. Kim, a seamstress, describes the atmosphere in the factory in which she works: "Sometimes our boss distributes boiled pork, which according to Korean folk culture gets rid of accumulated dust. And we workers take turns bringing homemade snacks including special dishes."[6] I also observed workers enjoying Chinese glutinous rice cakes, "Chinese tamales," brought by a Chinese woman worker at one Korean garment factory in Elmhurst.

Despite all these work problems, several ideological factors combine to thwart the growth of class consciousness among Korean immigrant workers. These include fears about joining labor unions; the Korean "familism" that permeates organizations, including small businesses; and the strong desire by many workers to start their own businesses. As Safa analyzed, job instability among women garment workers also appears to have weakened their resolve and their capacity for collective action (1987: 265).

The ideology of establishing one's own small business as the route to success is prevalent in the Korean American community. Immigrants hear repeatedly that, if one works hard, beginning one's own business is almost guaranteed. Therefore, an immigrant considers working for another Korean to be a transitional status. By the late 1980s, however, the goal was more likely to remain a dream than a reality. Today, new Korean immigrants arrive in a different economic context, and more and more will remain workers despite their American dream.

Today, a more complex hierarchical structure seems to be emerging in the Korean community. Garment factories or vegetable stands have managers who are neither owners nor workers; at Korean restaurants, there are chefs and skilled workers above unskilled kitchen workers and waitresses. In Korean construction firms, there are skilled and unskilled workers. Cab drivers may be either self-employed or work for a Korean cab company. Among the several hundred "Koreatown" wholesalers in Manhattan is an elite group of large, capital-rich importers, some of whom own factories in Korea and supply Korean small businesses throughout New York City and the rest of the United States. Still, in Queens, the ideology of anjong remains strong among professionals and workers as well as small business proprietors. Other occupations are still defined as transitional to reaching the goal of small business ownership.

6. *Korea Times Los Angeles* carried an article titled, "Eat Pork against Heavy Metal Poisoning or Dust" and claimed that "you can also clean rusted brassware by rubbing it with lard" (May [date missing] 1993).

PART II

# Consequences of Gravitation to Small Business

# [4]

# Establishment and the
# Domestic Cycle

In this chapter, I examine the impact of immigrant small business on the organization of domestic life. As Korean immigrants seek to realize their American dream as self-employed small business proprietors, they discover that one of the most important means to success is the use of family and kin labor. Because most immigrants begin their businesses with limited capital, the labor of family members is critical. Most scholars have discussed the Korean immigrant family in relation to either the tradition/modernity debate or an acculturation perspective. Others have paid more attention to changing gender relations in the Korean immigrant family (see Chapter 5). Min (1988b) is exceptional in pointing out the importance of the family in explaining so-called successful entrepreneurship. He does not, however, explain the critical role that family labor plays in small businesses throughout the entire establishment process.

Overall, studies of the Korean immigrant family have been largely structural-functional, ignoring internal family dynamics and developmental processes. The functionalist model tends to treat social change as a succession of structures and emphasizes the description and ordering of structural types (A. Smith 1973: 30). Hence, most empirical research is preoccupied with identifying elements of family structure and concomitant value systems as either continuations of tradition or developments of the modern system but do not explore how any transition is occurring or how modern and traditional elements are related. Such research often assumes that the Korean family, sooner or later, becomes similar to the American family as a part of a larger process of acculturation. Min (1988b) states that in many of its characteristics the Korean American family is

[71]

more traditional than the American family but more modern than the family in Korea. By the logic of his criteria, however, the Korean American family is, in fact, more modern than even the American family. Korean American women have a higher labor force participation rate and a lower fertility rate than other American women. Yet these statistics need to be understood in relation to household transformations over the anjŏng or establishment cycle.

## Historical Studies of the Korean Family

Historical evidence shows that the major features of the traditional family and kinship system in Korea did not emerge until after 1600 and did not take root, even among the elite, until well into the eighteenth century. For example, it was not until the eighteenth century that daughters were excluded from an equal share of inheritance of family property (K. K. Lee 1977: 360–89). Before this traditional system was well established, men often lived with their wives' families (Deuchler 1977: 15–17).

The family as the basic unit of society is called *chip* in Korean.[1] In its most common usage, the chip is a household unit formed of agnatic members who may or may not share a residence but have some moral obligation to collective income pooling and a claim to collective consumption (Yoon 1989: 79). The chip as a household (*ho* in legal terms) was a basic political and administrative unit of the local community and the larger society from the Chosun dynasty through the colonial period (the fourteenth through the twentieth centuries) (T. Kim 1969: 328). Yet the chip was not exactly a household or a self-liquidating domestic group created by conjugal union and dissolved by divorce or death. According to Tu-hon Kim, "the Korean word chip signifies more than the house. It means the family (*ka*), which exists conceptually. It is a collectivity of common life and a chain of ancestors and descendants. Chip is not a house or household or home. It is more than that and includes family manners, family ways, family teachings, family laws, family customs, family estate, family property, and family lineage and so on" (1969: 643, quoted in E. Yi 1993: 97).

On his marriage, the eldest son brought his wife into the household and continued to live with his parents and unmarried siblings. He inherited ancestral rituals and the largest share of family property. The younger sons

1. *Chip* is the Korean indigenous term corresponding to the Chinese character that symbolizes family, *ka*.

and their wives remained junior members of the chip. They were expected to set up households of their own within a few years of marriage and start a branch family line (K. K. Lee 1975: 218; Sorensen 1981: 313; Janelli and Janelli 1982: 29, 104–6; E. Yi 1993: 103). The younger sons' households were called "little houses" (*chagŭn chip*); and the eldest son's household, which was also the parents' household, was called "big house" (*kŭn chip*). This branching was called *punga*, which meant "division of the house."

The big house and the little house(s) formed a solitary group, which was also called chip (K. K. Lee 1975; Janelli and Janelli 1982; E. Yi 1993). When the younger sons established their own households, they were usually located close to the eldest son's household (kŭn chip) in the same village. The eldest brother represented the chip, which included the younger sons' "little chip" in the wider kin group and had the prerogative to perform ancestral rituals (*chesa*). The eldest son supported aged parents and looked out for younger siblings.

For the Korean immigrants I studied, households were larger and more inclusive than the number of family members resident within them. For 90 households, membership varied from one to seven individuals; the mean household size was 4.2. The mean family size was 3.7. Of my 91 informants, 17 lived with people who were not family members. The modal forms of household organization included 57 composed solely of nuclear families (husband and wife with or without children), and 17 stem families (two married couples of two adjacent generations with or without other unmarried children). See the Appendix for more information on these households. Adult couples with young children make up the typical post-1965 immigrant family. From a demographic sense, the structure of the Korean immigrant family appears to be more stable than that of other American families. In my study (based on census information), the percentage of children under eighteen living with both parents was 89.4 percent for Koreans compared to 82.9 percent for whites and 45.4 percent for blacks. Often a grandparent or grandparents lived with the immigrant family or close by.

Statistics, however, do not tell what is actually going on inside the Korean immigrant household as it passes through the stages of business establishment. Sorensen, in discussing the developmental cycle of Korean and Japanese traditional families, notes that "any particular sequence of structural types . . . was not a fundamental feature of the system, but was rather the result of the intersection of principles of family organization with demographic and economic variables. The average life span, age at marriage, and fertility of marriage affected which of the culturally allowed structural possibilities would actually be realized" (1984: 310–11).[2] I develop this framework by emphasizing that the Korean immigrant household consists of more than demographic and economic variables.

As Korean households in Queens metamorphose, they "exist within a political-economic context of employment structures, relations to the control of production, and classes" (Sanjek 1982: 99). Small business formation and the stratification associated with it mold the Korean American household in terms of form and composition and produce a predictable, culturally recognized set of transformations, similar to a snake shedding its skin in autumn. Korean immigrant families and households continuously reorganize according to the necessities of immigrant life. Family and kin, even those who were not close in Korea, tend at first to live together. Over time, individual family members leave to form new households by marrying or joining another family. According to American immigration law, people can come to the United States if they have relatives here or a sponsor. Because migration for Koreans is normally a family decision, not an individual one, it has been typical for a couple in their twenties or thirties to bring their children and later invite their parents and siblings to the United States. Koreans who come to America have no choice but to rely on family members in a foreign environment. Even in the two-decade-old Korean community of New York, there are few channels other than family, kin, or friends to which a recent immigrant can turn for help.

We must also relate immigrant household forms to housing conditions. Many immigrants live in apartments or rent single-family homes. In Korea, many of these middle-class immigrants remember that it was more common to live in private houses.[3] Moreover, because immigrants invest more money in business than in housing, the proportion of home ownership is lower for Korean immigrants than for Americans in general. In Korea it is possible to find housing by *chŏnse*—that is, by paying a large refundable deposit on occupancy but without monthly rent. Such arrangements are not possible in America.

American housing differs from Korean housing in construction style and room arrangement. Immigrants who lived in apartment buildings in

2. For studies of family developmental cycles in Korea, see Sorensen (1988) and Janelli and Janelli (1982).

3. In reality, it is increasingly popular for middle-class Koreans to live in apartment complexes. See Un-shil Kim's dissertation (1993) regarding lives in an apartment complex.

Korea are disappointed by the small size and poor maintenance of apartment buildings in Queens. They find walls are thin compared to those in Korea. The smaller housing impedes the traditional norm of co-residential living for two or three generations of people. Few find it comfortable to live together in a small space and still maintain proper social distances. In addition, they often find themselves living with non-kin roommates or housemates. Yet even non-kin roommates share cooking, dishwashing, cleaning, and other tasks. In these arrangements, people apply the standards of Korean domestic organization.

The Korean notion of household co-residence implies the sharing of meals, no matter how many families constitute a household. In the American context, immigrants organize households of unmarried persons who share all domestic activities. Often the oldest household member is responsible for paying rent and making decisions about other household expenses. Kin-related roommates may share finances; but if a male immigrant works for his kin without pay but with the promise of support for the establishment of his own business, he will be given free room and board. One of my informants co-residing with his sister did not pay rent while he worked for her husband in the Bronx. After he found a job on his own in Manhattan, however, he was expected to pay his sister rent for the room. (Nevertheless, he is still pressured to help his brother-in-law in the business after he finishes his own job.) Meals for Koreans involved in small business, either as employers or employees, are taken at the workplace. Many co-workers thus share three meals a day (see Appendix).

My data show that most immigrants work for kin members during the initial settlement period. This creates a more exacting, but also more ambiguous, work situation for kin than it does for paid workers. New kin employees are trying to save for themselves, hoping to gain business information and assistance from their relative-employer. Once independent, the former employee will in turn establish a labor supply of his own kin members.

For Korean immigrants in Queens, the organization of domestic life is connected fundamentally to their new activities in small business. Yet try as they may, only a few households are able to complete the full cycle of establishment (that is, owning one's own business; bringing parents and siblings from Korea; establishing a home in the suburbs; sending children to good schools; marrying children to fellow Koreans). Many are not able to pass through all of the stages due to business failure, a mismatch between their labor needs and the available pool of relatives and immigration law, expenses for education, and other factors. The critical question for each immigrant is, how soon can he start his own business? When a man invites a family member to the United States, he must be ready to accommodate him or her. This decision will be influenced by how established he is and how this is perceived and evaluated by fellow Koreans.

A woman immigrant who is single and has been unable to find a spouse in Korea is forced to search for a husband in New York. (Single women immigrants are said to be contaminated by American ideas and are less welcome as wives by men in Korea.) After marriage, the couple enters a stage similar to that experienced by single men. In this case, however (and also for war brides married to Americans), the wife plays the more important role through chain migration in deciding which relatives are going to be sponsored and when. One reason for this enhanced power of women is that more Korean immigrant women than men hold U.S. citizenship. Until 1976, women, primarily as nurses and war brides, migrated in greater numbers than men and initiated the developmental cycle. In recent years, however, more single men have been initiating the cycle. In either case, after several years of struggle, when the couple feels secure, they invite either or both sets of parents. Next, the parents invite their other children, the siblings of the initiators of the cycle. These siblings move out into their own households as soon as they marry. (This follows Korean ideals of household composition.)

The parents tend to go through periods of residence in each of their adult children's homes, forming stem households. This pattern differs dramatically from the cultural norm in Korea, where parents live with the eldest son. As each child arrives in the United States and marries, the parents may move into the new household. In many cases, parents rotate first through the homes of their daughters, then the third and second sons, and finally the eldest son. This sequence reflects the order in which the children have immigrated and has much to do with marital status, army service, educational status, and each child's cultural orientation toward American life. It is easier to invite children who are unmarried yet have finished army service in Korea. Those who are most reluctant to emigrate to America, frequently older siblings, tend to come last if at all. Daughters usually come first, and the eldest son is the last to emigrate, often due to ancestor worship duties.

Domestic decisions about household composition and location are based on the varying ideological understandings of each generation and its experiences in Korea and America. In Korea the eldest son often migrates first from the countryside to the urban areas for higher education. Later other siblings join him; and after these siblings have married, their parents move from the countryside to live with their urban-based children. In urban Korea the daughter's family may try to live near her parents' household, but in America it is the parents who are eager to live with their daughter. Their daughter-in-law is often reluctant to accommodate her immigrant parents-in-law in her new house.

In this context, the American welfare system may play an important role in domestic decisions. In the United States, unlike Korea, parents do not have to live with their married children to guarantee their support in old age. With SSI (Supplemental Security Income) or housing in a senior citizen residence, elderly parents may remain in the Queens Korean community, living by themselves even after their children achieve suburban establishment. Contrary to their original intentions, neither parents nor children may feel comfortable living together over a long period of time, because of the smaller living space in U.S. apartments, parents' dislike of suburban isolation, or changed expectations from both sides. Even when the original couple is about to buy a roomy house in suburban Long Island or Bayside, the parents may prefer the company of other elderly Koreans and the convenience of shopping and social life in Flushing or Elmhurst, where newly immigrating Koreans continue to arrive. As parents living independently, they may rely on a combination of welfare, their children's support, and their own employment. When they do live with children, parents in the United States tend to live in their daughters' households.

At the beginning stage, kin and families tend to cooperate with each other; but as each family member establishes his or her own business and forms an independent household, cooperation decreases. Nevertheless, I have come across few Korean families in which *all* the children are fully established. It is common for parents to keep moving to the households of their less established children, usually providing child care and other household services.

## Five Stages in the Cycle of Establishment

In this and the following sections I explore in more detail the stages that the Korean American household passes through in its American transformation. As they struggle to realize their dream, Korean immigrants elaborate on the key symbol of establishment (anjŏng). As if composing their own Horatio Alger myth, they develop a detailed scenario for how establishment occurs. In this quest, however, each immigrant seeks to move through five successive stages in a domestic organization cycle. At each stage, persons are influenced by opinions of others and their own evaluation of whether they are able to move on to the next stage. Serious discussions are held to analyze whether a man or a woman—and later a couple—are doing well enough to get married, have babies, invite parents and siblings from Korea, buy a business, buy a house, financially support their parents, or sponsor other relatives.

For a single man, anjŏng primarily means marriage and beginning a family. At the next stage, for a couple, anjŏng means establishing their own business. By the time a couple is operating business successfully, anjŏng means having children and inviting parents from Korea to join them in America. At the final stage, anjŏng means buying a house in a good suburban neighborhood, possibly sending their children to Ivy League schools, and marrying their children to fellow Koreans.

## Single Life

Here being single means those who are single due to immigrant circumstances. For instance, even a married man is called an "L.A. bachelor" (ch'onggak) if his family is not in the United States. Being single also means not having established one's own business. In my fieldwork, seventeen of the households were at this stage of establishment.

Mr. Lee works at a grocery in Elmhurst and lives in Sunnyside. A community college graduate, he came to America in 1983 for further study and stayed. He lives with four male roommates, all high school graduates, in a two-bedroom apartment. He occupies the living room, which has no curtain for privacy, and pays $90 a month toward the rent. Roommate A is fifty years old, roommate B is forty-one, roommate C is forty, and roommate D is thirty. Mr. Lee is twenty-seven years old and unmarried. He eats rice and *kimch'i* at home for breakfast and eats both lunch and dinner, mostly Western food, at the grocery where he works. His employer is his mother's sister's husband. At home, the oldest roommate does most of the cooking. Other housework, such as dishwashing and cleaning, is done by each roommate in turn. No one does any ironing. Mr. Lee said: "I never did housework in Korea, as my family members did it for me. Here, as it is necessary to do it, I feel annoyed, sometimes reluctant to do it."

Mr. Yun is forty. He came to America in 1982 and lives in Corona, where he is a manager at a vegetable stand. He lives in a rooming house— four very small rooms for rent. His wife, two daughters, and a son are still in Seoul. He stated: I take *namyŏn* [instant noodles] with my colleagues at work and eat excellent Korean food for lunch. I either cook at home or eat takeout food for dinner. Often my colleagues and I get together to drink after work. As I do all my housework, because of my situation, I think Korea is more convenient for me. Here, I do not even eat properly. However, I admit that household facilities are more convenient here." Most of the families of these men are still in Korea. Many of the men are undocumented. But whether they come legally or not, they dream of establishment. Until they are recognized by other Koreans as having made enough money, they cannot think about conjugal co-residence or marriage. When single people are better established, others come to them with marriage proposals or at least are eager to introduce women as possible spouses, often at church. The men sometimes delay marriage until they have begun their own businesses. Until then, they are very clear about working and saving money. Once a man is married, however, he is considered trustworthy for business loans.

Those single immigrants who are married but who left their families in Korea belong to varying age cohorts. Their situation is worse than that of the unmarried men because they are under more pressure to send back money to Korea to support their family members. In some cases they send virtually all they make, leading very frugal lives alone in America. Even when a man is able to invite his family here, he must usually go through long period of single life first. He will wait until he and others feel he is well enough established.

With no women available to do their housework, for the first time in their lives single Korean men have to do dishes, clean kitchens and bathrooms, vacuum, dispose of garbage, and wash laundry. These tasks are conducted either individually or by a division of male household labor. As a result, there is both a growth in independence for men, who now handle housework, and a rising communal life-style among them. To a Korean woman, it is intriguing that single Korean men can develop these domestic skills relatively easily, often as a result of their unique living situations. Some older men or young single males have confessed that, although they started to do housework out of necessity, they found it interesting, a new field to plow. At the same time, many single men do rely on instant food such as namyŏn or buy prepared foods at Korean groceries. Often single men eat most of their meals at work. To a lesser extent, this applies to single women too. But single women give little attention to cooking for themselves and often skip meals. Some women informants stated that, when their husbands are away from home, they neglect to cook or eat very simply.[4]

To conclude, this first stage of domestic organization is common among workers, particularly men, and those who have not lived long in America. People at this stage are struggling to save money. They are eager to move on to the next stage by inviting family members from Korea. If they are not married, they are under social pressure from family and the community to prepare themselves to marry.

## Married Couples

According to E. Yi (1993), at the heart of the conceptualization of chip as an entity in Korea is a hierarchical division of two gendered spheres: the outside, which represents the family to larger society—the male domain, and the inside, the female domain. The husband is called outside master and the wife inside master. This hierarchical division is still found in Korea among urban middle-class families.

My study, in which thirteen households were at the married-couple stage of establishment, shows a disruption of this cultural rule. Regardless of gender, most Korean immigrants are engaged in so-called outside activities, such as small businesses. In addition, there seems to be some change in the way they conduct inside activities. Mr. Pi is a Yellow Cab driver in his early thirties. His wife is a waitress at a Korean restaurant. They live in a one-bedroom apartment in Elmhurst. It is two years since he immigrated to the United States at his wife's invitation, after they fell in love and married in Korea. His wife came to America through her sister's invitation three years earlier. According to Mr. Pi, "while I work from five in the evening to five in the morning, my wife works from eleven in the morning until eleven at night. We therefore have little time to see each other. As another consequence of this busy schedule, I also participate in housework, at least cooking rice and warming up dishes already prepared.

4. Many Korean women think of cooking and preparing meals for other family members but not for themselves, which they think is too selfish.

I also wash dishes. The rest of the housework, such as cleaning, is done by my wife."

Generally, the burden of housework is left to the wives. Men participate in meal preparation as far as cooking rice, a fairly easy task. In America most of my interviewees cook rice in an electric rice cooker, while in Korea they use the rice cooker only to keep rice warm. Here technology helps those men who share housework. For dishwashing, some women get help from husbands because it is considered more of man's job than cooking is. But the male contribution will decrease when there are other female family or kin members in the household.

In my study of Queens Korean conjugal households, 61 percent of ironing was done by women only; 11 percent by men only; and 25 percent by both, although male informants made comments such as "Do you think we need to iron? We wear only casual work clothes here. Unlike Korea, I hardly have any need to do ironing. Here it is only when I go to church on Sunday that I have a chance to dress up." Washing clothes is done exclusively by women in 53 percent of the households, in 9 percent by men, and in 35 percent by both. About 63 percent do laundry in public places such as laundromats or basement laundry rooms in apartment houses, and 37 percent do it at home. It is a new experience for immigrants to use public laundromats, which are not yet available in Korea.

At this stage both husband and wife are eager to work as hard as possible and to save for their future small business. As a result, some couples leave their children in Korea or with other more or less established relatives in the United States. Others delay having babies until they feel themselves established here. This stage is as difficult as any other for wives, who must do most of the housework. Women do not yet have any help from other family members or kin. It is a much more difficult stage than the first years of marriage in Korea, where women, mostly those of the middle class, get housework assistance by employing household workers as well as help from nearby family or kin.[5]

### Couples with Children

In my fieldwork, thirty-six households were at this stage of establishment. Mr. Paik, for example, is in his mid-forties. He came to America in

5. Assistance from kin may come also in the form of instruction. I owe this observation to Laurel Kendall.

1972 as the manager of a New York branch of a Korean company. In 1976 his wife joined him. After that they lived in Elmhurst for three years and now live in New Jersey. Every Sunday they return to their old neighborhood to worship. They run a fish market and live in a rented apartment. In addition, Mr. Paik owns a vegetable stand that he has asked his brother-in-law to run for him. At home, he said: "most of the housework is done by my wife. My children do the dishes and help their mother with laundry. We have three daughters—fourteen, thirteen, and three years old—and a one-year-old son. On weekends our children help us in the store. We give them an allowance. As far as day care is concerned, we pay the Korean Episcopal Church in our neighborhood $230 a month, and they pick up our three-year-old daughter. We also hire a Korean baby-sitting lady to take care of our one-year-old baby, paying her $400 a month."

Families at this stage also include some who immigrated to America with their children. If children are very young, families who have their own business can afford to hire a baby-sitter. In other cases, the parents of the couple come to visit from Korea and become baby-sitters. Sometimes children stay with other relatives in America who are established enough to take care of them. Older children who live with their parents contribute their labor to the family business in the ever-more-competitive conditions of Korean immigrant life.

My 36 families at this stage included 14 families who had two children, 13 families with three children, 7 families with one child, and 2 families with more than three children. These numbers accord well with the substantial drop in fertility that accompanies Korean immigration. The 1980 U.S. census reported 2,097 children per 1,000 Korean immigrant women between the ages of thirty-five and forty-four. The comparable figure for women of this age group in Korea is 4,036. (For native-born American women the figure was 2,652.) In other words, a Korean immigrant woman has an average of two children in comparison to four children for the woman who remains in Korea.[6] The rate, however, is also dropping in Korea (see U. Kim 1993).

Why the lower fertility rate of Korean immigrants? Min (1988b) relates this to two factors. First, immigrants are in many ways a select group whose fertility would remain lower than average even if they remained in Korea. Second, the difficulties of adjustment for immigrants is a restrictive

6. In Korea, the number of children for each married woman has now been reduced to fewer than two.

force on fertility. These two factors undoubtedly play a role, but we also need to recognize immigrants' quest for establishment and their desire to realize the Korean American dream. Many immigrants will not have babies until they become more established. And those who already have children may leave them with their parents in Korea, postponing a united living arrangement (and more children) until a later stage of establishment is reached.

The impact of this quest for establishment on family life is greatest when we consider the use of child labor by immigrant entrepreneurs. In Korea, children in middle- and upper-class households (including college students) are prohibited from doing anything beyond their studies. In America, however, parents find themselves facing a different norm. They see American parents paying their children for their labor (in allowances or rewards for housework). They also see other Korean immigrants use their children's labor as a simple and cost-free way to save wage expenses in businesses. A few immigrants adopt an orphan or other people's children for the specific purposes of using their labor in small business.

Because they usually speak English better than their parents do, Korean American children play a key role in family businesses. In some cases, the youngster takes care of the cash register after school and on weekends while the middle-aged parents manage other store activities (such as attending fruits and vegetables, in the case of a greengrocery) and the grandmother remains in the kitchen behind the store. In some extreme cases, parents force their children to work long hours in the store because they are obsessed with the idea of making money quickly and accelerating their establishment. Still, there are other parents who do not want their children to do anything other than study.

Because many parents at this stage are so preoccupied with business, they have limited time, energy, or emotional reserve to give to their children. In middle-class families in Korea, the mother stays home and takes care of the children. In the United States, it becomes difficult for parents even to communicate with their children because of hard work and long hours, not to mention the language barrier. Another factor that affects the parent-child relationship is parents' expectation that teachers should educate their children in both knowledge and morality. In Korea, teachers are expected to do so, following Confucian influences. Immigrant parents are soon disappointed by the lack of moral education provided in American schools. To make matters worse, parents tend to lose authority over and respect from their children because they have to rely on them for English-Korean translation.

As far as daytime baby-sitting and child care are concerned, parents are dependent wholly on elderly Korean women. If they cannot afford to hire a baby-sitter and do not have their own mothers to help out, the couple brings the children to the shop. In a few extreme cases, my informants reported they saw parents give their babies sleeping pills and leave them in a van while they worked. I personally observed children playing at a beauty salon and in a restaurant.

Child care outside the immediate household is best conducted within the kin network. Babies or young children are taken care of by the wife's mother or mother-in-law (see plate 4) or by non-kin older women encountered through kin connections. Some also send their children to kin in Korea, usually their mother or mother-in-law or a brother or sister. The few paid Korean baby-sitters are mostly old women from the local community. Some parents prefer old men as baby-sitters for boys. Most baby-sitters live nearby. Some move in as a member of the household. If they live with their husbands, old women tend to confine child care to their grandchildren. But if they are widows, they tend to work as paid baby-sitters. This situation is new to Koreans; in Korea no elderly women earn their livelihood in baby-sitting. The only thing that comes close to this situation are those middle- or upper-class households that hire a young woman *yumo* (nanny), *ch'anmo* (cook), or *sikmo* (household worker).[7]

In my interviews, I asked about the specifics of child-care arrangements, jobs such as dressing, feeding, bathing, putting to bed, disciplining, supervising homework, and giving allowances. Of course, many older children do these tasks themselves, but almost half of child-care work is done by the children's mothers. The other persons who do child-care tasks are primarily co-resident paternal or maternal grandmothers. Fathers assist to a lesser degree. One-third of my interviewees still needed some assistance in their child-care arrangements. I suspect that in America, because of language and cultural problems, more husbands are concerned about their children's education than they would be in Korea. Despite this trend, monitoring homework is done mostly by mothers.

Giving an allowance is something new to most Korean immigrants. Some see it as a cold and calculating practice. They think that it is wrong

7. It has become increasingly difficult to hire women for domestic work. By the late 1970s, the practice had disappeared.

*Plate 4.* Elderly woman carrying her grandchild outside an apartment complex. Photo author

to give children money in this way because it develops a financial side to the parent-child relationship. Others try to adopt this American custom with the hope that their children will learn how to manage finances. Allowances are mostly given by the mother. Even in Korea, it is usually the wife who is in charge of family finances, a practice that seems to continue in America. Men here will say that the paycheck is too small for them to deal with or that women are inherently good at money matters.

As I mentioned in Chapter 2, in contemporary Korean society one's social status is largely determined by one's educational attainment. It is a thoroughly internalized belief that more educated people deserve better treatment than less educated ones. Academic achievement has practical importance for launching a successful career, although this is largely restricted to males. The better the university a child attends, the more prestigious a company (*chaebŏl*) he is likely to work for. Hence, the child's academic performance is extremely important, not only for the child's future career but also for the status of the family. When the child fails to enter a good college, the parents lose face.

To which schools do my sixty-one Queens Korean parent informants send their children? About 45 percent send them to public schools, 30 percent to nonreligious private schools, and 25 percent to parochial schools. Some scholars state that, because college in Korea is very expensive, many Koreans immigrate to the United States to provide their children with opportunities for higher education (Hurh and Kim 1979; Min 1988). Some people pay $30,000 or $40,000 for their children's education at elite colleges.

According to the 1980 census, Koreans show the highest level of suburban residence of *all* ethnic groups. They are eager to buy houses in affluent suburban areas where they can send their children to private schools to prepare them better for good colleges. Some who send their children to parochial schools (in particular, Roman Catholic schools) are Protestants, but they believe such institutions emphasize moral education. A few families also send their children to after-school instruction at Buddhist temples even though they are Protestants. This decision is made out of the conviction that Buddhist education imparts training in Korean culture, including its moral values.

Mr. Um is critical of Korean children in America; he feels that they do not seem to pay attention to keeping the language alive: "I see children who came here at the age of four or five who, when they are seven years old, have already forgotten Korean. Chinese children first of all try to learn Chinese, and then, later, English. If our knee-high generation does not speak Korean, they won't get jobs at American workplaces looking for bilingual staff." Mr. Kong points out what he feels are the bad effects of Americanization on children: "Unlike Korean children, American or Korean American children do not appreciate what parents do for them, supporting their studies and so on. They think of it just as a parental duty." He is furious about his own son's attitudes. Although he works hard to support his son, his son says, "You supported me because you are supposed to do so. That's your matter; I have nothing to do with that." Mrs. Shin balances her views with a sense of the difficulties that Korean children go through at school: "Adults here do not seem to change a lot. But children here have lots of problems: their parents are always at work; they do not know how to deal with the stresses coming from their new life in America. They begin to make bad friends and may not pay attention to their studies."

## Families with Co-Resident Adult Relatives

Most households with co-resident adult relatives are characterized by a division of labor. Twenty-seven of the households were at this stage of establishment. For example, Mrs. Kim and her husband are pharmacists. They live in Elmhurst with their nine-year-old daughter and Mrs. Kim's sixty-one-year-old mother. Her mother does baby-sitting and most of the cooking. Her husband does dishes, most of the ironing, and occasionally the laundry. Most housecleaning is done by Mrs. Kim or her mother. "Before my mother came, my husband used to cook simple things that required boiling water and do the dishwashing. But now, he does less and less."

Mr. Choi, in his late thirties, runs a fish market in Washington Heights, Manhattan. He also bought a shoe repair shop in the Bronx for his father-in-law to run with a Latin American helper in order to earn pocket money. He lives in a rented apartment in Sunnyside with his wife, two sons, and his parents-in-law. Mr. Choi came to America in 1974, his wife in 1980, his parents-in-law in 1982. Most housework is done by his wife or his mother-in-law; he or his father-in-law take out the garbage. His wife and his mother-in-law do laundry and together take care of the four-year-old boy and the one-year-old baby.

Some couples residing with children and co-resident relatives are closer to establishment than others without such arrangements. In some cases, a couple may invite their parents to join them even before their first child is born. Others invite siblings, uncles, or aunts after children are in their teens and the couple's parents already have been sponsored. By this stage, the family already has a business. In some cases, other brothers and sisters are even more established and own houses.

In these cases, we see Korean families becoming more complex, adding both lineal and collateral household members. The relationship between grandparents and grandchildren is particularly important for those who are able to reach this stage of the domestic cycle. Most grandparents do baby-sitting; only 25 percent do not. In addition, grandparents contribute housework and in some cases work in family business. For households at this stage, only 3 percent of baby-sitters are non-kin among my informants, and none used formal day-care centers. Mothers preferred grandparent baby-sitters; however, the women who do this work complain that they are forced to take care of their grandchildren and that other people try to exploit them by not paying decent wages for their services. Another significant problem is generational difference between a Korean mother-in-law or mother (or elderly sitters) and daughters who have adopted American child-care standards. In families with adult relatives, cooking is still mostly done by women. In only 7 percent of such households do men participate at all. The women involved are mothers, grandmothers, sisters, daughters, and aunts. Clearly housework is managed by more women than the wife-mother.

During my research, many informants read their own meanings into my questions about housework and gender. A few even seemed to be embarrassed. More often than not, while women seemed to take pride in answering questions about housework, men hurried to explain why they could not do more. For instance, when I was interviewing Mrs. Chung in front of male household members, she seemed to be proud of her household work. The men were subdued. Then they started to argue about who was or was not committed to a democratic division of household labor. I didn't know what to say. Although I was primarily interested in learning the facts, the informants went beyond merely answering the questions. They were very sensitive about their own norms or ideals.

Many women seemed to feel that these questions put them in a good light. And both men and women knew that I was a woman and would be writing about Koreans in America for a broader audience. But a few women did not understand why I asked such questions. In their mind, it is only to be expected that women do the housework, especially cooking. In other cases, a few men explained why it was *less* difficult for them to contribute to housework in America than in Korea. According to them, Korean culture and the arrangement of housing there made it difficult for men to do so. In Korea, most men get together with their colleagues after work, and they have little time to help their wives or mothers. In addition, the kitchen facilities in Korea made it less convenient for men to help their wives. They contend that here in America the facilities make it easier for men to take part in housework.

In a mail survey study of men's changing family roles, Ahn (1986) compared families in Korea with immigrant families in the New York metropolitan area. He found that immigrant husbands' increased participation in household work was correlated with their wives' employment outside the home and the lesser availability of other adult females in these households. My research certainly confirms this. Ahn concluded that the use of American-style housework technology was not significantly related to husbands' housework before or after immigration. He also concluded that husbands' Western values had a stronger impact on housework participation in Korea than in the United States.

In general, I found that males of lower socioeconomic status tend to do more housework, principally because they live alone or in male-only households. Otherwise, I could see little difference in terms of any criteria other than age or family developmental-cycle stage. Some elderly men and single men confessed that, even though they started to do housework out of necessity, they found it satisfying, a new challenge for them. This scenario might arise in households where the labor of older women is more valued in the family business than in the household, leaving elderly males alone at home to do the necessary housework.

Gendered division of labor is somewhat spatialized. While the kitchen and the bathroom are the female domain, the garage is considered the male domain. In these households vacuuming is done by men more than any other category of housework (see Appendix).[8] Still, in 42 percent of households vacuuming is done by only women and in 37 percent only by men. I suspect the reason explaining why vacuuming is done more frequently by men than other tasks are is related to traditional notions of male and female roles. Vacuuming is regarded as a job needing physical strength and is machine-related, factors both considered more typical of men's work than women's.

Even though a bathroom is cleaned after each use by family members democratically, it is women who in most cases sweep up hairs or scrub the bathtub. Heavy cleaning of the sink, bathroom floor, and bathtub is done by the housewife more often than by other household members. Some of my informants recalled interesting episodes regarding Korean use of American bathrooms. One man remembers how he regularly flooded the bathroom because at first he washed his body outside the bathtub as he used to in Korea. On the other hand, I heard stories about Korean American children who, while visiting Korea during the 1970s, refused to eat out due to their fear of going into Korean-style bathrooms.

## Established Families and the Korean Elderly

When a family becomes established enough to buy a house, there is usually a change in the living arrangements of co-resident household members. In many cases, the elderly grandparents' generation moves out to live independently. My research was conducted in the core Queens

8. Hurh and Kim found in their survey of Koreans in Los Angeles that, in one-half or more of the families, it is the wife who actually bears the heavy burden of performing four tasks: grocery shopping, housekeeping, laundry, and dishwashing. "In two task items, disposal of garbage and management of family budget, the burden of performance is evenly distributed between the husband and wife, although they are not so expected" (1980: 211).

areas of Korean settlement, so I did not include established families in suburbs. I did, however, learn about their lives from those who continued to maintain businesses and attend church in Elmhurst and nearby areas and from their elderly parents.

When adult children buy a house in a suburban neighborhood of Queens, the family group sometimes continues to live together. If the house is in New Jersey or on Long Island, however, where there are few other Korean elders, the elderly face a big decision—to put up with suburban isolation or live by themselves in a rented apartment, cooperative housing, or a condominium. Sometimes another choice is to move in with other adult children who are not yet established and live in Elmhurst, Woodside, or Flushing.

Each kin-connected household may be in a different stage of establishment. But for all households cultural values of filial piety emphasize that children should care for parents at home. Ideally, when a father reaches age sixty, the eldest son assumes responsibility for the patrilineal stem-family estate and ancestor worship (Janelli and Janelli 1982; K. K. Lee 1975, 1984). Neglect of parents is considered immoral, a breach of traditional values (J. Choi 1964; J. Park 1975). A 1981 Asan Foundation study in South Korea found that only 4 percent of the elderly lived alone and 93 percent lived with family members (Koh and Bell 1987). Another study found that 79 percent of South Korean elders lived with their adult children (Park et al. 1984). Korean immigrants bring with them cultural values that stress multigenerational residence, especially for the elderly.

Kiefer et al. (1985) studied 50 elderly Korean immigrants in San Francisco using both open-ended interviews and psychological assessments of morale, self-concept, and symptomatology. In terms of residential arrangements, they found that "elders living in two- and three-generation households often had problems of crowding, overwork, and strained social relationships, yet they tended to exhibit more positive morale and better self concept than those who lived alone or with a spouse only. Apparently the stresses of social life were less devastating than the stresses of loneliness, helplessness, uselessness and boredom" (1985: 480). Koh and Bell (1987) interviewed 151 Korean elders in New York City, asking about their living arrangements, service needs, and formal and informal social support. The major problems they identified were "lack of proficiency in the English language; health conditions; loneliness; transportation; income; and housing" (1987: 60). While 82 percent had adult children living in New York City, only 51 percent resided with their children. The rest lived alone, with a spouse, or with non-kin.[9] Unlike the situation in Korea, but like that of older people in America in general, the majority actually *preferred* to live alone regardless of current residence patterns (Troll et al. 1979). Most also had weekly telephone contact with or received visits from their adult children. These studies confirm that residence patterns in the United States are diverging from cultural practices in Korea.

My research in Queens revealed considerable cultural disruption for many elderly immigrants. Some felt useless because they were not employed as they were in Korea. They found their advice unwanted, and less respect was paid to them by the younger generations. They were disappointed to see "knee-high" and second-generation youth smoking and acting loose. With longer residence in the United States, however, they have come to regard their immigrant lives positively.

Many immigrants are critical of how Americans treat the elderly. Mr. Paik, a store employee in his twenties, said: "When I was living in Sunnyside, all of a sudden I no longer saw the white old man who lived near me. At his funeral, no one showed up. Next to my apartment, when the super rang the bell, another old man was found dead. How horrible it is! The American old people seem to lead very lonely lives. Of course, that's partly due to the American social structure and partly because those old people want to do so. However, I know that in fact the elderly want to be with someone."

In immigrant households, the most difficult relationship is between grandparents and grandchildren. While the grandparents speak only Korean, grandchildren speak only English. There is a communications breakdown. The grandparents also have problems with their own children, including disputes provoked by the traditionally volatile mother-in-law and daughter-in-law relationship (see Chapter 5). Although adult children sponsor their parents' immigration in order to live together and take care of them in their old age, all generations encounter difficulties living together in America. Nevertheless, some elderly are sympathetic toward their children who are fully occupied in small business activities.

I identify four strategies by which elderly Koreans try to make the best

9. Immigrants who are sixty-five years old and over constitute only 2.6 percent of total recent Korean immigrants (U.S. Bureau of the Census 1984: 12), whereas the elderly category forms 3.9 percent of the South Korean general population (Korean National Bureau of Statistics 1984: 41). Koh and Bell report that in New York City 19 percent of Korean elderly people live alone and another 25 percent live only with their spouses (1987: 66–71).

of their lives during this final stage of the domestic cycle, with each strategy dependent on the particular individual's access to friends and public services. First, some continue to live in three-generation families, as in Mr. Pang's household. He is a medical technician living in Elmhurst with his wife, three children, and his seventy-six-year-old father and sixty-five-year-old stepmother. Mr. Pang's household is established; he sponsored his parents' immigration from Korea. Since then, they have all lived together. He has not moved out of the Korean community in Elmhurst because his parents get along well with their older Italian neighbors there. They garden together and sometimes exchange foods such as Italian spaghetti and Korean miso casserole.

In the second strategy, the elders set up a separate household, as in the families of Dr. Mun and Mrs. Pai. Dr. Mun lives on Long Island with his wife, two sons, and a daughter. He is fifty-three years old. He and his family came to America in 1974. They lived in New Jersey for seven years and then moved to Long Island. While they lived in New Jersey, his parents lived with them, but they decided not to move into the Long Island house. Instead, they moved into a condominium apartment that Dr. Mun bought for them in Elmhurst, where his medical office is located. His wife works at the office as a secretary. His father also helps—for example, by running errands to the bank. Dr. Mun and his wife eat lunch with his parents in Queens and dinner with their children on Long Island.

Mrs. Pai came to America in 1981. For a few months she stayed with her adult son and his family in Forest Hills, Queens. Then for two years she lived with a roommate in Elmhurst and has recently moved into a co-op there. She works as a baby-sitter for two children, which is not easy for her. The root cause of her move was that her daughter-in-law wanted her to move out of the Forest Hills house, but now the daughter-in-law cannot ask for her help with child care. Mrs. Pai said cynically: "Well, my son used to be a devoted son in Korea. I sold everything to get money for my son. Then they bought a new house. There, I thought I could live with them. However, it did not work out that way. My son bought a co-op apartment for me. At first he paid the monthly $500 mortgage and maintenance cost. But now I pay one-third, considering that he needs to support his own family." Now Mrs. Pai sees her son only once a week.

A third strategy falls somewhere in between the two previous ones. Some elderly couples rotate residence periods with several adult children, usually with those who have not yet established their own businesses. Mr. Chung is twenty-seven years old and lives with his father and mother, who are seventy-two and seventy-one. His parents came to America in 1981. Three years ago, he and his parents lived with his brother's family in a house in Elmhurst. Next year Mr. Chung's wife will immigrate to join them. He works at a greengrocery run by his brother. His parents receive SSI, and he also contributes his own salary to household expenses.

In the fourth strategy, elderly women develop new ways of organizing domestic life, living separately from their husbands. This is quite unconventional in Korean terms. Mrs. Chung came here first, in 1977, and her husband followed in 1978. On their arrival they lived in Brooklyn. At first their children lived near them. Their eldest son immigrated first to Argentina and then to the United States. He then sponsored and supported other siblings who were beginning businesses. After all the elder Chungs' children left Korea, the parents had to come as well. Now the old woman stays with her daughter's family in Elmhurst taking care of her grandchildren. She occasionally visits her husband in Brooklyn but no more than once every several months.

Even though they still have a cultural preference for multigenerational co-residence, it is evident that Korean immigrants are not always able to realize such traditional cultural norms in the American context of Queens. The overriding organizational factor in domestic arrangements is now the drive to establishment, to achieve the Korean American dream. This entails a new domestic cycle of household composition. The Korean concept of chip has been remobilized in realizing the new immigrant ideology of establishment. If the traditional Korean family structure is understood in terms of branching between "big house" and "little house," the immigrant's domestic cycle runs according to a completely different logic. The new process does not involve a cycle of nuclear and stem families. It involves nuclear, stem, joint/extended, and stem families but with specific reference to the criterion of establishment, regardless of birth order or gender. Ultimately, the immigrant chip includes parents and childrens' families, including the daughters' families. Thus, there is little distinction between "big house" and "little house," unlike the case in Korea. This transformation of Korean domestic organization has led to the development of a new kinship structure, which will be discussed in Chapter 4. In the immigrant community, Korean values and norms have not vanished, but they intersect with the emphasis on establishment.

# [5]

# The Rise of Sisters in Korean America: The Shift to Women-Centered Kin Organization

As I explained in Chapter 4, the ideology of establishment and its accompanying social practices surrounding small business activities influence the way in which Korean immigrants organize domestic life. This leads to a new kinship structure, the subject of this chapter. Familial connections are one of two important channels through which Koreans can come to America; and since 1976, when occupational preference was restricted, kinship has become the principal channel. Among most Korean married couples in Queens, members of the wife's family in the United States outnumber those of the husband's family. More significantly, wife's kin's contributions to a family's small business establishment are very visible.

The immigration process has resulted in a new sibling hierarchy of gender and birth order: The old hierarchy has been turned upside down. The eldest son, who has most power in Korean culture, is likely to have least in America. Among the sons, status often depends upon who came to the United States first and who became established there first. Moreover, a sister is often at the top of the sibling hierarchical order in America.

In this chapter, I analyze the form and content of immigrant kin relations. First, I look at kinship in terms of exchange, identifying the conditions and channels by which kin are in contact with each other. Then I examine conflict among kin. Finally, I focus upon some of the distinctive characteristics of Korean kinship in America.

[94]

## Studies of Kinship in Korea

Previous research on kinship and family in Korea adopted an evolutionary model, studying the transition from the kinship-based society through the patriarchal extended family to the democratic nuclear family in industrial society. What has been called the Korean kinship and family system is largely discussed within the framework of lineage theory or the British structural functionalist theory of kinship, which treats kinship as an organizing principle of discrete groups (Ch'oe 1966; K. K. Lee 1975; Janelli and Janelli 1978, 1982; E. Yi 1993: 19). Most discussions focus on lineage and stress the extreme importance of kinship in premodern Korea. Researchers generally agree that the main function of lineages (*munjung* in Korean) is the assertion of *yangban* (high-born, hereditary elite) status (for example, Ch'oe 1966; Janelli and Janelli 1982). Kwang-kyu Lee, who has studied various aspects of Korean kinship, points out that the rules of descent in Korea are characterized by the priority of the direct lineal descendant and symbolized in the transmission of ancestor worship responsibilities from father to eldest son. The custody of family property and succession to family headship follow this basic rule (K. K. Lee 1975: 400).

When members of chip commemorate the common father's great grandfather, this practice is called *tangnae* or *sochong*. Members gather at the house (big chip) of the direct lineal descendant (*chongson*) to perform chesa several times a year. The attendants at tangnae also make up a formal mourning group and have an obligation to wear mourning clothes. Within tangnae, the foremost big household (*chongga*) or the chip of the direct lineal descendant of the father's great-grandfather (chongson) commands respect from other junior households and is expected to take the lead in family group activities.

The concept of the family as a moral domain culminates in the idiom of filial piety. Filial piety requires one to love and obey parents. Yet this filial love in Confucianism is different from love as understood in Western culture, which emphasizes sentiments and affective feelings. Rather, in the native view, great moral value is placed on filial piety on the grounds that "the man's 'love' of parent comes from his moral endeavor to suppress his sentiments and affection toward his wife and children" (E. Yi 1993: 133).[1] In general, relationships with paternal relatives are formal and obligatory. A tangnae is primarily a ritual assemblage and much more

1. There are many folktales in which a heroic man sacrifices his own child and wife to save his parents.

[95]

important among gentry rather than nongentry families. The relationship between the wife's natal chip and the husband's chip is characterized by great formality and courteous treatment. In comparison to relationships with paternal relatives, relationships with maternal relatives are usually informal, intimate, and carefree.

From the male point of view, a man's relatives consist of members of his paternal chip (tangnae), his maternal chip, and his wife's chip. These relatives are called *ch'inch'ŏk* in Korean. Although scholars have translated the English word *kin* as *ch'injok*, in everyday life ch'inch'ŏk is used to refer to individual relatives of the male through his father, mother, or spouse. Genealogical distance between parent and child is one *ch'on*. Genealogical distance between two persons can be calculated by adding the number of parent-child links between them.

After the lapse of four ascending generations, the ancestral tablet—a wood or paper marker—is buried and ritual service performed only once a year at the grave. This ritual group is commonly called *munjung* or *chongjung*, meaning "lineage." Unlike tangnae, munjung has a formal organization called *chonghwe* and may own corporate property to finance ancestral rituals. Seniority of family lines is also important in munjung.

In urban settings, lineage consciousness (the idea that one is a descendant of a prominent ancestor) does not define social identity as in traditional yangban village. In addition, the growth of the Christian church has contributed to the decline of Confucian family rituals (E. Yi 1993). The church in Korea has grown rapidly during recent decades (see Chapter 9). Nevertheless, not having chesa on the death-day anniversary for the parent of the head of a chip is unthinkable in most non-Christian families.

In Eunhee Kim Yi's study of urban middle-class families, among thirty-seven families (the husbands' chips) in which parents were alive, parents in thirty families (81 percent) did not live with the eldest son, which testifies to the declining trend. In this way, parents lose their claim on not only their son's economic contribution to the household but also their daughter-in-law's domestic labor, which they relied on in the traditional extended family. Unmarried brothers or sisters now tend to live separately from the married eldest brother. In the traditional system, the eldest brother's wife was expected to care for younger brothers and sisters like a mother.

In the modern period married daughters have close relationships with their *ch'injŏng* (the wife's natal family), and neolocal residence allows newly married women to have close relationships with their mothers and sisters. It is an increasingly common pattern for working women to live close to, and often eat at, their ch'injŏng (E. Yi 1993: 328). Yet too close a relationship with the ch'injŏng is considered a problem (330).

It is apparent that urban Korea has changed. Newly married couples tend to live near the wife's family, and increasing importance is given to the wife's kin as well as the husband's kin. Nevertheless, Korean American kinship shows its own development of new forms and patterns, some of which converge with trends in urban kinship in Korea. With the development of women-centered and sister-initiated kinship, we see that kinship in immigrant families is greatly modified under the specific conditions of life in the United States.

## Women-Initiated Migration

Beginning with the Korean War, immigration entered a new period of female-initiated migration. During the 1950s most Koreans who came to America were war brides married to American servicemen. Since the 1965 Immigration Act, women have continued to play an important part in immigration. Under occupational preference many more women than men came to the United States as nurses or members of other health care occupations. And since 1976, when restrictions were placed on occupational preferences, the important role of women in immigration has continued. Through family reunification, it is more often women than men who invite family members to come to America.

Women who came as war brides (or military wives) or nurses and then became American citizens often sponsor their kin. Because the Korean government does not allow dual citizenship, the immigrant husband or wife has to decide who will be naturalized. More often, wives rather than husbands obtain U.S. citizenship. And among those who come here temporarily, perhaps sent by a company or coming to visit, it is more often women who want to stay in America. "If Korea is a country for men, America is for women," Koreans in Queens frequently comment. In addition, in those cases when an immigrant family returns to Korea to stay (*yokimin*), it is often only the husband who returns while his wife and children stay in America, thus forming a divided family—*isan kajok*.[2]

2. This term has been used for those who have family members in North Korea and have been separated from them for more than forty years.

In the New York Korean community, people call those who come to America through a wife's connection *ch'ŏgajok* (kin who have immigrated to the United States through a wife's connection) (see Chapter 6). This phrase is frequently used by men, with the implication that they have too many relatives who have come through their wife's sponsorship. Men often complain, "The wife's family, they try to influence or undermine my authority as the head of the household. I don't feel comfortable dealing with them. And yet obviously I cannot ignore them."

Until recently, Korean immigrant men revisited Korea to be introduced to a woman for marriage. These men were considered desirable prospects by young women in Korea. Many women hoped to go to America, where they would be better treated by men. Women thought of emigration as a wonderful idea. But since the mid-1980s, many immigrant men are being rejected by women in Korea. Women have come to know from kin or friends that, if they immigrate, they can expect hardship in the form of long working hours at stores or factories. Today, women from middle- or upper-class families are reluctant to join a new husband from America. Yet those from working-class backgrounds are still willing to go to America, ready to experience the hardships that await them.

## Exchange among Kin and Small Business

Small businesses provide a major arena for interaction among kin in the New York City environment. Often brothers and parents work in their sister's and daughter's businesses, or one brother works for another brother, or a father or a mother works in a child's business. Many other complex permutations also occur. Koreans recognize that in the United States kinship relations become stronger because of shared business interests and one has more opportunity to relate to one's kin than in Korea. Business activity may even lead to firmer ties with particular kin who are still in Korea. Mrs. Park, who runs a craft store, makes frequent trips to Korea in order to import clothing and craft items. While in the United States, she leaves important business decisions to her sister-in-law in Korea. As a result, the two women are in close contact by telephone between Mrs. Park's visits.

Work schedules here influence contact with kin. If one's work hours are similar to a kinsperson's, one can develop deeper or thicker relations (*tut'ŏun kwangye*) with that person than with others. For example, Mr.

Shin runs a sewing machine store in Elmhurst and lives with his family in Flushing. Because of similar work schedules, he and his family see his brother's family every week. He can visit his brother-in-law's family less often, however, because one man is usually at work while the other is free.

Those who are established here are able to offer crucial help to their kin in Korea. This is especially important for those who are not well off in Korea and cannot immigrate without sponsorship and material assistance from kin in America. Once such an immigrant arrives in America, the newcomer and his or her family will be helped by their established kinsperson. Typically, newcomers will stay with their relative for some time until they gain their bearings in American society. They receive free room and board and help in finding their own employment and housing. The help provided also depends on the receiving kinsperson's resources and living standard in Korea. For example, Mrs. Shim's family, now in America for more than twenty years, began to send money to Mrs. Shim's sisters in Korea after seven years of immigrant life. According to Mrs. Shim, her sisters were in need, unlike her husband's sister, who married a rich man. As a result, she said, the Shims became close to her sisters but not to Mr. Shim's sister. It is noteworthy that, once the Shims were sufficiently established, they offered help to the wife's kin rather than the husband's. If they had established themselves earlier, however, they might have received pressure from Mr. Shim's kin in Korea to assist his sister before she married her well-to-do husband.

A dense network ties together kinspersons in the United States with those still in Korea. These ties include telephone calls, letters, visits, money, gifts, taking care of property, supporting children or older persons, and offering rituals in the name of absent kin. Interestingly, clothes are presented by kin in Korea to those in America, not vice versa. This is because Korea is said to produce better-quality clothing in terms of price than America does. (In addition, Koreans find it difficult to buy what they like in terms of design, size, and material in America. Many Korean immigrants make special visits to Korea primarily for shopping.)

There are several Korean companies that specialize in sending gifts from Koreans in the United States to friends and kin in Korea. On Korean holidays, in particular, these services are in great demand. On such occasions exchanges of money and gifts and expressions of personal concern are obligatory. It is a daughter-in-law's duty, especially to her *sidaek* (husband's family, including the families of his brothers), to send money and other gifts. This, however, is a more important obligation toward relatives

[99]

still in Korea than to those in the United States. Should any immigrant fail to meet proper kin obligations, other kin will indirectly apply pressure, making the shirker well aware of what he or she is supposed to do. The people most scrupulous in maintaining these proprieties are those who, before they were established, had left their children with kin in Korea.

## Contact among Kin in the United States

Korean immigrants maintain active social interaction with their kin. In a Los Angeles study (Hurh and Kim 1984: 90), about half of the respondents reported at least weekly contact with kin beyond household members. I found daily kin contact among my Queens informants. Contact depends, of course, on distance and particular relationships. People follow Korean kinship norms, but contact is affected by residence and involvement in small business.

If a kinsperson lives beyond the New York area, regardless of genealogical distance, Koreans will call them at least annually on special occasions or with the change of seasons. But if kin are one's parents, children, siblings, or direct relatives of a spouse, monthly telephone calls are proper. Parents or children receive weekly telephone calls, even if they live in Los Angeles. For close kin living in New York City, especially in Queens, a person makes at least weekly telephone calls. For kin in the same neighborhood, a person makes daily, or at least every other day, contact, regardless of genealogical distance. My informants generally met these culturally articulated norms of kin contact.

Such patterns of contact are maintained with both the husband's and the wife's kin. This is in great contrast to Korea, where a man does not usually think about his wife's kin as relatives in the same way he considers his patrilateral kin. According to a study in Korea by E. Yi (personal communication), couples and their children are frequently in close contact with the wives' kin; but husbands find it difficult to include such kin among their relatives when conceptualizing kin obligations.

In terms of face-to-face contact, Korean immigrants will see their own parents and children daily, making visits if they live in separate households in the same neighborhood or the same New York City borough. Siblings who work in the same business, even though they live in different neighborhoods, have daily contact. Other siblings make either daily or weekly visits. I also found that close ties to a mother's kin, such as a mother's sister or brother, often form when those kin live in the same neighborhood. These kin also make weekly visits to each other. This is also novel in terms of the patrilineal Korean kinship structure. In the case of a man's other in-laws, visits are less frequent, but telephone contact with both patrilateral and matrilateral kin are fairly equal in occurrence. If a wife's siblings also live in Queens, the family will usually make either weekly or monthly visits.

## Contact with Kin beyond the United States

Kinship contact with relatives still in Korea depends more strictly on genealogical distance and patrilateral norms. Closest contact, of course, is maintained with a man's wife and children when they are still at home. Close contact is also maintained first with a man's parents and then with his wife's parents. For young adults, long-distance telephone calls to parents are made as often as every third day or at least weekly. For middle-aged immigrants whose parents or parents-in-law are old, contact may be monthly, seasonal, or twice a year. With siblings in Korea, contact is less frequent than with parents or parents-in-law, often just a few times a year or annually. Of course, when children remain with these relatives in Korea or plans concerning immigration or business are being arranged, contacts are more frequent.

Families in which a wife or child remain in Korea are called isan kajok (divided family), the same term used for families separated during the Korean War. In such cases, one is in close contact by telephone, as often as daily or weekly. Letters are written to children or parents in Korea, either weekly or monthly. It is often a married woman's duty to write letters to her in-laws. The immigrant male sends money, as much as $10,000 per year, which is frequently the total income that the family receives. If immigrants have parents or parents-in-law still in the homeland, they will send gifts of money as well as make monthly telephone calls and send letters. My Queens informants, at different stages of establishment, send their parents and parents-in-law varying amounts, from $150 to $600 per month. Remittances to siblings in Korea varied from $500 to $10,000 per year.

The greatest obligation to send money home falls upon immigrant men who are eldest sons. In Korean society, they have the principal rights of family inheritance yet the heaviest obligation toward other siblings in terms of support for education and living expenses. I even noted a case in which one eldest son in America supported an unmarried sister in Korea and expected to do so throughout her life.

The appropriate and common occasions on which Korean immigrants tend to send monetary gifts to Korea are New Year's Day, *kujŏng* (lunar New Year's Day), *ch'usŏk* (the mid-autumn festival), *ŏbŏi nal* (parents' day), and *ŏrini nal* (children's day). In particular, lunar New Year's Day and the mid-Autumn festival are near the beginning of the Korean school year and graduation time, respectively, and people often choose these dates to send money to kin. People also send money to kin in Korea in celebration of their birthdays, *paegil* (a baby's first one hundred days), *tol* (a baby's one-year birthday), *hoegap* (a sixtieth birthday), *ch'ilsun* (a seventieth birthday), an engagement, a wedding, and *kiil* (in memory of a relative on the anniversary of the day of his or her death). In addition, when a kinsperson is ill, one sends money.

In these monetary gifts, immigrants do not give priority to the wife's kin, and this differs from the way in which kin relations are being reorganized in the United States. But they do give more importance to the wife's kin than they would had they never left Korea. Nonetheless, Korean immigrants do try to fulfill the patrilineal kinship norms (chip or tangnae) that mark Korean social organization—for instance, by sending money to one's father's brother (*samchon*).

In America, those kin ties activated in the process of immigration often become most significant. If one receives substantial help from a kinsperson, the relationship with that person will be strengthened. For example, in the case of Mrs. Chung, her own parents and siblings live in Chicago, but she and her husband have far more contact with his family in Korea. This is because they have received financial support from her husband's family for his education. They call her husband's parents in Korea two or three times a week, but they visit her parents in Chicago or New York only two or three times a year.

## The Clash between Generations

It is usually necessary to receive help from kin if an immigrant wishes to realize the dream of establishing his or her own small business. This sometimes leads to friction among kin, particularly among those of different generations. In extreme cases, the older generation might leave for

Korea while the younger generation stays, thus causing family division. In Korea, Reverend Won's father was in charge of medical supplies in the air force and retired as a lieutenant colonel. In the United States he hoped to become a pharmacist but failed to complete his internship. He then started to run a dry-cleaning store. Because Reverend Won's mother, a doctor, could not work at her profession either, both parents returned to Korea. Now Reverend Won feels that his parents were too old to adapt to America because of the language barrier and other differences. When they left, he and his sister were still in school, and his sister married an American. The Won children both decided to remain in America.

The grandparent generation also has problems with adult children, the parent generation. One example can be found in the volatile mother-in-law/daughter-in-law relationship. On the one hand, daughters-in-law still suffer from the tyranny of their co-resident mothers-in-law. On the other hand, even in Korea (T. Lee 1981), increasing numbers of older women complain about hardships caused by rebellious daughters-in-law. Of course, if a woman's parents-in-law are still in Korea, she and they have much less of a problem. This is often a major reason explaining why Korean women do not want to return to Korea.

Jenny compared her life with a friend's. Both see themselves as "knee-high" generation members, having immigrated as children. Jenny's parents-in-law live in California, which makes it easier for her to deal with them. Her friend has a very difficult time with her mother-in-law, who also lives in Queens. Her friend recently came to visit Jenny and cried for a whole evening. Jenny said: "My mother-in-law was well educated, but she was forced to stay home to help in farm work in those days. My father-in-law is a respected church minister but very patriarchal. When I saw her offer him fruit after peeling it—very politely, like a slave serving the master—I was surprised and disapproved of the whole scene. At home, I have never seen anything like this. We daughters did the work, not my mother."

Alice divorced her husband, partly because she did not get along with her mother-in-law, a second-generation Korean American. She recollected, "When I lived with my husband and my mother-in-law for a year, we fought each other all the time. For example, she did not like the way I cooked. I also answered back to her. I could not understand why she did not like the way that I was brought up by my family. Finally, my husband could not bear our conflict at home any more."

Mrs. Lee lives with her son's family and takes care of the housework and her grandson. Her son is a financial analyst, and her daughter-in-law is an attorney. Mrs. Lee said, "These days, a mother-in-law lives under a daughter-in-law's oppression. In fact, young people have become kings. I have problems with my daughter-in-law over our different ways of raising children—she argues for a more scientific way." Although children invite their parents in order to live together and to take care of them in their old age, both generations find it difficult to live under the same roof.

## Characteristics of New Kinship System

In the transition from Korea to the United States, traditional concepts of kinship ties have become diffuse, sometimes even overturning genealogical distance. In Korea, people have definite ideas about whom they consider to be close kin—those within tangnae. With the emergence in America of ch'ŏgajok, a person who is related to either the wife or the husband is considered to be a kinsperson because he or she can potentially work for the family's small business. Moreover, relationships that traditionally were avoided—those between mother and son-in-law or brother-in-law and sister-in-law—may now be close. Blood is thicker than water, the proverb says. Thus, remote kin may be more reliable than a total stranger. It is common for an established immigrant to provide newcomer kin (sometimes even non-kin from the same locality or those related through a school friendship) with free room and board for several months, up to a year. Without such assistance, it is difficult for immigrants to save money and establish their own businesses.

The nature of kin relationships in the United States is more substantial than formal compared to those in Korea. As I have discussed, in Korea, despite the emphasis on kin ties, kin relations are based on rules of propriety in contrast to relations involving friends or neighbors. This is not the case in the immigrant community. As kin members work together in family businesses and socialize together, people find their kin to be critically important for practical matters.

## The Rise of Women-Centered Kinship

Effective kinship ties in the United States tend to be bilateral. Kinspersons on both sides of a married couple's family become important. In contrast, kin norms in Korea are weighted to the husband's side: On the mother's side only those up to four ch'on (the basic unit of genealogical distance) are technically counted as immediate kin; on the father's side, those up to eight ch'on are so recognized. (But how Koreans actually accord recognition to their relatives is not well documented by anthropological research.)

In America, kinship is more horizontal than in Korea, with more emphasis on sibling ties. In Korea, vertical ties between father and son play a more important role than they do in the United States, due to inheritance and ancestor worship. In America, immigration and productive activities are usually organized around horizontal sibling ties. The sister (*nui*) in a sibling group plays a much more central role for all siblings than she does in Korea. She sponsors her other family members and directs the beginning of their pathways to establishment. There seems to be little explicit cultural recognition of this sister-initiating kinship structure. By and large, my analysis is based on ethnographic knowledge; nonetheless, this pattern applies to nearly half of the kin groups I studied.

Mr. Yi represents a typical case in which women not only initiated immigration but also directed and supervised what the rest of family members could do. Mr. Yi and his wife came to the United States in 1980 and lived with their daughters in Manhattan for two years. After that, they moved to Elmhurst. Since then, their third and fourth sons have joined them. They now live in a house in Woodside, registered under the names of Mrs. Yi and their second and third sons. Mr. Yi explained, "That is because my daughter advised us to do so." It is remarkable to a Korean to see immigrants acknowledge the advice and contributions made by daughters. As Mr. Yi put it, "she is really clever to know everything in the United States. She is *ttosuni*" (meaning very tough and bright).

At first Mr. Yi opposed the immigration offer from his daughter in America. He could not think of leaving his motherland. But his wife liked the idea, he believes, because she is younger than him. Their children still at home said that, in order to join their family members, they were ready to immigrate to America. Yet Mr. Yi still was not sure. His daughter then suggested that she would help him to establish his own business. He finally decided to come. As his daughter promised, the Yis were presented with a greengrocery in Manhattan owned by the daughter. It was a good business and interesting to run, he recollected. His daughter worked in the store as cashier and later bought a house after selling the store. Mr. Yi was paid weekly and given extra pocket money when he needed it. It is evident that this ttosuni played a significant role in her family's life. She persuaded the rest of the family to immigrate, helped her parents establish their own business, and continues to guide the family in their adjustment to American life.

Mr. Choo's case is similar. In Korea his eldest daughter, a typist, married an American and moved to the United States. His eldest son then came to Arizona in 1978, invited by the eldest daughter. Within a year, the whole family was in America. After two years in Los Angeles, they came to New York. Now Mr. Choo and his wife live with his eldest son, third and youngest daughters, and youngest son. The eldest son runs a Chinese fast-food restaurant in lower Manhattan with the third and fourth daughters. Mrs. Choo does the family's housework.

Mr. Chung runs a fish market. He migrated to America at the invitation of his wife's sister, who also married an American. Only his wife's kin have ever stayed in his household; his own family members have not migrated. Mr. Chung's mother-in-law, brothers-in-law, and wife's cousin all live near his home and often visit each other. All have been sponsored by his wife's sister, who now lives in Albany. The Queens relatives visit her twice a year and telephone her as frequently as they need to.

In Queens we often encounter what is for Koreans an asymmetrical situation: the wife's kin live in America, while most of the husband's kin are still in Korea slowly trying to immigrate one by one. The women-centered, sister-initiated kinship values are also evident in co-residence; such kin tend to be given household accommodation. In Mr. Park's case, his in-laws stayed with him for more than a year. Usually the wife's kin stay more frequently and longer, and a daughter's children become more integrated into their mother's parents' household. (In Korea, the increasing importance of the wife's family also has been documented; see Cho and Koo 1983; Kendall 1985; Yoon 1989.)

It cannot be stressed too much that for Koreans such arrangements overturn the traditional mode of living with the eldest son's family. Mrs. Park, for example, runs a craft store. Her family immigrated under her daughter's sponsorship. Now she and her husband, son, daughter, and father-in-law all co-reside with her grandson, the son of the daughter who invited her. In accommodating a daughter's child, this household deviates from traditional Korean residence norms. Elderly Mr. Zion's case is also untraditional in that he lives with his daughter's family and takes care of her children but works with his son.

Mr. Park, a worker at a greengrocery, resides in his wife's parents' household with his wife and six-month-old son, a very un-Korean uxorilocal residence pattern. His wife came to America earlier than he; and when he married, he moved in with her family. As a result, his life is centered around his wife's relatives. They frequently call his wife's father's sister (*komo*) in Washington D.C. and his wife's mother's brother (*oesamch'on*). Even the neighbors they see are primarily his wife's friends, most of whom are Korean (though five are Latin American). The Parks' friends include his wife's schoolmates, whom she sees once a week. Moreover, she belongs to a rotating credit club (kye) for $30,000 with ten members; they meet either in a restaurant or at his home. Every Saturday, his parents-in-law host a meeting of their friends at the household. Mr. Park's kin are all in Korea. He calls his parents twice a month. In the future, once he is established in his own store, he intends to send money to them.

We also observe the influence of women-centered, sister-initiated kinship networks in the frequent contact among people living nearby. For example, Mrs. Shim's brother lives upstairs with his family. Reverend Won's wife's mother and his brothers-in-law also live upstairs in the same apartment; in that way his mother-in-law is able to take care of her grandchild. This situation is also occurring in urban Korea, where a newly married couple tends to look for a house near the wife's parents in the same neighborhood. In America, however, this trend appears to be even more developed, with the wife's family or kin trying to find a newly married couple a house near their own or even offering them space in the same house.

## Lowered Status of the Eldest Son

Another noticeable change in Korean kinship in the United States is the decreasing importance of the eldest son. Because he is often the last to migrate, owing to his duty to continue ancestor worship in Korea, the hierarchical order among siblings is reversed as sisters and younger brothers adjust first to immigrant life. In Korea, it is imperative that the eldest son take care of the parents, usually by living with them. Because of primogeniture or partial primogeniture inheritance, siblings have differing amounts of power in the family depending on birth order, marital status, and gender. Until it was revised in 1989, Korean family law stipulated that the eldest son could claim one-and-a-half shares in family property, the other sons one share each, unmarried daughters a half share, and married daughters a quarter share.

In America, this customary arrangement changes. A sister, alone or as a wife, usually arrives first. Unmarried and younger brothers and sisters are invited next, before the married siblings. Immigration regulations also make it easier for unmarried persons to migrate rather than those already married. Parents usually live first with the more established children and then take turns living with those who arrive later. As a result, the later-arriving eldest son assumes a lower status.

Mr. Nam's family is representative of this new family situation. His sister initiated the family migration after marrying an American army man and now lives in New Jersey. She first invited her second-oldest brother and his family, and he is currently Mr. Nam's employer. Next she invited his youngest brother and his family, and now the Nams' mother lives with this brother in Queens. Mr. Nam is the eldest son but was the last sibling to immigrate to America.

Of course, there are exceptions. If the eldest son himself came first to America as a student or a professional, he often initiates the family immigration. Or if a set of related families all migrate to South America and later remigrate to the United States, the eldest son's family might be included in this group. In some cases, only by passing on inheritance rights and the obligations of ancestor worship to another brother can the eldest son migrate.

As a result of the immigration process, we often see a new sibling hierarchy in terms of gender and birth order—the old hierarchy turned upside down. The eldest son who has most power in Korean culture is likely to have the least in America. Among the sons, their status and position often depends upon who came first and who became established here earlier. Moreover, it is often a sister who is at the peak of the sibling hierarchical order in America.

## Importance of Locality

Another change in the nature of kin relations is the increasing importance of locality. Regardless of genealogical distance, people form closer ties with kin who live nearby than with those who live far away. Locality contributes affective ties to a genealogically diffuse set of kin. In Korea, kin often get together regardless of physical distance, which is not possible here in the United States.

Most immigrants tend to settle in the core settlement neighborhoods, such as Elmhurst and Flushing, and then, as they become established, move to other parts of Queens or to the suburbs. Kin of the wife often tend to live in the same apartment building or in the immediate neighborhood. After moving away, some people commute to stores, churches, or community events in the core areas and maintain kin contacts much as before. Others, however, especially professionals, move out to suburban areas, and their frequency of contact dwindles. Thus, the effective kinship networks may become less genealogically complete or homogeneous over time. Newly arriving wife's kin may replace patrilateral husband's kin. If kin live far away, they are as remote as they were before they immigrated.

In the immigrant situation, then, Koreans in Queens form close relations with kin, regardless of genealogical distance, who live nearby. Even remote kin ties may be effectively activated by immigration. Mr. Kang, a grocery worker, sees his mother's brother's family every week. They live in the same immediate neighborhood in Elmhurst. He feels very close to his mother's first and second brothers (oesamch'on) and has received many gifts of clothes from them. His maternal grandfather, who lives with his mother's first brother, is also someone to whom he feels very close. Ms. Choi has a cousin here whose degree of kinship is beyond third cousin. Although she lives in Queens and he lives in Westchester, they call each other almost once a week and both participate in activities at the same church.

## Evaluations of Kinship Relations

The longer they live in America, the more immigrants perceive change in their kinship relations. Initially, many experience a more or less positive feeling on arrival mixed with a sense of distance from kin still in Korea. Mr. Chun recalled his wedding here, about which he feels horrible because so many of his kin were not present. He married for love. When he and his wife married in church, they had no kin to celebrate their wedding ceremony with them.

Over time, there are two different routes pursued by Korean immigrants in reorganizing their family and kin relations in the American context. The first is to somehow continue to maintain their kinship networks, now at a distance. Such persons rely heavily on family and kin, both materially and emotionally. Like Mr. Chung's family, they spend considerable amounts of money to telephone people in Korea. They often feel lonely without their kin network around them in American society, as Mr. Chun felt at his wedding.

Others build on the importance of family and kin ties here, especially in the establishment of their businesses. As a result, many at first reify the importance of family and kin ties as the key to success in immigrant life. "Emotions are socially constituted and are not only the expression of experience but also the determinants of experience and practice" (Medick and Sabean 1984: 3). But once the beginning stage of establishment is reached, the honeymoon period is over. As business prospers, family or kin ties play a less important role. People perceive family and kin relations as increasingly cold, rational, calculative, even inhumane, and alien to the traditional Korean notion of domestic life. The turning point comes in their realization that their children need something more than a pool of family and kin ties in order to succeed in America.

Mr. Yi's case reveals conflict between father and adult son, which is considered the strongest tie in the Korean kinship system. In running his business in America, Mr. Yi's son does not find it useful to listen to his father's advice. Mr. Yi complained that his son didn't listen to him but to a friend and therefore failed in business. His son bought a store in Elmhurst on the friend's recommendation. Without any experience, he relied on what the friend told him. Half the capital was provided by money that Mr. Yi and his son had brought from Korea. Now the son runs a fish-frying store in Manhattan.

Mr. Choo described kinship relations in his immigrant family:

> As I have an American son-in-law, I have come to know a lot about America. In America, brother and sister borrow or lend each other money. They do not just freely give and take. This is very good. Children don't rely only on parents. I plan to leave two-thirds of my property to my children, in Korean style, and donate one-third to charities, American style. I am going to pass my property in equal shares to my children, unlike the traditional Korean way. Here Koreans try to adopt the American way—for example, smoking in front of their seniors and making no concession to their parents. They do not take care of, or serve, their parents politely, which has been the way in Korea for a long time. However, most Korean immigrants have to work hard to survive. Otherwise they starve.

He also noted that elderly Korean women invited to the United States by their daughters take care of young children so that a husband and wife can work together. Nowadays, if they do baby-sitting for others, they can earn $600 per month. In caring for their own grandchildren, they never used to be paid. But now even grandmothers are given some money for taking care of their grandchildren.

A newcomer told me that he was surprised at and disappointed in his mother's sister. His mother had immigrated some time before, but her sister, according to him, was a millionaire who laughed at his idea of working very hard and striving for small business establishment, implying that he would be better off turning to welfare.

In the United States, Korean kinship undergoes considerable change. Old norms are less honored, but new patterns of kinship behavior can nonetheless be identified. In general, changing productive activities in immigrant small businesses, not factors of relocation or acculturation, account for these changes. For many people, kin plays a key initial role in their total evaluation of life in America. Korean immigrants see kinship as a necessary ingredient to achieving their dream of establishing their own business. Here, we see a reification of kinship: Kin relations become fetishized, seen almost as a factor of production like capital or labor. But once an immigrant establishes his or her business, it becomes less important to mobilize family labor. Kinship relations may then cool.

I emphasize a new characteristic within the Korean American kinship structure—the rising status of sisters. I argue that under the specific conditions of immigrant life in the United States, Korean kinship structure has been transformed to stress sister-initiating kin mobilization and women-centered kin organization, which influence small business activities. In short, I argue that it is kin mobilization, rather than socialization inside the family that partly explains the success of Korean American small business activities. More significantly, in this process, gender plays the key role. The Korean immigrant family is witnessing an inversion of kinship structure in both gender and birth order, with the rising influence of sisters in relation to brothers.

There is an emerging body of literature regarding the key role of women-centered kinship structures in urban industrial societies. For example, Yanagisako emphasizes the existence of closer interpersonal relationships among female kin than among male kin and the consequent matrilateral bias in groups committed to bilateral kinship norms. This asymmetry has been studied among working-class and middle-class Londoners, New York families of Eastern European Jewish origin, nonfarm families in Finland

and Sweden, and middle-class and lower-class families in the midwestern United States. "In these groups, the female bias in both intragenerational and intergenerational kin relationships manifests itself in patterns of co-residence, residential proximity, and mutual aid, and in the frequency of interaction and the strength of affective ties among kin" (Yanagisako 1979: 207).

My treatment of women-centered kin organization among Korean immigrants follows Yanagisako's distinction. "The term women-centered kin networks refers to the centrality of women in the web of kinship linking together sets of households" (Yanagisako 1979: 208). In the case of Korean American women-centered kin organization, the causal factor can be found in women's critical role in their new productive activities—that is, in small business. While it is true that immigration policy and demographic characteristics of the Korean immigrants facilitated this trend, the small business activities have made possible the rise of sister-initiated kin mobilization and women-centered kin organization. Korean American women-centered kinship goes beyond traditional Korean categories and discourses on the gender division of activities. These new networks do not necessarily fit into division of gender roles in terms of the private and public spheres, home and workplace, love and money, and expressive (or affective) and instrumental domains in the American capitalist system.[3] For example, work in the Korean American family is understood as an extension of family. Moreover, in this process, work itself redefines the family and kinship structure. In this way, increasing numbers of Korean Americans recognize and appreciate the significant role played by their female kin who have indeed become ttosuni (very tough and bright girls).

3. For a critique of this Parsonian interpretation based on a theory of universal family/work, private/public, love/money, and expressive/instrumental opposition in capitalist and industrialist societies, see E. Yi (1993).

# [6]

# Women's Changing Viewpoints: The Pursuit of Human Dignity

Korean women's immigration has brought for many a delayed industrial revolution: For the first time in their lives they are entering the paid labor market. They are thus freed from some traditional social burdens and constraints, just as new industrial workers were fired from traditional constraints nearly two centuries ago in England. At the same time, their new status in America creates possibilities for exploitation. In this chapter, I explore how Korean women live and evaluate their new lives in America, focusing on the ideology of anjŏng—the dream of setting up their own business. I discuss how gender and "establishment" interact. At issue is how women make sense of their involvement in "establishment," including their changing gender roles and politics. First, I discuss gender in Korean society and critiques of traditional roles. Next, I examine women's employment and analyze how marriage is tied to economic arrangements; thus, I clarify the relationship between immigrant women's productive and reproductive activities. Then I discuss the influence of American gender ideology on women. Finally, I look at women's viewpoints toward their jobs and their responsibilities for housework and the new choices they face in struggling with the Korean American dream.

## Problematizing Gender in Korea

The specific form of patriarchy in Korea is crystallized in Confucian ideology. Korean men cite the Confucian homily "Namjon, yŏbi": "Men are honored, but women are abased." Accordingly, Confucianism eliminated women's participation in society outside the family and restricts them within the family. However, as Kendall (1983) points out, the missionaries and travelers who gave the West its first glimpse of Korea inverted this image of Confucian womanhood: the Korean woman became the wretched and depraved product of oppressive patriarchy.

These have been the working assumptions, but they are now being challenged. Many new studies have shown that "most of the social patterns we now associate with 'traditional Korea' did not take firm root until the sixteenth or seventeenth century, a scant three centuries ago" (Kendall 1983: 11).[1] " 'Traditional Korean women,' as they have been recorded in the past or observed in present-day rural villages, seem often to confound the Confucian idealization of passive and sequestered womanhood. That image, and the tension between image and reality, is a part of the twentieth-century Korean woman's heritage" (16). I argue that this conclusion applies even more so to Korean immigrant women because of their drastically increased participation in the paid labor force in the United States.

In 1948 the Korean constitution granted women's suffrage; nevertheless, women still experience gender inequality and sexual discrimination. According to Korean patriarchal logic, women are not secure until they become ancestors in their husbands' lineage. In reality, as Chungmoo Choi (1992) notes such discriminatory logic colors a wide range of socioeconomic issues, including marriage and divorce, inheritance and distribution of wealth, labor and wages, and education. Such was the logic codified in the family law. For instance, in the case of the property inheritance law, it was not until 1989 that a revision eliminated all the discriminatory measures against women.

Contrary to widespread belief, Hye-jong Cho (1988) maintains that the vast majority of Korean women have always participated in economic activities in addition to their domestic duties. Moreover, the labor of women underwrote South Korean's "economic miracle" in the 1970s (see S. K. Kim 1990). The number of women in the work force increased from 34 percent in 1963 to 41 percent in 1989. The majority of women wage workers are concentrated in manufacturing, particularly in labor-intensive textile, chemical, electronic, shoe, and garment industries. Women workers composed about 32 percent of the white-collar work force in 1979, up from 25 percent two decades earlier (E. Yi 1993: 242). Nonetheless, in 1986 an average woman worker received 49.6 percent of the pay of a

---

1. See two volumes on Korean women: Mattielli's *Virtues in Conflict* (1973) and Kendall and Peterson's *Korean Women: View from the Inner Room* (1983).

average male worker. Furthermore, there is a wide gap between the employment opportunities of men and women. For instance, in 1991 some sixty major industries in South Korea together allocated only 1,200 positions to female graduates (Choi 1992: 111). And women office workers often complain of forced resignation when they marry or become pregnant. With this background in mind, I discuss Korean immigrant women's lives.

## Migration and Gender

Different views have been advanced regarding the impact of international migration on women and their families. According to one view, migration results in the emancipation of women from unequal relationships with their husbands, mainly due to their new cash income-earning status (See Pessar [1987] on Dominican women in New York City and Foner [1975] on Jamaican women in London.) According to another view, however, this new status does not necessarily lead to women's emancipation. Despite some changes in decision making and the household division of labor, most immigrant working-class families continue to adhere to a family ideology that emphasizes male authority (Lamphere 1986; Safa 1987).

Nevertheless, these studies ignore other important dynamics. First, emancipation should be interpreted from the actor's point of view. Second, analyses of changing gender relations should not solely emphasize the new economic activity of women. What other changes occur with migration, and how are women affected by these changes? What happens when the immigrant women are from urban areas and arrive with high levels of education but lack experience as wage earners—like the majority of Korean immigrant women? Third, how does an immigrant woman's new economic status translate into emancipation? Is the new status gained through economic independence, or is it mediated through other factors such as control over the household budget? Does this increased economic independence lead women to different ideas and practices regarding gender relations?

## Women in Small Business

Korean immigrant women's work is organized around the goal of establishment. In Queens, most of these women work in sewing factories or small family businesses. A smaller percentage work as professionals such as nurses, pharmacists, and doctors. It is true that some women in Korea do work in the paid labor force; but as far as my informants were concerned, few had been so employed, especially if they were married. While the 1980 U.S. census showed 54 percent of Korean immigrant women in the paid labor force, in Korea only 29 percent were employed outside the home (Korean National Bureau of Statistics 1984). (In 1980, 51 percent of all American women were in the paid labor force.) The contrast was even greater for married women. In 1980, 56 percent of married Korean women in America were in the paid labor force, while in Korea only 19 percent of married women worked outside the home. (Married women's employment is slowly increasing in contemporary Korea; see S. K. Kim 1990.) In the United States, then, their likelihood of paid employment is three times greater than it is in Korea.

When immigrant men plan to open a business, Korean patriarchal ideology plays a role, and wives and other kin are expected to cooperate in whatever way they can. The business is directed by the male household head. Whether they have professional training or not, women most commonly start to work in either factory jobs or as employees in small businesses, and later join their husbands' businesses. Mrs. Choi worked first as a nurse; as had her colleagues, she later joined her husband to run a grocery. "At first, in Philadelphia, my husband worked at an American-owned automobile body shop, through a Korean pastor's introduction. I worked as a nurse at a hospital for two years. Then we opened a Western-style grocery with $10,000 in savings brought from Korea. We have run this store for seven years."

Mrs. Park shows a more typical profile, first working for an American electronics company, then working in a garment factory, and later joining the family's vegetable stand business. She got her job at the electronics company in Brooklyn only because she was accompanied by her husband, who could translate. She explained: "What I did was to try to read a person's face, not expressing any opinion because of my difficulty with the language. As I worked hard, my boss liked me. I could at best only greet my co-workers. I worked there for a year. Then I found work at an American garment factory, through a friend's introduction. It was also in Brooklyn. For three years, it was very difficult for me. Then I ran a fish market with my husband. It was very nice to have my own store. It was a tough job, though. For five or six years I worked cutting fish."

Among the varieties of Korean immigrant business, most are male-initiated. Although they depend upon their wive's labor contribution, men usually register the stores under their own name when they open their businesses. This makes it difficult for either men or women to give fair recognition to the woman's contribution to a family business.

Until recently, vegetable stands and fish markets were usually started by men. Men bore the physical demands of buying in the wholesale market and transporting produce to the store. But because many owners have come to use delivery services or employ a market buyer, they no longer need to go to the wholesale markets themselves. It has thus become possible for women to run these stores. Still other businesses are initiated by women—for example, beauty salons, nail salons, and fashion stores. Korean nail salons now form up to 80 percent of the nine hundred nail salons in New York City. Just as immigrant couples first found their economic niche in running vegetable stands or fish markets, women entrepreneurs now find their niche in nail salons. Such businesses require a relatively small initial investment, a simple command of English, a readily available supply of labor, and no certificate or license.[2]

In Korea, Mrs. Nam, a beautician, had worked as a hairdresser for three years. In Manhattan, she had to start as a sweeper and only later was promoted to hairdresser. She worked in a large beauty salon, and worker turnover was low. Although she had to work hard at first and faced communication problems, the customers were agreeable. She recollected: "In Korea, once you were a professional skilled hairdresser, you did not have to do all the work by yourself. There were always plenty of helpers for each skilled hairdresser. After four years of experience here, I wanted to set up my own beauty salon. I became interested in a store in Elmhurst. It was run by a Greek. My husband [who already had his own business] and I have invested all of the savings we made throughout our immigrant life in that store, investing $10,000 at first and then later the same amount again [in the mid-1980s]. It was possible only through my husband's cooperation." This case illustrates a variation that some women experience on the way to establishment. Like most women, Mrs. Nam started as a worker for someone else. But rather than join her husband's business, as many women do, she continued to earn wages. Then she opened her own business with her husband's cooperation. As other couples reach the Nams' stage,

2. Unlike other states, New York does not require a license to open a nail salon. This is one reason explaining why Koreans have easily entered the business. Although there is currently a state campaign to require licenses for nail salons, Korean operators are lobbying against the measure.

some women continue in the family business, while others, depending on their children's ages and the household composition, stop working. Nurses and other professional women usually join a family business after working at a non-Korean workplace. Beauticians, after working in a non-Korean beauty salon, may open their own businesses. Of course, there are exceptions to these general patterns; and other women continue as workers for many years in America, still stages away from establishment.

## Factory Workers

In a family business a woman's economic contribution may be taken for granted by her husband and even by herself. But women who work continue the family business are aware of their own separate pay check and therefore of their potential economic independence.

Almost from its inception, the New York garment industry has depended on immigrant labor (see Chapter 3). Irish, Swedes, and Germans formed the first flow, and by the turn of the century Jews and Italians made up the majority of the industry's labor force (Fenton 1975; Waldinger 1986). Black women from the South and Puerto Rican women began to enter the apparel industry in the 1930s (Fitzpatrick 1971). With New York's transformation from a production center to a spot market and the need of employers to remain competitive within the entire global organization of apparel production, the exodus of key labor force groups has always posed a serious threat. From the 1960s on, new immigrants were drawn into this labor vacuum. They included Chinese, Dominicans, Colombians, Haitians, Central Americans, Ecuadorans, and Koreans (Pessar 1987: 108).

Garment factory work is the most easily available job for Korean women (sere plate 5), as it is for women of other immigrant ethnic groups. This is true regardless of a woman's age or social background. A typical Korean-run sewing factory is owned and operated by a group of family members. Male workers are hired for pressing, packing, shipping, and other odd jobs; and women work as seamstresses. Ms. Kim works as a seamstress at a garment factory in Long Island City. There are thirty to forty people working there, one-third of them Korean and the rest whites and Latin Americans. She said, "At my factory we usually make one-piece dresses, and sometimes we make pants, quilted clothes, and winter coats. For example, I sew scores of pockets or hundreds of shoulder holders. We are supposed to sew each part of both sides. Sometimes we sew darts. I am very proud of what I am doing. When I saw clothes made by me, labeled with a brand name in a good

*Plate 5.* Seamstress listening to music while sewing garments in a Korean-run factory. Photo author

department store, I was very satisfied. Here I make very good quality-goods, whereas in Korea they make cheap clothes."

Ms. Chung works as a Merrow operator at a Korean garment factory in Elmhurst. She makes $400 per week. She said, "I cannot breathe because of too much dust in this basement. As I am a skilled worker, the manager gives me only the most difficult part to sew. This factory produces men's clothing. My legs and shoulders hurt because of the long hours of sewing. However, when I receive my weekly wage on Saturday, I can forget how painful it is."

Mrs. Gu compared work as a waitress with sewing at a garment factory: "It is much better to work at a garment factory, particularly for a house-wife. There are set working hours. But in the restaurant there was no particular closing hour. If there were customers for a party, they might go home later than the usual time. Besides, many immigrant single men customers proposition waitresses. But then when I work on T-shirts, I have to breathe cotton dust. I think I earn fairly good money. A man can make the same amount of money only if he works till eight in the evening. When it is very slow, like summer vacation around August or September, I work part time somewhere else. Autumn, around October, is the best season to work at a garment factory."

*Plate 6.* A client receiving a manicure in a Korean-run hair and nail salon. Photo author

## Service Workers

Among service workers, young women more often work as cashiers or saleswomen in small shops and middle-aged or older women work at nail salons (see plate 6) and salad bars. Older women also work as baby-sitters or cooks.

Mrs. Park, in her early thirty's, immigrated to America in the early 1980s. She and her husband have two children. Once she had settled in Forest Hills, she went on her own to a nail salon. She was hired immediately. She had to adopt an American name, and her employer chose "Grace" for her. Because most customers are American women, Korean manicurists call each other by American names but add *ŏnni* (sister) to such names among themselves. If one wants more contact with a broader society, it is preferable to work in a nail salon rather than Korean-run small businesses or garment factories. Grace-*ŏnni* explained how she became a nail salon worker:

> At first I observed how pedicure is done, and also learned from my *sonbae* [a more experienced worker]. In doing pedicures, first I soak the feet in water and then cut the toenails. Next, I remove skin which has become hard. Finally, I color the nails beautifully. I did pedicures for two months,

and then I moved on to manicures. Depending on the size of the salon, one will have to do pedicures for some time. Basically, a manicurist takes care of nails, including cleaning and coloring. If a customer needs skin waxing, we pull out hairs from eyebrow, leg, face, or armpit. If there is more to be done—for instance, if nails are weak or split—we will have to wrap the nails with cloth gauze. In some cases we will do all ten fingers and attach artificial nails. If necessary, we attach linen or silk for further strength. Moreover, we may add acrylic powder and glass jelly. A "full set" means to do all ten fingers, including glass jelly treatment.

There were twenty Korean women of different ages and educational levels working at Grace-*ŏnni*'s nail salon. Seven or eight workers were beginners. At first, Grace worked six days a week and earned $180 for a ten-hour work day, from 10 A.M. to 8 P.M., and often worked later. In tips, a beginner earns another $150. Regular customers come at least every one or two weeks. The most inexpensive treatment costs seven dollars. The more often a customer comes, the more she wants done. After about a year, two-thirds of customers will want a full set. Customers are assigned to each worker by the manager, who considers each worker's capability and skill. Most Korean manicurists are in their thirty's, but some are high school students and others are in their fiftys. Many of them are college graduates.

Women cashiers at a greengrocery are paid for their official activities but are also expected by the Korean community to remain in a "women's place." The assumption, in other words, is that all domestic matters belong a priori to the nearest woman.[3] The store's housework is heaped on them; they are expected to cook meals, do dishes, and clean up for their employers and male employees. Ms. Chun has worked as a cashier at a greengrocery. "I could get $200 or $250 per week by working twelve hours a day. On top of that, I had to cook for the male workers at the greengrocery. My legs were so swollen from overwork that my foot muscles cramped up."

Ms. Choi, in her early thirties, worked as cashier at a coffee shop located in lower Manhattan. Most customers were white American office and bank workers. "I earned $180 for five days a week. At that time I was not healthy, so it was very difficult. I had to work harder, as I had known

3. This notion is related to gender ideology in Confucianism and is equivalent to the idea of domesticity, a nineteenth-century Victorian concept that devotes the household as the proper sphere for women. These ideas, according to Humm (1990: 55) are less a description of women's reality and more a way of structuring a masculine ideology of women's lives.

the manager before. Sometimes I had to help with kitchen work. [I asked why only women, not men, work as cashiers.] If it doesn't pay well, no men will be interested in it! They usually find better jobs. I do not feel discriminated against in terms of sex because men and women traditionally were supposed to do different jobs."

Roughly more than one-third of immigrant women work for their family businesses, and another third are employed as either manufacturing or service workers. The two categories are closely related for many women often work in these jobs before joining their family businesses. Less than one-third of the women are professionals. (See Chapter 3 for more about female professionals' work and lives.)

## Influences from American Gender Ideology

In America, as Koreans see it, not only are women in a better position economically, but people have different ideas about male-female relations, including the proverbial "ladies first" attitude. In addition, both immigrant men and women are exposed to existing stereotypes of Asian American men and women, such as the short, ugly, unconfident, clumsy, arrogant Oriental men and small, long black hair, gentle, obedient, loving, soft, very womanly, quiet, and beautiful Oriental women (see Tachiki et al. 1971).

Women hear before migration that in America gentlemen treat ladies as if they were fragile dolls and follow a medieval European spirit of chivalry. Many soon realize that this behavior is only a formality and not as important as they had imagined in Korea. If Korean men in America change their attitudes toward women, it is due less to acculturation to such American formalities than to women's economic independence. Korean men, and even conservative women, are still ready to criticize a woman for speaking up or acting more assertively than she would in Korea. "Women sound so ugly when they raise their voices. Probably they have learned something from American culture, but not in a proper way, only in their own distorted way," one man told me.

As Ortner and Whitehead (1981: 23) aptly put it, "although the complex of meanings surrounding any particular kin role will vary greatly from culture to culture, one can anticipate certain very general repercussions on the image of women depending upon which type of cross sex bond— wife, mother, sister—is highlighted by prestige concerns. . . . Because wives are normally sexual partners, and mothers and sisters normally are not, an emphasis on wives will tend to give more ideological prominence to the sexual aspects of women in general." In America, woman as wife is more strongly emphasized than woman as mother, as it is in Korea. This American ideology of gender places immigrant women under pressure to pay more attention to appearance and beauty. In addition, the Korean American dream now defines both the attractive wife and the successful husband as partners who enjoy the fruits of establishment. (I am indebted to Laurel Kendall for this insight.) In Korea, if a married woman is preoccupied with her appearance rather than with taking care of her family and household, she is criticized and socially ostracized.

Many of my informants have learned to apply the American concepts of "ladies first" and "going out." This process creates gender tension. Still others, however, do not enjoy the pressures of American culture on their marital relationships, including the drive for an active sexual life. Ms. Suh's statement reveals the female interpretation of "ladies first": "Americans in general lack deep affections [*chŏng*]. However, American men behave better as gentlemen toward women than do Korean male students, who do not care about female students. They usually do not open a door for girls, a lack of gentlemanly manners. Well, other Asian students are the same."

Mr. Ha said that it took him some time to understand "going out." He had to ask his American friends again and again in order to get a clear idea about it.

> According to their explanation, once a man and woman start to go out regularly, they ought to be faithful to each other; at least they should not see anyone else. Two individuals make a serious decision about going steady. Yet they seem to break up so easily. In Korea there is no concept of friends who are of opposite sexes. Once a girl starts to see a boy, they make decision about marriage. To a Korean mind, it seems that even after going steady the breakup can be very quick and easy. I see it among those knee-high or second-generation Korean American young people, too. They do not seem to have any difficulty with seeing each other steadily and then breaking up. With no shyness! This is not possible for Asians.

In America, women are respected more than in Korea, he added; but American men do so because women are weak, not because they really respect women. At work, he observed, when a capable person is needed, men are preferred to women because men do the job better and faster. In addition, in the American family, it is still the wife who cooks, even if husbands help a lot more with housework.

Ann, a nurse, spoke of new pressures in terms of sexuality. She feels considerable pressure here to become sexually active. "As a single unmarried woman, I feel less social pressure on me to marry in America than in Korea. However, I feel that in America people pressure me by asking how my love life is and assuming that I have to have an active sex life."

Korean women in America ask their husbands to wear wedding rings. While they grumble about it, many Korean men do so, even though they did not wear them in Korea. They understand that in the United States men and women actively approach each other, regardless of marital status, owing to the high divorce rate and the instability of male-female relationships.

Aware of American ideas about human relations, including the concept of noninterference, Mrs. Nam worries about bothering her husband: "As Americans are self-centered, Korean Americans here learn to adopt that attitude. It becomes difficult to handle feelings between husband and wife or parents and children because they have different expectations of each other. For instance, I worry whether I bother my husband, but I do want his concern. . . . Life here is too bitter, and everybody is too busy with their own affairs. . . . At first my husband used to help me, but not now." She said he now spends his free time at a newly established Korean chess parlor in the neighborhood.

Sunyoung told me, "It was not until 1980 that I came into contact with other Koreans. As far as I could see, in the past Korean immigrants suffered and were not successful at all. But now the Korean immigrants are not only rich in the material sense but also in culture. For instance, in the past I would rarely see Koreans enjoy cultural performances at such places as Lincoln Center or the operas in Central Park. I used to go to concerts alone. Sometimes I tried to take my friends whom I came to know through church. They were scared and viewed my actions as wrong. Concretely speaking, if one is said to have 'been to Greenwich Village,' they do not see you as a 'good girl.'" In this case we see that immigrant women are subject to two different gender ideologies in America—public pleasure seeking and Korean Christian conservatism—in addition to gender expectations from Korea.

Such views can clash in the same household. For example, a middle-aged Korean woman showed off a new, fashionable pair of boots to her son, who was in his late twenties. The son was silent for a while and then told his mother indignantly, "Pass them to me. I'll throw them away. They are proper for young girls, not for you." After hearing this, his father asked him, "Son, guess who bought them? I bought them for your mother. Who is the boss in this family?" Here American ideas of female beauty and enjoyment were opposed by a son influenced by Korean notions of the proper mother. It is also interesting to see that the son's opposition was blocked by his more American-oriented father.


## Women's Views of Life in America

Korean women's viewpoints are formed within a particular constellation of workplace, household, culture, and demography. In addition, we need to understand the subjects' point of view: women's self-evaluation of their new immigrant lives. Unlike men's, women's self-evaluations have less to do with their changing class status than with changing gender relations.

Korean women in America show a high rate of labor force participation and, as we have seen, work under harsh conditions. U.S. census data in 1980 showed that in California more than 25 percent of Korean immigrant women held low-paying jobs, with the greatest concentration in the opera-tor category, where they are nearly four times as numerous as white women (Chu 1988: 203). Despite high levels of education, many suffer from a language barrier, 51 percent said that they do not speak English well or at all, which is a higher percentage than for any other Asian immigrant group (Gardner, Robey, and Smith 1985: 28). Demograph-ically, there is a severe imbalance in adult sex ratios: overall there are seventy-one men to one hundred women and only fifty-three men to one hundred women in the twenty- to thirty-nine-year-old age group (Yu 1986: 19). (Chapter 2 discusses demographic characteristics in relation to immigration history.)

After living for some time in America, Korean immigrant women seem to react in one of two ways. Especially after revisiting Korea, some regret their decision to come here, realizing they live a hard life. They imagine that, if they had not come to America, they could have enjoyed a peaceful, less stressful life as a housewife, perhaps even hiring a maid due to the low cost of labor in Korea. But others, who also might envy the comforts of life in Korea, do not regard the life of a housewife as desirable. On the basis of their own experience, they now say that it is important for women to work outside the home and thereby be independent in an economic sense, and they find this more possible in America. In short, this new understanding relates to their pursuit of human dignity. They recall that in Korea they were not able to work and felt useless in confronting financial crises in the household. Thus, in describing their new understanding, I use the term *human dignity* rather than the much favored *autonomy*. Feminists often stress the concept of autonomy—that is, a sense of self-direction and self-determination that grows through affiliation and connection with others rather than through competition (Humm 1990: 14). My interviewees, however, hardly ever relate their new status to autonomy, freedom, or equality. Instead, they refer to dignity, (*chonŏm*) or human liberation, (*ingan haebang*) and stress that they are now able to make an equal contribution to the household as a full member of society. Ms. Kim works at a sewing factory: "I think that it was a good decision for me to come to America. Everything that women need is available to us. What is more, women can have better jobs in terms of pay than in Korea. If I stayed in Korea, I would only have suffered a lot."

Significantly, both men and women perceive that women change much more than men do in this immigrant society. Men's behavior also changes, as my data reveal, but it is interesting that few people see things this way. Mr. Han, a worker at a greengrocery, said: "While Korean men don't seem to change greatly, Korean women seem to change completely. They become more frank and open. There then seem to be lots of problems. As they want to do things differently, it doesn't fit with a Korean way of life. For instance, they even may look down on their husbands, which women didn't do in Korea." As Deaconess Ahn sees it, "here, as Korean women can work and thereby support themselves, we can have greater pride in ourselves. By working, I can give an allowance to my children. How nice this is! In Korea, when I needed more money than my husband's salary in order to pay tuition for my children, I didn't know what to do. So now I thank God. On the contrary, my husband, like many Korean men, didn't like American life at all at the beginning of our life here. He regretted his situation and felt lonely and tired of his life. Almost every day he complained, I remember. I figure that's because he is addicted to the life of a Korean gentlemen."

## Women's Perceptions of Work

In Korea, women tend to stop paid work upon marriage. In addition, many workplaces have age restrictions on women's employment. For example, in the Masan Free Export Zone, most electronics factories only hire women who are between seventeen and twenty-two years of age (S. K. Kim 1990).

In America, the birth of a child rather than getting married, stops Korean women's employment. What accounts for this difference?

Once they migrate, women often join husbands who are earning an average of $1,000 a month in small Korean firms. Women soon realize that this is not enough to support a family; in New York City they spend at least $600 to $700 a month for rent. So women have to work to help the whole household, not only to satisfy their personal financial needs. More is involved, however, than simple calculation of necessity. Some women do decide to migrate in order to improve their economic independence. And as one of my informants put it, even if you try to stay home, you soon find yourself isolated with nobody at home to talk to. This is quite different from Korea, where housewives are rarely the only person at home. There are also more important considerations arising from the Korean American dream. In the United States people work in order to make money, no matter who they are or in what condition they find themselves. Thus, women who do not work begin to feel foolish or useless.

In the immigrant community, everybody knows that women can make a significant contribution to the family economy—as much as men do, in fact. Gender ideology has shifted from Korea. It is clear to Koreans in the United States that if a man remains single, it is impossible for him to save enough to start a business. Thus, wives are considered to be economically valuable assets. But unexpectedly, after finally establishing a family business, women often find that they are more occupied with running the store than their men are. Mrs. Lee, who runs a greengrocery with her husband, is tired of doing both store work and housework. She said, "Even if you don't work, staying home and doing housework will also make you tired. I feel that I take better care of the store than my husband. He says that he needs to have his own time, getting together with his men friends. It seems that women do not have similar needs. So he often goes out, asking me to take care of the store. Sometimes he just rests at home, making excuses about his advancing age. He leaves no room for my needs, thinking that I am never too tired to take care of the store."

It is true that most immigrant women take jobs outside the home, a radical change from life in Korea. But if we look at the kinds of jobs they get and how they are treated, we do not find a rosy picture. Only by adopting the Korean American dream can women feel they are on the way to establishment and avoid feeling ashamed in these jobs. They would never engage in such occupations in their home country, and the jobs themselves do not provide any positive self-esteem. As with immigrant men, there is downward mobility, which is particularly poignant for professional women. Meanwhile, they experience a new place in the hierarchy of gender and racial or ethnic categories that segment the U.S. labor market. Women, they learn, have less chance to be promoted, get a raise, or ever become a manager, whether in American or Korean-owned firms. Mrs. Chung, who works at a Korean vegetable stand, earns $300 a week. She began as a cashier with a starting salary of about $220. At her level, however, she is more likely to be fired than to be promoted. A male greengrocery worker starts at around $240 a week and in two or three years can earn $400 as a manager. Men's work—taking care of the fruit and vegetables—is considered more important and a harder task than women's work at the cash register. In offices, a woman is supposed to work only as a secretary, a receptionist, or a typist regardless of her education. Men have more chance of advancing in more rewarding business arenas.

## Women's Reevaluations of Housework

Depending on their experience with housework in Korea, women immigrants evaluate housework differently. Older women who have lived in rural Korea are likely to feel that housework in America is easier than in Korea. Mrs. Chung, in her sixties, asked, "How can you say that it is even work at all to clean a kitchen or bathroom here, compared with cleaning a kitchen in Korea? There it is a tough job, but not here. Even in the case of ironing, are there any clothes here which really need ironing? For me it is next to nothing to cook three meals and to make *kimch'i* and *panch'an* [side dishes] here, compared with the labor in Korea." Ms. Suh remembered having to make a wood fire: "It is much more convenient here. Since I lived in the countryside, I had to make a fire in order to cook. Here, we can save time by cooking with gas. I can have hot water at any time. In addition, I can take a shower as often as possible. How nice it is to live in America!"

Mrs. Lee, who runs a greengrocery, has developed a "superwoman" self-presentation to deal with the multiple burdens of work and housework. "I don't have to sweep and mop by kneeling down, which is very inconvenient. Here, as we cover our floor with carpets, I don't have to bother to do that. We can wash our clothes by machine, which is fast and convenient. [I asked if she felt tired doing housework after leaving her business.] If you think of it as work, you feel more tired. It is O.K. if you can just manage it sensibly. After all, it is what women are supposed to do. I always consider how I can do both my store work and housework more efficiently."

Men and women seem to have quite different opinions about housework (see Chapter 4). This stems from circumstances related to immigration: reduction in the absolute volume of housework, change in terms of quality of housework, and aid from machines and technology. But all of the changes are not beneficial. With immigration, there is also the loss of help from kin and relatives and the lack of an affordable household worker, readily available in Korea. With the new employment situation some women find it more difficult to handle duties at home. This causes some men and women to feel that Korean women are too quickly Americanized and therefore lazy in the home.

As more women work outside the house, some try to live up to the superwoman image while others gradually neglect housework. This follows the usually brief period when Korean men tend to help their wives with housework, generally in the beginning stage of immigrant establishment. Once they are secure enough to start their own businesses, men end these contributions. At this point, their wife's labor power in the firm also becomes less critical; and if they are successful, they begin to use wage labor as well as family labor. Some men do acknowledge that women have a substantial burden in this immigrant society and provide some help. But many other men do no housework at all.

Mr. Chung owns a fish market in Elmhurst. At home, either his wife or his daughters do most of the housework. He said: "Only a silly man, like someone without a gall bladder, would do the cooking for his wife. Well, it might be good to alternate such work, but, you know, a man's job is very difficult. Men get tired out. Anyway, housework is easier here. That's because we eat a simpler diet. People care less about eating formal meals. The cooking facilities are better, too."

In the case of Mr. and Mrs. Ho, we see a modicum of sharing. Mr. Ho, in his late fifties, told me: "As far as cooking is concerned, most is done by my wife. As far as doing dishes and cleaning is concerned, 30 percent is done by me. Vacuuming and garbage disposal are done jointly or by me. Although most housework belongs to women, here it is inevitable for me to help my wife with household chores. Besides, my wife has a problem with her health, so I help her more. To me it is much more convenient

**[129]**

here, since we can use the vacuum, oven, and the more conveniently designed bathroom."

What is debated now by women in the Korean American community is not so much equal sharing of housework as men's effort to help with it at all. This finding is consistent with other literature on the immigrant family (Lamphere 1987; Grasmuck and Pessar 1991). As Lamphere found among Portuguese and Colombian families in Rhode Island, many immigrants maintain a family ideology that "values the husband as head of the household, emphasizes respect by children for parents, and stresses gender differences between males and females in the face of considerable changes in the allocation of productive and reproductive labor" (1986: 129). In some exceptional cases, where men do more housework than they did in Korea, a more positive marital relationship often develops. Mrs. Park, a pharmacist, elaborated: "In Korea I did such things as putting out garbage, ironing, and washing clothes, and my husband merely took care of the charcoal briquettes [for cooking and heating.]⁴ Cleaning was done by the maid. Here, since I can share some of the housework with my husband, I feel much better, and he also seems to feel good about his involvement in it."

## New Gender Consciousness

With life in America, Korean American men and women develop different attitudes about each other. Some men view women with sympathy (although this does not always mean they share the housework burden); others think that women lead an easier life than in Korea; still others object that women in the United States become rebellious. According to women, men in America are relaxed in their attitudes and withdraw into playing golf. Some women think that young men, especially those born in the United States, tend to treat women better, while older men almost never change. The experience of Japanese American immigrants before World War II supports an argument that women's entry into the labor force leads to realignment of gender attitudes in the household. Farming and small-business families engaged in household-based enterprise reproduced traditional Japanese gender relations in the household. In contrast,

4. Many female interviewees referred to charcoal briquettes, *yŏnt'an*, when they recalled domestic work in Korea. Women's domesticity was evaluated according to their tending of charcoal briquettes, partly because the briquettes play an important role in heating and cooking in the home and partly because they require constant attention.

*issei* (first-generation) families who shifted from these economic activities to multiple wage-earning displayed greater discontinuity (Glenn 1986: 216). In the Korean American case, the pattern is somewhat different. Most women begin as wage workers and shift to family businesses after their husbands establish them. With this stage of establishment as their initial goal, their distinction between wage and family business work is less sharp than it was for Japanese women. The variety in male-female attitudes does not have any single determining cause. Class, age, and experience are all involved. In a few cases, professional couples develop mutually positive gender viewpoints. But there were only a few professional couples among my informants. Mrs. Park is from one of these marriages: "In my view, what is good about America is the fact that women can argue for their opinions and can have jobs. Personally I don't have any complaint. My husband, unlike the typical Korean husband, listens to me a lot and always tries to help. Be that as it may, it is true that women get a stronger voice in America when they make money on their own."

Older women, now in their sixties, often refer to how it used to be in Korea; younger women, even if born in the countryside, have only the experience of an urbanized Korea in the 1960s and 1970s. Overall, women do tend to adjust to life in America. It is more often men who do not. Mr. Ha explained, "While my mother feels very comfortable about life in America, I don't." He also believes that Korean women in America have become spoiled to the extent that they consume money without considering how much they earn. When they see a new immigrant, like himself, carefully consider spending even ten dollars, they laugh at him, saying this is typical of new immigrants. "If I have a wife in the future, I don't want her to work. I have seen too many cases of women's employment leading to failure in married life. If a woman becomes independent economically, she is liable to divorce her husband, even over something minor."

Interestingly, young women do not necessarily see any change in men of their own generation. Older women, such as Mrs. Choi in her fifties, may be more observant: "I think that Korean guys tend to be dependent on their parents or parents-in-law. They are usually authoritarian, especially toward women. To make matters worse, if their wives work, they like to stay home. How naive they are! On the contrary, young guys educated in the United States, if they are properly educated, are very thoughtful and considerate. So, to be honest with you, I would like to have a U.S.–educated son-in-law. However, these young guys should also have a strong belief in God."

Terry, a young woman, works as an organizer for the International Ladies Garment Workers Union. One of her Korean female union members told her, "My son is also knee-high generation like you. But it would be unfortunate to have one of these useless young women as my daughter-in-law." Terry felt insulted. She said: "Those women brought from Korea to marry a knee-high generation man, like my sister-in-law, are no good either. She thinks only about her appearance: how to dress in full feather. She is an extravagant person. She has a bossy manner, which I hate. However, it is true that Korean girls who grow up here make difficult wives. Although most of them prefer to marry a Korean, they are not looked on with favor by Korean men."

## New Choices for Women

The new situation of husband and wife as co-workers greatly influences their marital relationship. Bonacich has stated that small business puts stress on the husband-wife relationship (1988).[5] Min, on the contrary, argues that it reinforces conjugal ties (1988b; 1990). Hong (1982: 130) reports that Koreans in Los Angeles appear to be less happy with their marriages than the general married population of the United States, even though a substantial majority describe their marriage as "happy" or "very happy." I argue that we should go beyond this dualistic framework. Instead of asking whether immigrant life makes a positive or a negative impact on family/kin and gender relations, it is more productive to identify those aspects of family life that are changed by small business activities.

Because Koreans enter the segmented labor markets of New York City, they face limitations in the kinds of jobs that men and women can get. One ironic result is that it is not rare for women to earn more than men do. Mr. Yu, thirty years old, expressed this point: "Korean women try to live as human beings equal to men. As a result of this, some women go too far: They are too frank and easygoing. In Korea, they were extremely good at thrift, but not here. On the contrary, males are the same here. As women become independent in the economic sense, there are many problems

5. According to Bonacich, small business contributes to family breakdown in the following ways: First, it typically absorbs most of the time and attention of both parents, leaving little time to spare for children; second, small businesses can put stress on the relationship between the husband and wife; finally, and perhaps most important, the hardships of immigrant entrepreneurship are undertaken on the presumption that the family will accumulate capital and climb up the social ladder (1988: 125).

related to this. For example, if a wife earns $400 per week by working at a garment factory and a husband earns only $300 working at a fruit stand, she is liable to have a sense of her own superiority."

Mr. Pai is a Yellow Cab driver, and his wife is a waitress at a Korean restaurant. He also pointed to difficulties in marital relations due to women's employment: "It is meaningless to maintain a married life here. Look at my family. My wife and I work at different times. I do not see my wife's face except on Saturday. Besides that, I cannot see friends. Nor do I even see any acquaintances as often as I did in Korea. [I asked about Korean women here.] They get bold. As they get economic power, they seem to laugh at their husbands. I expect a more respectful attitude from women. And that includes my wife." Although his case is extreme, the problem is typical in the immigrant family.

Mr. Won runs a garment factory in Elmhurst. As he sees it, Koreans living in America experience profound changes in family life. He believes that the stresses of work create a very difficult situation between husband and wife.

> When both husband and wife work together, there seems to be conflict between them. When both of them come home, tired from work, each can ask the other to share housework. The wife doesn't have great respect for her husband any more, since he does menial jobs, such as working at a greengrocery. All family members are sullen, full of complaints toward each other, and toward their work. Many Koreans don't act to the best of their ability because of the language barrier. They find they are trying just to maintain their daily lives, without remembering the original dream of what they wanted to do in America. They are too frustrated to do anything about their dead-end situation.

Some couples develop a new dimension to their marital life by discussing business matters. Husbands in Korea work and come home late after socializing with their colleagues; wives stay home and take care of housework. There is little time for verbal communication between them. Commitment to a shared relationship, which many couples experience in the United States is only one of the new choices facing immigrant women. Choice also occurs in another context: a growth in the number of women remaining single, an increase in the divorce rate, and a rise in cases of marital separation for older women. Similarly, Grasmuck and Pessar reported in their study of Dominican households in New York City that for many women "the struggle to gain greater parity has not led to a more egalitarian household but, rather, to the dismantling of the union" (1991: 156). The divorce rate for Korean women in the United States has increased dramatically. In Korea, 6.2 out of 1,000 women over fifteen years old are divorced, but in America the figure for Korean women is 36.8, a sixfold increase. This figure includes divorces by women who were not married to Korean men, such as military wives. Real figures may be even higher; this figure is based on cases formally reported at the Korean consulates. Meanwhile, for men, the figure is 3.6 divorces in Korea per 1,000 men, which increases to 15.0 when they immigrate to the United States (Korean National Bureau of Statistics 1984; U.S. Bureau of the Census 1984). This figure is still well below the figure of 93.7 per 1,000 for other American men. Note, however, that Korean divorce law is different from American law. It was not until 1989 that the Korean family code was amended to make divorces easier.[6]

## The Context of New Marital Decisions

When a young Korean immigrant man is about to marry, he will usually make a trip to Korea because he or his family thinks that most young women in America are contaminated by American culture. With money he has saved, the young man will first purchase several new suits. Then, over several months, he is introduced to woman after woman until he finds his intended spouse.

Mr. Han is twenty-eight years old and works for a Korean greengrocer. His new wife is still in Korea. She quit her job as secretary in her father's company four months ago in order to prepare for her journey to America. Mr. Han met his wife through a friend of his mother and it took only ten days to make his decision. Mr. Chung is twenty-seven years old and works in his brother's greengrocery. Next year his wife will arrive in the United States. They married a few months ago. It took him four months to find a wife after numerous introductions.

Korean women in America complain, "There are already more women than men in the Korean American community, and yet the guys bring more and more girls from Korea. Who can guarantee that girls in Korea are virgins? People don't realize that girls are apt to be less [romantically or sexually] experienced here, because of the lack of opportunities to meet Korean men." Nonetheless, I found that single women in the United

6. For detailed discussion regarding Korean women's low legal status, see Yoo (1985).

States, whether not yet married, divorced, or widowed, tend to exhibit greater self-confidence than those in Korea largely due to their greater economic independence. Single women make more decisions about their lives than they would in Korea. Ms. Choi made it clear that it is less difficult for single women to live alone in America than in their homeland: "There are many good aspects about life here from my point of view. I don't have to hear those worrisome statements, such as 'Why aren't you married yet?'; 'It's a big disaster'; 'There must be a problem with you'; or 'You must be lacking something.' As I can be independent economically here, I feel wonderful. As to negative aspects about America, I would list drug addiction, immorality, and the high divorce rate." Now she feels that she was once excessively searching for love, which did not deserve such energy. It is nothing in comparison to love of God, she asserts.

Youngmi is a divorcée in her late thirties. She said: "When my husband, a third-generation Korean American man, and I divorced and he left for Hawaii by himself, I felt that the sky was going to collapse [*hanŭli munŏjida*]. However, I feel fine now. This decision should be made more by one's own point of view than by social considerations."

Jenny is twenty-seven years old and came to America when she was twelve years old. Recently, she broke off an engagement with her fiancé. She talked about him:

> Fortunately, he was looking for an active and tough [*walgadak*] woman. However, as I saw him more and more, I found him to be very traditional, a mere mama's boy. He is a formalist and cares about good family background, education, and professional background, what Korean seniors [*ŏrŭn*] like but which I hate. I used to wear clothes indecently on purpose as a kind of social protest, which he used to criticize a lot. I think he is lacking in practice, considering his theoretical ideal. He is indecisive. After all, he might be a victim as an *ilchŏmose* [those who came as children from Korea to America]. He lacks strong ideals and will, unlike men in Korea, but neither is he in the mainstream of American society.

## Interracial Marriage

I encountered a few cases of interracial marriages (see Kitano and Chai 1982). In Korean, *kukche kyŏrhon* (international marriage) refers specifically to Korean brides of American GIs. It is commonly held that many of these marriages end in divorce (see S. D. Kim 1979). In fact, at a military base near Seattle, 80 percent of the marriages between white servicemen and foreign-born Asian women ended in divorce (Hoyt 1974: 123). In Queens, people nowadays try to distinguish young professional Korean American women who are married to white professional men from Korean GI brides, some of whom, whether still married or not, are part of the Queens Korean community.

Mrs. Kwon talked about how difficult it was for her to approve of her daughter's marriage to an American man:

> I sent my eldest daughter to study here. Although she was good in her studies, she married a British student. I was terribly disappointed. It was not easy for me to support her financially. I had my own dreams for my daughter. So I told her that I would never come to America, and I didn't attend her wedding. I would not let her come to Korea, where she would be treated as a war bride and held in contempt. My daughter's father-in-law was a veteran of the Korean War; in fact he was a general in the U.S. Army. He felt bad that his son and daughter-in-law could not visit Korea, as if a white married a black in America. However, my daughter eventually visited Korea, bringing her daughter. After seeing her, and my grand-daughter, I felt better. But I couldn't get rid of the feeling of betrayal.

Mr. Um also married an American, but his marriage did not have a happy ending: "In my fourth year in America I met one woman. After four months, we decided to marry. However, I felt that, although she was ready to marry me, at some point she would divorce me. Her daughter from her first marriage didn't like the idea of her mother's marriage to me, an Asian man, so she left home. She used to say, 'I understand if you have him as your boyfriend, mother, but why do you have to have him as a husband? I don't understand.' Although the daughter came back in two months, we felt awkward. Finally my wife did divorce me."

### New Decisions in Sexuality

Young Koreans in America constantly compare American male/female relationships to Korean ones. Some young Korean couples are even brave enough to live together before marriage. In Korea, this is rare among the middle class, although it is common in the working class.[7] In America, Korean men take advantage of both American and Korean dating cultures

7. S. K. Kim (1990) and U. Kim (1993) report that some of their women worker interviewees in Korea were living with a man before they were married. Laurel Kendall reports similar findings (personal communication).

by asking women to be faithful to them, following the Korean mores, and at the same time adopting what women see as the American reluctance to make a commitment to one woman. In Korea, if a man does not actually marry a woman to whom he promised marriage, and with whom he then had sexual relations during courtship, he can be taken to court and jailed.

There are also changes in sexual relations among middle-aged couples, according to Mrs. Lee, a greengrocer: "So far I know little about the real world. I didn't even know how to use birth control, which surprised my gynecologist. But unlike me, most Korean women I see are crazy about leading a luxurious life. They are vain creatures. They become very aggressive toward the opposite sex by paying so much attention to their physical beauty. In my case, I have never bought any clothes or jewelry at a department store. So I don't want to make friends with those women. As a result, I don't even want to go to church." Mrs. Lee also spoke of what is seen by many Koreans as a pathological aspect of their new community: the penetration of massage parlors into the immigrant family environment. According to a gynecologist I interviewed, many wives are under great stress, taking care of both job and home. Often their sex lives are adversely affected, resulting in reduced interest or desire. They worry that their husbands will turn to a bar hostess or a massage parlor for sexual attention. In Korea it is not uncommon for men to visit bar hostesses or even prostitutes, but it is new for wives in the United States to seek professional advice about marital relations.

The next generation has its problems, too. Korean girls who have grown up in America have difficulty finding husbands. They prefer to marry a Korean man because they more easily understand each other and share the same culture. Yet some of these women are not seen as desirable by Korean men.

In this chapter, we examined the relationship between Korean immigrant women and emancipation in the context of their dream of establishment. Scholars who study immigration, women, and work in general agree that the new cash-earning status of married immigrant women provides them with a strategically better position vis-à-vis their husbands. But scholars have focused on the workplace without paying equal attention to the changing role of women in their families. Despite their new economic status, immigrant women do not seem to gain much in negotiating their gender roles (Lamphere 1986, 1987; Safa 1987).

My study also stresses the need to look at the impact of American gender ideology on new immigrant women. Korean immigrants are influenced by both Korean and American gender ideologies and by their daily experience as husbands and wives. As I have discussed, gender plays a vital role in realizing the Korean American dream of establishment. More significant, however, are the changes that occur in reproductive activities. Although many Korean immigrant families adhere to an ideology that emphasizes the husband's authority, respect for parents, and differing roles for men and women, increasing numbers of women are developing new attitudes.

The employment factor is revolutionary for most Korean women. Because they are economically independent, many develop a new self-confidence and creative ways to deal with their daily lives. Overall their new gender consciousness manifests itself in a growing sense of human dignity. This concept can be defined in terms of improved self-esteem, self-confidence, autonomy, freedom, and equality; however, it also relates to the feeling that women have become full members of society by making equal contributions in their families. This new gender consciousness helps women negotiate their gender relations. Some decide to divorce, separate, or not to marry at all. When women stand up for themselves, many men feel that their wives have become less obedient, less "Korean," and more "American." Thus, American realities do not match American dreams for those still struggling for establishment, or even for many who find it.

# [7]

# Conceptions of Race and Ethnicity: Workplace Encounters

Koreans arriving at J.F.K. International Airport are impressed by the diversity of people in America. When they settle in the multiethnic community of Queens, questions arise. Who are these other people? Who are we? In "Poem by a Yellow Woman," Sook Ryul Ryu (1996) considers their ethnic dilemma:

> When colored friends are making a rainbow coalition,
> my yellow people wonder whether yellow is on the
>    rainbow.
> They think the lighter the skin, the closer to heaven,
> the darker the skin, the closer to hell.
> They decide yellow is in between.
> So they smile at white and frown at black.
> They make money in the hope of becoming a majority
> and forget about the minority.
>
> And now here I am torn between
> my own self-flattery and my own revolt.

In this chapter I explore how Koreans answer questions of ethnicity as they meet people of other ethnic backgrounds. In general, their experience in small business enterprises appears to structure emergent ideologies of race and ethnicity. In addition, neighborhood, school, church, and other settings provide contexts for building relations between Korean immigrants and other ethnicities. (For more about ethnic encounters in the neighborhood, see Chapter 8.)

Barth provided the classic formulation for the study of ethnicity: "The critical focus of investigation . . . becomes the ethnic boundary that defines the group, not the cultural stuff that it encloses" (1969: 15). In other words, an ethnic population often is better understood as a category rather than a group; and analyses of ethnic interactions should focus on reciprocal relations occurring between individuals of different ethnic categories, not on those between entire ethnic groups (Vincent 1974).

## Being Asian in America: *Tongyanggye Mikukin*

Perhaps the most jarring change for Korean immigrants in America is their awareness of being Asian. Their experiences in New York offer opportunities to build common understandings with other Asian immigrants, particularly the Chinese in Queens. As Korean immigrants spend time in a racially divided America, they learn that being Asian American and immigrant, *tongyanggye mikukin* (people in the United States but from the Asian continent) is a stigma.[1] Historically, however, Asian Americans in the United States have been treated sometimes like blacks and other times like whites, making the racial meaning of "being Asian" ambiguous. Many Korean immigrants had little consciousness of their skin color before they arrived in the United States. Moreover, it is one thing to hear about racial prejudice and quite another to experience it as a fixed part of one's daily existence. Indeed, the movement from a society where being Korean is taken for granted to one where Koreans are a minority lumped with other Asians has sharply heightened Koreans' consciousness of their racial and ethnic identity.

Most of my informants assign Asians a status higher than that of African Americans and lower than that of white Americans (which reflects the dominant ideology of race in America). Whether Asians are higher or lower than Latin Americans varies among Koreans in Queens. Some also point out that, in terms of individual or household income, Asians may rank higher than African Americans; however, in terms of language fluency, familiarity with American culture, and political power, African Americans are better off than Asians.

1. Literally, it means those Americans who can be traced to Asia. *Tongyang* means "east," indicating countries such as China, Korea, and Japan. It is unclear if this term also includes Indians, Filipinos, Thais, and so on.

If Koreans continue to believe in the American dream, they never forget that even the most successful immigrant still belongs to an ethnic minority in American society. Nonetheless, they can aspire to middle or upper rank inside the Korean community, and the drive for establishment in these terms continues. But their reassessments of the American dream usually begin with the question of how they are treated by others in America.

Discrimination and prejudice toward Koreans are now widely discussed in the community. In addition to cases of police brutality, many Korean merchants complain about harassment and exploitation by city law enforcement officers (see Chapter 8). A beer distributor talked about his difficulties: "I feel that we tongyanggye are subjected to cold treatment. For instance, when there is a quarrel, the police, who are supposed to be evenhanded, support and argue only for whites. If an inspector from the City Department of Sanitation notices garbage improperly placed in front of my store, which is in fact the overflow from the white storeowner next door, still they ask me to pay a fine."

Korean retailers or garment industry subcontractors also feel the bite of discrimination, often at the beginning of their relationship with their jobbers or manufacturers. Mr. Won, the owner of a garment factory in Elmhurst, said: "When I had not yet lived in New York for a long time, a man whom I was asking for trucking information told his colleagues that I was hopeless because I am a colored person. This humiliated me. Due to my poor English, I suppose, they laughed at me. I felt so bad."

Customers often falsely accuse Korean business proprietors of insults or shortchanging on work or money. Sometimes resentful customers cause damage on purpose, bring false charges, or provoke a shopkeeper by verbal or physical attack. Mr. Kim, an automobile body shop owner, told me: "Well, when I could not communicate with customers, often I was falsely charged. For example, when customers argued and complained to the police that we had not done the job properly, there was nothing we could do. I think this is a kind of racism. Even a small kid came to me and told me to go back to my country. If I had command of English, I know they would treat us differently."

Korean consumers also encounter difficulty while shopping. Although it may appear minor, this is a common complaint. In these cases, salespeople or merchants give Korean customers a hard time and show that they are not pleased to wait on them. Mrs. Choi, a grocery owner, said: "When I go shopping, they look down upon us, and they do not greet us. They never do this to others, especially to whites. Whenever I call a repairman for my refrigerator, they usually do not come quickly. If I call a Korean repairman, they come immediately." Ms. Choi feels there is much racism in America. At first she did not realize it, but now she experiences it everywhere. For instance, when she goes shopping or to a restaurant, she feels that she is not served properly. One day she went to a café in Greenwich Village. She was not permitted to sit outside and saw that all the Asian customers were inside. She said that other Koreans have told her similar stories about racist attitudes of restaurant workers.

Some even experience racist name calling in the street. Mr. Lee, who runs a Korean restaurant in Elmhurst, said: "I think that I have lived my life in vain. In America I am not treated well. People laugh at me, calling me *Chino* [Spanish for Chinese]. Therefore, we Koreans should stick together. I think that Koreans are at the bottom of the American social structure. Hispanics are poorer than us but have more power."

Individually, Koreans experience ethnic antagonism in a broad span of daily life, including shopping, dating, schools, and court appearances. Mr. Kang, a real estate broker, told me that at school he was always rejected by white girls when he asked them for dates. Once he asked out a German girl who was willing to pursue an Afghan man, but she turned down Mr. Kang. He got angry and attributed the incident to racism. According to him, racism and discrimination are also part of the American court system. A landlord since 1976, he has gone through many legal proceedings. He said: "Even if you are bitten by a white's dog, still you will lose. Ethnic discrimination is widespread. For example, in 1983 I was sued for lack of heating. In that case, if you are white, you will be fined only $25 or $100, but $2,000 or $3,000 if Chinese, and, if Korean, you will be fined $4,000. This reflects community power in the justice system. There are already many Chinese judges. So we badly need second-generation Korean American judges, a district attorney, and lawyers in the future."

## Race, Ethnicity, and Class

Korea has been a country with one homogenous population for more than a millennium. Partly borrowing from the Chinese conception of the world, Koreans believe themselves to be more civilized than any other nation except China. Thus, they dismissed whites as *yangi* (Western Barbarians) until the late nineteenth century, when Korea was confronted by the military power of the supposedly inferior yangi and the *waenom*, a derogatory term for the Japanese (J. Yi 1993). Since that time, Koreans' racial framework has developed in a global context. As Sanjek asserts, "race is the framework of ranked categories segmenting the human population that was developed by western Europeans following their global expansions beginning in the 1400s" (1994: 1). From the turn of the twentieth century, whites occupied a higher position in Koreans' conception of the world racial hierarchy, reflecting their realization that whites controlled the world with superior military, economic, and political power. Since 1945, the predominance of U.S.–educated Koreans in government and business and the presence of the U.S. Army in South Korea has also contributed to this conception.

Meanwhile, blacks came to occupy the bottom of Koreans' racial hierarchy, in accordance with the global view of races that Sanjek alludes to. As yet, no one has studied the precise evolution of Korean prejudice against blacks. Although some scholars contend that "The primary source of Korean American racism toward African Americans is the American racial ideology" (Abelmann and Lie 1995: 150), exposure to African Americans has been largely limited to Koreans' experience with black soldiers after the Korean War. What is significant is that through American media Koreans have learned that the dominant people in society are mostly white, while blacks are depicted as part of the lower classes or as criminals.

After immigration, the experience of running small business enterprises that appears to structure Koreans' emergent ideologies of race and ethnicity.[2] When Korean immigrants start businesses, they begin to refine their previous understanding of race in America. While some develop elaborate conceptualizations of this multiethnic society, others hold much simpler notions. All Koreans observe, however, that in America the lighter one's skin color, the better one is treated. They notice that there are white, black, and brown Latin Americans and also learn that the typical description of blond hair and blue eyes does not seem to apply to many whites in America or New York City. Overall, the numerous nationalities and languages and heterogeneous physical appearances of Americans cause Korean immigrants to shift from a narrow racial analysis of U.S. society to a

2. This generalization is based on my in-depth interviews with 109 Korean immigrants.

more complex ethnic analysis. Although they use the Korean term *injong* for race, there is no Korean term for ethnicity. Therefore, they use the same term for ethnicity, (injong or *minjok*) that they use for race or nation.

In analyzing the ethnic encounters involving Koreans in workplaces, I found that class differences produce different ethnic conceptions. The class segments of Korean Americans—worker, businessperson, and professional—are each associated with distinct ideologies of race and ethnicity derived from differences in their workplace interactions. For example, African American allegations of Korean racism apply mostly to small business proprietors; Korean American professionals and workers are almost never mentioned. These Koreans' ethnic attitudes, in fact, stand in contrast to those of small business proprietors. Professionals are more involved in the American mainstream and are more likely to experience direct racial discrimination by white Americans. Even more than professionals, Korean workers in American businesses experience discrimination. Nevertheless, small business proprietors are the pivotal group because they are the main agents in developing a Korean immigrant racial ideology.

## Small Business Proprietors

For Koreans in small businesses, ethnic encounters arise in their day-to-day operations. For the most part, these businesses provide a setting in which Koreans serve non-Korean customers. Both business proprietors and workers are aware of their subordinate position to white Americans in the U.S. system of ethnic stratification. They understand their role in replacing white American small business proprietors via "ethnic succession" and know that whites are aware of this as well.

After the Immigration Reform and Control Act of 1986, Korean business proprietors began to hire more non-Koreans, the majority of them immigrants from Latin American countries, who now compose more than one-third of their work force.[3] These circumstances have made Koreans more aware of which ethnicities they can consider subordinate to themselves. Korean small business proprietors also encounter various ethnic groups at their workplaces as suppliers and customers. White Americans are said to be problematic—difficult to please and sometimes even threat-

3. This is due to more availability of Latin American undocumented workers than Korean workers as well as changes in immigration laws, such as employer sanctions.

ening lawsuits. Some shopkeepers are too ready to suspect African Americans of being potential shoplifters, primarily because of rumor or bad experiences. This has created situations of conflict.[4]

## Latin Americans As the Best Customers

Many Korean small business proprietors in Queens say that Latin Americans are their best customers. Some express it even more precisely: They define the best business area as half Latin American and half African American. It is evident that their choice of business neighborhood is by and large restricted by their amount of capital; however, it is unclear why they prefer these minority neighborhoods. They admit that one can make more money in a white neighborhood but say that they prefer the friendliness of Latin Americans and African Americans. They do not feel the same warmth from white customers. Another reason I have heard is the claim that Latin Americans and African Americans are easier to deal with as customers. They do not take as much time to buy goods, are not difficult to please, and make fewer complaints than white customers do. Clearly most Korean/African American relationships are seen by Koreans as cordial rather than hostile.

In the following examples, I reproduce ethnic characteristics as they were presented to me. In Elmhurst, most white customers are older persons and in many cases less prosperous than new immigrants. Two Elmhurst Korean business operators identified Latin Americans as the best customers and whites as the most difficult, but each has a different explanation for this opinion.

Mrs. Choi runs a grocery. Among her customers, she said, "Latin Americans are the best. They are easier to deal with, without complaints. I have customers such as Colombian, Puerto Rican, German, Italian, and Jewish. Colombians just buy what they want, whereas Germans are very particular

4. Since the early 1980s, there have been increasing complaints, tensions, and dissatisfaction toward Korean immigrant merchants in African American neighborhoods. Some residents have initiated boycott campaigns against Korean stores in New York, Philadelphia, Washington, D.C., Chicago, Atlanta, and Los Angeles. (See E. Chang [1990] for details.) The 1990 African American boycott of Korean grocers in Brooklyn is the most widely publicized example: "Since January, 1990, Brooklyn's Flatbush section had been embroiled by a black boycott of two Korean grocers that began after a Haitian woman accused the Koreans of assaulting her in an argument over a dollar worth of fruit" (*Time*, 28 May 1990).

and bargain over even one penny." Mrs. Lee runs a dry-cleaning store. She said:

> Seventy percent of my customers are Latin Americans, and the rest are Asians. Spanish people are good customers: They behave as gentlemen and are kind and friendly. They are people with whom I feel intimacy. Among Asians, Indians are difficult: They bring filthy clothes; they bargain over prices. Filipinos are clean. There are also some Chinese and Japanese. Among the Latin Americans, Colombians are a majority. But those elderly whites who could not leave this neighborhood—they are very difficult to please. They are stingy. At first they ignore you. Later, if you perform well, they accept it but even give back advice. In the past I was made to feel inferior to them because of their racism. Now I do not care any more.

Mr. Chung who runs a fish market in Washington Heights, Manhattan, and lives in Sunnyside, shared his experience: "Now I have hired two black workers. Both of them are very good. Because my store is in Washington Heights, 60 percent of my customers are Dominican; 25 percent are Puerto Rican; 10 percent are black; and the rest include Chinese, Japanese, or Korean. From my observation, Dominicans are a little richer than Puerto Ricans. Dominicans are moody people. There are a few Greek and Jewish customers, but I do not like to deal with them because they are very particular."

Mr. Kim, who has operated businesses in different neighborhoods on his trajectory to establishment, mentioned his wariness in dealing with both white and African American customers: "I used to run a shoe repair shop in the Bronx. I could make $500 or $600 per week. However, as it was in a Jewish neighborhood, people were very stingy. Even now, I do not want to run any business in such a neighborhood. After that, I ran a general merchandise store in an African American area in Brooklyn for one year. Although it was a good business area, I was always worried that they would quarrel with me and that someone would attack me. Now I operate an automobile body shop in Corona."

### Differences in Business Practice

In some cases, Korean business proprietors arrive at their evaluations of various ethnicities through their experiences with customers in different types of businesses. For instance, Koreans do not ask for discounts at beauty salons, but they do at drugstores. Accordingly, Koreans are considered the best customers by hair stylists but the worst by pharmacists. Perhaps this is due to the history of different business practices in Korea. In general, merchants have a positive view of customers who are big spenders. There is no doubt that Koreans buy much more than any other group at Korean groceries, and in those stores they are the preferred customers.

Mrs. Nam, a hairdresser who owns a beauty salon, commended on ethnic differences: "Seventy percent of my customers are Korean, and the rest are Hispanic, Jewish, Chinese, and Indian. Among them, the Jews are usually elderly, and Hispanics are both young and old. [When I asked more questions, she clarified that most Hispanics are Colombians.] Koreans are the best customers because they are very generous, and they are not difficult to please. Hispanics are fine, too. Jewish people often bargain over the price. Those who bargain over the price also tend to complain a lot about other things."

I asked Mr. Kim, who runs a drugstore, why Koreans are good customers at Korean-run beauty salons yet the worst at Korean-run drugstores. He shared his experiences: "Eighty percent of my customers are Korean, and the rest are Hispanic and white. In my opinion, there is little difference between any of them. However, Koreans are used to bargaining over prices and want to buy things on credit. If it is too high, Koreans simply do not buy it. Other ethnic groups accept my price. Besides, Koreans ask for medicine without a doctor's prescription. They do not know that in America there is a strict division of labor between doctors and pharmacists. My suppliers from pharmaceutical companies and medicine wholesalers are Jewish or Italian."

Mr. Rim, who runs a Korean supermarket, noted: "Eighty-five percent of my customers are Korean, and the rest are Japanese, Chinese, Indian, and Hispanics. Non-Korean customers do not tend to buy a lot, unlike Korean customers. But they do not complain and greet me in a friendly way."

Another situation is more complicated. Korean sewing factory owners often ask, Why don't Latin Americans work as hard as Koreans do? Asians, they say, are better educated than non-Asians. Mr. Won remarked:

> At the present time, there are forty-five workers, including those who do homework only, who are around ten. Among them, thirty are Korean, eight Chinese, five Spanish, two Indian. Usually those who want work

come directly to us, and then we screen them. I hire workers of different ethnic groups. Chinese are very diligent, working patiently. Spanish do not seem to accept heavy pressures of work, working exactly eight hours a day and five days a week. They do not seem to be quick in understanding the work either. On the contrary, in my experience, Koreans are very quick to learn the work, making fast progress. But they are not faithful: if it is no longer in their interest, they leave this job immediately. However, as members of the same ethnic group, they are sympathetic to their employer, working more than they are required.

Mr. Pai sees economic interests as more important than primordial attachments in defining his relations with other Koreans. What matters to him is profit, not ethnicity. "I distribute beer and other drinks to 150 or 200 retailers. Half are American stores, and the other half are Korean ones. If I make a comparison, although there seems to be a little difference, more Korean store owners tend to write bad checks, buy on credit, or get nervous about prices. This is because of their lack of capital."

## Workers

Workers have ideologies of ethnicity markedly different from those of their employers. Among other things, they emphasize the differences between Korean and American workplaces (see Chapter 3). They often state that Korean employers exploit their workers more than Americans do. Nevertheless, they experience paternalistic or more reciprocal relationships with their Korean employers. One important reason to work for Korean employers is to learn how to run small businesses.

### American Workplaces

Although most Korean immigrants work in Korean business establishments, an increasing number work for other Americans. In addition to experiencing language and cultural barriers, Korean workers often feel that they are not trusted by white employers. Mr. Chun, who worked at an automobile body shop, and recalled: "I was skilled and worked hard, so they treated me well because they needed me. I had both white and black American colleagues. The whites were very cool and suspicious of me as a tongyanggye. The blacks were very friendly and got along well with me. In my analysis, white Americans only know themselves and their own kind, and they are ethnocentric and arrogant."

To make matters worse, some Koreans feel that they are not respected when working for non-Koreans. Mr. Chung, now a fish market owner, told me: "When I was working at an American business, the boss lost something. From then on I was treated peculiarly. I was investigated three times. That did not happen to the other workers. I felt dishonored. And I was very upset. Finally, I called the police and asked them to investigate me and search my residence. How else could I clear myself from dishonor? Eventually I quit the job."

Although some report bad experiences with other minority workers, many Korean workers describe friendly relations. Mr. Nam is an example:

> Ordinary Americans seem to be backward. They have too many payments to make and concentrate on trying to enjoy their weekends. On the contrary, Koreans toil sixteen or eighteen hours per day in order to build up savings. For this, Americans make fun of us. At the bakery, I saw a second-generation Puerto Rican who had both a strange inferiority feeling and American pride. When I used to work hard, including overtime, he used to say, "Damn Chinese, you never know how to rest." But on the weekends he would spend all his money. Then he would ask me to lend him $10 or $20. I did, but I used to say, "You see, I am not a slave to money. I make an effort to work hard in order to save for the future. Don't you understand?"

### Korean Workplaces

In many Korean workplaces, employers hire non-Koreans, usually for specific jobs. There is, however, a difference in wage scales based on ethnicity as well as gender (see Chapter 6). One often observes job hierarchy: Koreans and sometimes white Americans hold a more central position than other workers do. Korean workers frequently become sympathetic to the lives of their non-Korean co-workers by talking about problems of immigrant life and sharing work, meals, and leisure time. One Korean worker expressed relief that he was not born a Mexican because they are paid less and exploited more by employers. At the Korean greengrocery where he worked, he and his Mexican fellow worker shared the 8 P.M. to 8 A.M. night shift, six days a week. While he was paid $350 a week as a cashier, the Mexican worker was paid $200.

Mr. Ha told me that there are different job descriptions and wages based on gender and ethnicity at the Korean wholesale store where he works. "Besides the employer and his wife, there are twelve workers:

**[149]**

Three are Spanish, and two are [Korean] female accountants. [All were paid less than Korean male workers.] Whereas Spanish workers only do sales for Spanish-speaking customers, Korean workers do many tasks. I am supposed to do various jobs, such as sales, shipping, and arranging stock."

Mr. Kim explained the different pay systems for Koreans and non-Koreans at a Korean garment factory, where he worked after leaving an American firm: "Americans are fair about working hours and payment. But in my opinion, Koreans just try to exploit other Koreans, taking advantage of them. As soon as I started to work, I was immediately covered with cloth dust. Koreans are too cold toward each other, compared with the Chinese and Japanese I see on the subway. As I see it, Korean women seem to remain at garment factories almost forever. I see that Spanish workers work only for an hourly rate, not piecework. Although they are less enterprising, they are kinder than Koreans. As I spoke English better, they became friendly to me."

In Korean small businesses, Korean workers are often directed by their employers to deal with suspected shoplifters. Ironically, customers often believe that these workers have negative attitudes toward them. These Korean employees often complain that their employers force them to watch customers more than is really necessary. Some workers do not see any ethnic or racial differences in the behavior of customers. Mr. Lee's first job was at a greengrocery in Brooklyn, where most customers were African Americans. After that job, he worked for his uncle in a grocery, doing odd jobs. At this store, most customers were Italian. When I asked him to compare these customers with the African Americans at the other greengrocery, he said there was little difference. He complained only that he had to work harder for his uncle than he did at the other store.

**Professionals**

Interestingly, two doctors I interviewed, a pediatrician and a physician, arrived at differing evaluations of their Korean and other patients. This may be related to their specialization. While the pediatrician deals primarily with mothers of babies and young children, the physician deals with adults of both sexes.

The pediatrician, Dr. Choi, said that 80 percent of her patients are Korean and 20 percent are "American," which she said included whites, Indians, Latin Americans, and others. According to her, "American" patients tend to ask why they have to take a prescribed drug, but Korean patients do not. Korean patients do not directly question their doctors, even if they have questions. In her analysis, Koreans are deferential to authority, unlike her other patients.

About 75 percent of Dr. Park's adult patients are African American, 10 percent white, and the rest Korean and Latin American. Comparing his non-Korean patients with Koreans, he said, "They do not call the doctor for matters other than treatment, whereas Koreans call me for personal advice." Thus, he has to spend more time than is medically necessary with Korean patients. This is also no doubt true for Korean professionals such as lawyers, accountants, and teachers. Due to the language barrier, however, Dr. Park also needs to spend more time treating non-Korean patients. For a thorough examination, he has to ask more questions and examine them more carefully than he does Korean patients. Ironically, his non-Korean patients like Dr. Park's predicament because they feel they are getting a very careful examination.

Many doctors run their own clinics catering to fellow Koreans. Dr. Song, a gynecologist, is one such case. He came to America in 1974. Three years ago he opened his own office in Elmhurst. Now he works both at his office and Flushing Hospital and Medical Center. His wife helps him with work in his office. They have hired a Korean receptionist and Korean nurses. He compared his work at the hospital with his office work: "As I work at my own office, I take more responsibility, besides being kind to patients and more diligent." He described Korean patients that he sees in Elmhurst: "They are not punctual. They should follow the American way, for example, making appointments about seeing the doctor. Nevertheless I feel bad about patients without health insurance. I cannot hospitalize patients or give adequate medical treatment without insurance.[5] In Korea I could do everything, including operations, by myself, and I could take their circumstances into consideration. Here I am limited by the system." In his overall evaluation about his life in America, he stated, "I can have my own private life as a medical doctor. Life here is rather simple. In Korea my family and I were bothered a lot due to complicated social life, particularly social expectations for a medical doctor, such as service to the community."

5. In Korea, unlike the United States, various efforts since the Park regime (1961–79) have been were made to respond to health needs. Finally, in the late 1980s the Korean government adopted a mandatory national health insurance program (personal communication, Sung Joo Ko, 22 July 1994).

Dr. Lee, an herb doctor and acupuncturist, finds Korean patients to be more argumentative than his non-Korean ones. This situation reflects doctor-client interaction in the Korean system of medicine, where patients are expected to interact with their doctor. This dialogue, however, seems to be limited to Korean folk medicine. His non-Korean patients, who usually present neck and back problems, respond well to his instructions and keep returning for treatment. But, his Korean patients do not pay enough attention to what he says. They also stop treatment suddenly or arrive at his office without any appointment. Like Korean lawyers and insurance brokers, who also complain that Korean customers are more argumentative, he now prefers non-Korean clients.

Ms. Ahn works as a registered nurse for a private Queens hospital. She commented on her job:

> My colleagues are quite international: five Indians, three Filipinos, two Koreans, one Thai, one Jewish American, one Irish, one Israeli, one black American, two Italian Americans, and one Cuban. I have worked for five years as an operating room nurse. Half of my colleagues are very experienced. Most nurses work in the ward, taking care of patients in need of intensive care. They have a shift from seven to three. Nurses in the operating room have a nine-to-five shift. Nurses with the same shift socialize together. In terms of hierarchy in the nurses' world, there are supervisors (always more supply than demand); head nurse (it takes several years to move from staff nurse to head nurse); staff nurses, who are R.N.s; nurses' aides; and porters, who are male. For operating room nurses, promotion is very slow. Besides nurses, there are M.D.s, physicians' assistants, surgeons' assistants, and medical technicians.

She has no problems with her supervisor. Regarding M.D.s, she said, "If they get on my nerves, I try to get on their nerves." Because of their high status, the doctors socialize only among themselves. At her hospital, 80 percent of the M.D.s are Jewish. Many medical technicians are U.S. citizens, some Latin American immigrants, and a few Chinese immigrants. About 70 percent of her patients are white. "In general, Asian patients are passive and more cooperative and have a good reputation at the hospital," she stated.

James, a certified public accountant, commented that Korean clients expect more than just his professional services; and for the extra service that they demand, he accordingly charges higher fees. Most of his clients are Koreans; only a few are not. He estimates that more than half the work he does for his Korean customers is beyond a certified public accountant's normal services—for example, helping them open a bank account or explaining the American educational system.

Korean professionals who work in large American firms, unlike those in private practice, often encounter ethnic discrimination from Americans— or what is called the "glass ceiling." Mr. Suh, a medical technician, ex-plained: "Although there is racism, things remain calm on the surface. Employers prefer Americans educated in the United States when they are considering promotion. Korean professionals tend to advance quickly, which makes people of other ethnicities jealous. However, other Asians who face less language difficulty, like Filipinos or Indians, get better treatment than Korean and Chinese professionals."

## The Importance of Practice in Constructions of Ethnicity

As Koreans in America modify their ethnic conceptions through experi-ence, some unfortunately transfer the negative treatment they receive from the white majority to other minorities. Others, however, are sensitive to the plight of other minorities. Some Koreans who have experienced racial discrimination from white Americans apparently transfer this racism to African Americans. Mr. Kim, a pharmacist, said: "From my own experi-ence, I feel a kind of discrimination as a minority, visibly or invisibly. When I lived in Yonkers, a white store owner assumed that kind of atti-tude, seeing me only as a tongyanggye. When I worked as a pharmacist at the hospital, I was treated as a professional but only in the workplace. Beyond that, they knew nothing about me. They even thought that Chi-nese, Japanese, and Koreans speak the same language. Now I feel that sometimes I myself imitate that kind of attitude toward black customers, suspecting them all of shoplifting, which is a shame."

Mr. Suh, a sewing machine store sales worker, had a negative opinion of Latin American customers because he was told they were potential thieves. Later, when operating his own store, he was helped a great deal by the Chilean former owner and also patronized by Latin American customers, whom he now appreciates. "The local Latin Americans here do not speak English well either. I have few problems dealing with them. Furthermore, I feel that Colombians are better customers than Koreans, who often bargain over price."

The move to New York has given Korean immigrants a new awareness of being Asian in America (tongyanggye mikukin), a heightened con-

[153]

sciousness of themselves as a minority enclosed within a sometimes menacing, sometimes friendly, world of more powerful whites. This racial consciousness provides a potential bond with other Asian immigrants. But Korean encounters with other ethnicities are complex, and their attitudes reflect diverse workplace experiences in diverse neighborhoods. These new ethnic encounters and ethnic constructions also depend on class. Different class segments within the Korean immigrant community develop different constructions of ethnicity.

# [8]

# Political Processes

When he received an award from the U.S. Department of Agriculture, Kim Sung Soo, president of the Korean American Small Business Service Center of New York, commented (1988) on some of the problems facing the Korean American community:

> There is an increasing degree of violence aimed against Asians. Pecking order, "Toyota fever," Reaganomics which cut back welfare benefits, bad impression of Asian fatherlands, and the aftermath of the Vietnam War are among the contributing factors. Another problem is conflict developing between Korean shopkeepers and their neighbors. These are intensified by poor understanding of other ethnic cultures, orientation of business which emphasizes the maximizing of benefits rather than considering the business as goal, and different legal cultures that the Koreans experience in the states. The third problem is low access to political power and government. Koreans are much more silent in articulating their interests and grievances.

Previous chapters have dealt with the consequences and implications on family, kinship, gender, and ethnicity of Korean immigrants' adoption of the ideology of *anjŏng*. In this chapter, I examine how that ideology influences immigrants' political participation. I argue that Korean Americans' political activities can only be analyzed by relating them to the centrality of small business in their lives. This is most evident in the role that business organizations play in the Korean community. Immigrants often begin to undertake political activity to protect small business interests.

Nakanishi (1986) notes that in studies of ethnic minority communities many researchers restrict discussion of political participation to activities such as voting behavior, money and other resources mobilized for campaigns, and appointments to office. He argues, however, that it is "premature to exclusively focus on electoral politics" (1986: 3). Anthropologists no longer view politics as only "the activities of elected officials and the workings of government, enterprises out of the reach of ordinary people." Politics is also seen as "those activities which are carried on in the daily lives of ordinary people and enmeshed in the social institutions and political economic processes of their society" (Morgen and Bookman 1988: 4). My research deals with how Korean immigrants develop ideas about the causes of their powerlessness in America and how they act to change the conditions of their lives. I focus first on how the community is organized, examine its historical development, and then analyze the political activities of the Korean Produce Retailers Association, the small-business foundation of Korean politics in New York City. I next turn to Flushing and Elmhurst, areas of both residential and commercial concentration for Koreans, and analyze how Koreans have become linked to local civic structures. Finally, I examine two case studies of Korean immigrant political mobilization at the citywide level: issues concerning stoop-floor regulation and commercial rent control.

## Organization of the Korean Immigrant Community

Korean immigrants, unlike some earlier immigrants to New York, do not live in territorial enclaves. In the absence of residential bonds, associations become the thread that weave together different segments of the Korean population into an "associational community" (I. Kim 1981: 226).

There are three major forms of organization in the Korean community in New York City: occupational, local, and religious. (Protestant churches are discussed in Chapter 9.) Occupational organizations are formed to promote the economic interests of their members; table 5 lists the principal ones among Koreans in New York City in 1990. Other associations (see Korean Business Directory 1990; Korean Directory of Greater New York 1990) include:

Korean Traders Association
Women's Apparel Wholesaler Association of New York

[156]

*Table 5.* Korean American community organizations

**Number and type of organizations in 1990**

| Types of organization | Number |
| --- | --- |
| Occupational | 37 |
| Professional | 8 |
| Locality | 11 |
| Alumni | 65 |
| Social and cultural clubs | 23 |

**Major occupational organizations and their memberships**

| Occupational organizations | Membership |
| --- | --- |
| Korean Dry Cleaners Association of New York | 1,200 |
| Korean Produce Retailers Association | 950 |
| Korean American Chamber of Commerce | 600 |
| New York Korean Garment Contractors Association | 500 |
| Korean Seafood Association | 450 |
| Korean Business Owners Association | 380 |
| Korean Grocery Association of Greater New York | 400 |
| Korean American Restaurant Association of New York | 87 |

Source: *Korean Business Directory* (New York: *Korea News,* 1990); *Korean Directory of Greater New York* (New York: Dae Han, 1990).

Korean Toy Dealers Association of New York
Korean Traders Representative Club of New York
Korean Garment Association of Greater New York
Korean Entertainment Association of New York
Taekwondo Association of New York
Korean Musicians Association
Professional Photographers Association
Korean Postal Service Association
Korean Yellow Taxi Drivers Association
Korean Association of Asbestos Handlers and Supervisors
Korean American Electronics Association
Korean Scientists Engineers Association of New York
Eastern Korean Nurses Association
Korean Dental Association of Eastern United States of America
Korean Medical Doctors Association

While most serve business owners or professionals, they also exist among construction workers, asbestos handlers and supervisors, and postal employees. The Yellow Taxi Drivers' Association is composed of owner-operators. As we shall see, during the 1980s small business proprietors showed the greatest level of activism in the Korean community.

## History of Korean Community Organizations in New York City

Until the 1960s, there were only a few Korean churches and a dormant umbrella organization known as Haninhoe (the Korean Association of Greater New York), whose precursor was founded in 1921 (see Korean Association of New York 1985). The first Korean church in New York, now called the Korean Church and Institute, was also founded in 1921 and located near Columbia University.

In 1967, when the first Korean newspaper, the *Korean Times*, began publishing, there were about three thousand Koreans in New York, but only 125 of them subscribed to the paper. Soon Haninhoe, which had been reactivated in 1965 by a group of articulate Koreans, celebrated Korean Independence Movement Day (1 March) and Korean Independence Day (15 August) and began its own newspaper, *Hanin t'ongsin* (Korean communication). At that time, Koreans came together principally in churches, particularly the Korean Church and Institute in Manhattan, the Brooklyn Korean Church, and the Korean Church of Queens. In genearl, Korean immigrants paid more attention to the situation in their home country than to affairs in the United States. In June 1968, Haninhoe held a benefit concert to establish a scholarship for students from Korea and collected money for thirty Korean sailors who needed funds to return to Korea after being stranded in the United Stat4es when their employer went bankrupt.

In the late 1960s, as the number of Korean immigrants grew, the first business concentration in New York City became visible—a short-lived boom in the wig business among Korean peddlers in New York City (see I. Kim 1981: Chap. 4). With the great 1970s influx of Koreans to New York, an increasing number became involved in retail businesses such as greengroceries, fish markets, and dry-cleaning stores. Occupational organizations soon came into being: the Korean Produce Retailers Association in 1975, the Korean Seafood Association and the Korean Chamber of Commerce in 1977, and the Korean Dry Cleaners Association and the Korean

Businessmen's Association in 1978. In general, these associations were organized to further members' interests as well as promote friendship and communication. More specialized organizations also were established: the Council of Korean Churches (1975), the Korean Restaurant Owners Association (1978), the Organization of Korean Professionals in Computer Science (1978), and the Association of T'aekwŏndo (Martial Arts) Teachers (1978). In addition to occupational organizations, other groups arose to deal with problems in the community, including the Women's Organization (Yŏsŏnghoe) in 1975; Korean Community Service of Greater New York in 1975, which dealt with juvenile delinquency and other social problems; and the Korean Senior Citizens Society (Sangnokhoe) in 1976.

In 1978 New York City had only 250 Korean greengrocers and 100 dry cleaners in contrast to 1,200 greengrocers and 1,500 dry cleaners by the late 1980s. In neighborhoods across the city, these and other Korean business proprietors often interacted with each other and became aware of common problems. From this interaction, the peculiar double structure of organizations among Korean businessmen arose—citywide organization by type of trade (*chigung tanch'e*) and local organizations (*chiyŏk tanch'e*) that cross trade lines. From 1980 on, several local organizations (chiyŏk tanch'e) came into being. These now include the Korean American Community of Sunnyside (first formed in 1970 but long inactive), the Korean Merchants Association of Flushing (1980), the Korean Merchants Association of Jamaica (1981), the Korean Merchants Association of Church Avenue in Brooklyn (1981), the Korean Merchants Association of Lower Eastside (1982), the Korean Merchants Association in the Bronx (1983), the Washington Heights Korean Merchants Association (1983), the Korean Merchants Association of Newark (1983), the Korean American Association of Mid-Queens (1985), the Korean Association of West Brooklyn (1985), and the Korean Merchants Association of Yonkers (1985).

At first, the major goals of the merchants associations (*sangin pŏnyŏnghoe*) were to prevent crime against Korean merchants, deal with the problem of overcompetition, and exchange business information.[1] These organizations have remained focused on business interests and problems. There has been an interesting evolution, however, in the nature of the local organizations. In Flushing and mid-Queens, these groups now serve Koreans in general, almost like a shadow government. The Korean Merchants

---

1. *Sangin ponyong-hoe* means "prosperity associations." A similar term has been used among rural migrants in urban Korea for their mutual-aid organizations.

*Plate 7.* Korean parade in downtown Manhattan, 1989. Photo author

Association of Flushing eventually transformed itself into the Korean American Association of Flushing, seeking to represent all Korean residents; and the former Korean Merchants Association of Elmhurst became the Korean American Association of Mid-Queens, serving a broader geographic area and wider constituency than its original purpose (in plate 7, the Korean American community as a whole is represented by a parade in Manhattan). In both cases, as we shall see, what started as merchant associations have become civic associations active within their multiethnic neighborhoods.

A parallel process has taken place in the case of the Korean immigrant community leader Kim Sung Soo. His career path reflects an evolution from working for an occupational organization to forming a broad small business advocacy group strategically located in Flushing, a center of Korean American community activism. From 1981 to 1985, Kim worked as executive director of the Korean Produce Retailers Association. He realized the necessity of creating a service agency that could advocate for issues beyond those of greengrocers, so he founded the Korean American Small Business Service Center of New York in 1986. In particular, problems with escalating commercial rent pushed him to organize an advocacy agency that represented broader immigrant interests (personal communication, Kim Sung Soo, 20 March 1995). Now more than thirty different Korean occupational and locality organizations belong to his group. He has also formed alliances since 1986 with non-Korean business groups, both immigrant and American. In 1995, he was elected chair of the Small Business Congress representing a crossracial alliance of small business owners. Kim's political evolution testifies to an increasing importance of class over ethnicity in this sector of New York City politics.

## The Korean Produce Retailers Association

Since the 1970s, the Korean Produce Retailers Association (KPA) has been one of the most powerful organizations in the Korean community of New York City. It was organized as a fraternal organization of thirty members in 1967. After 1974 it become more active, adding economic interests to promotion of friendship. The organizational tie is consolidated in members' everyday encounters with one another at the produce market in the Bronx, and its leadership comes from men who combine seniority and experience in organizational activities.

When Korean greengrocers first came to the Hunts Point wholesale market in the late 1960s and early 1970s, there were some wholesalers who were openly anti-Asian and refused to deal with them. Others overcharged. One Korean grocer recalled that Koreans were not allowed to open crates to inspect the produce they were buying. Another, who has a Ph.D. in nuclear physics and entered the business in the late 1960s, said that the wholesalers always yelled, "Chinks, go away! We don't want Chinks around here" (Harris 1983, quoted in J. Yi 1993).

The KPA has offices at both the Hunts Point market in the Bronx and in Brooklyn and has several paid staff members. The produce market today handles between 50 and 60 percent of the nearly 4 billion pounds of fruits and vegetables consumed annually in greater New York. There are thirty people on the KPA board of directors. Newsletters are sent to members, who also have their own group health insurance plan. Within the KPA there are many clubs for members, including a golf club, a gun club, and a Christians' club. The organiztion has gradually transformed itself into a political pressure group. In 1978 KPA leadership effectively won control of the Korean Association of Greater New York in an election open to all Korean immigrants in New York City (see I. Kim 1981).

In the early 1970s there were only 30 or 40 Korean greengrocers, and no one owned more than one business. In 1975 the number had grown to at least 200 and by the mid-1980s between 850 and 900. By the 1980s, some people owned several stores. According to the KPA's 1984 estimates, New York City had 900 Korean-owned grocery stores with about five workers each, meaning that at least 5,000 Koreans were employed at greengroceries. If these 5,000 people were members of households with three or four members, then a total of 15,000 or 20,000 Koreans depended wholly or in part on the greengrocery business.

In addition to providing business information to members, staff at the KPA offices seek to resolve members' problems. One of the biggest problems is competition and subsequent disputes between KPA members. In such cases, the KPA tries to mediate, an effort that does not always work. The organization also helps its members deal with the government and wholesalers.[2] If a member believes he or she has been unfairly fined by a municipal agent, the KPA investigates. If the fine does not seem justified, KPA staff attempt to get it reduced or dismissed.

The KPA lobbyed for a change in the municipal stoop-line regulation, which prohibits display of store merchandise (such as vegetables and fruits) beyond a four-foot distance from the building line. One greengrocer was fined $300 for displaying vegetables in boxes longer than five feet, which stretched beyond the legal limit. A grocer in Manhattan, Lee Yong-ju, received fifty-three tickets within sixty days. Mr. Lee got so upset that he struck a city inspector on the head. In court, however, his fifty-three tickets were voided with help from the KPA. A KPA staff member said:

> The old law, which was made in the 1930s, is outdated. Because of the old law, Korean greengrocers have had a hard time. City government inspectors have confiscated fruit and vegetables within the limit as well as beyond the limit and charged many greengrocers thousands of dollars in fines. Korean greengrocers were exploited because their goods were confiscated without warning and because the way in which the produce was confiscated was arbitrary. For instance, those who violated the limit by only a half-foot might be subjected to confiscation, while others who violated it by a lot more were not. To make matters worse, landlords were

2. For further discussion on the nature of relations between Korean retail merchants and white wholesalers, see J. Yi (1993).

not cooperative and didn't permit greengrocers to remodel storefront areas. The KPA took these incidents seriously and investigated each case. They even found that in Chinatown, where the limit had long been seriously violated, there were no confiscations, thanks to the political power of the businesses there. It is generally agreed that this stoop-line situation matters greatly to the amount of sales, the logic being that the more pedestrians can see fresh fruit and vegetables, the more they tend to buy.

When the KPA first tackled this issue, its efforts were not welcomed by all victimized greengrocers. Some preferred to accept the actions of city government passively. After gathering data, however, the KPA was convinced of the need to lobby for reform of the stoop-line regulation. Although it put up some resistance, the city eventually accepted the KPA's proposal to extend the stoop floor beyond four feet but asked for further data. In order to justify an expected drop in revenue from stoop-line violation fines, City Comptroller Harrison Goldin asked for data to prove that extension of the stoop line did no harm to pedestrian traffic. The KPA provided this data.

Similar types of negotiations occurred between other Korean business groups and city agencies. For instance, in 1989, after eight months of negotiations, the Korean American Small Business Service Center saved greengrocers $1.5 million when it persuaded the city's Environmental Control Board to halve $3 million in fines for dirty sidewalks and sanitary violations. Similarly, the KPA succeeded in locating a small-claims court within the Hunts Point Terminal market. This is important because much as 1 million dollars a year in fines are charged to Korean greengrocers. Before the change, owners who could not afford to spend a day in court had no opportunity to contest what they felt were unjustified fines.

## Korean Harvest and Folklore Festival

In addition to offering ten scholarships, a summer picnic, and an end-of-the-year party and cosponsoring and endorsing many other events, the KPA produces the annual Korean Harvest and Folklore Festival, *ch'usŏk*. Held in Flushing Meadow–Corona Park in Queens, this is the biggest holiday event for New York City Koreans (see plate 8). In Korea it is held on the fifteenth day of the eighth lunar month, but for convenience the KPA always celebrates it here on a Sunday. In 1984, this festival was also supported by the Korean Association of Greater New York, the Korean

*Plate 8.* Speakers on stage at the Korean Harvest and Folklore Festival in Flushing Meadow–Corona Park, 1988. Photo author

Consulate, the New York City Department of Parks and Recreation, seven Korean newspapers, two Korean broadcasting companies, and thirty-two other organizations. To me, it seemed more impressive than the mid-autumn festival in Korea, which is primarily an occasion for family and kin gatherings, not a public ritual.

In his opening remarks during the third ch'usŏk festival in 1984, the KPA president described it as a day for celebrating the rich harvest of the year and offering fresh crops and fruits to the spirit of one's ancestors. It is also a day for families, relatives, and friends to get together to share food, fun, and games. Although he emphasized the function of ch'usŏk in keeping Korean culture alive, he made it clear that its celebration should also encourage Koreans to fit into the culturally diverse society of New York City.

**[164]**

Among the programs at the 1984 festival were an ancestor worship ceremony; a memorial service for the 269 victims of the Korean Air Lines plane shot down by the Soviet Union in 1983, Korean folk dances (farmers', fan, drum, Buddhist, and shaman dances), games (Korean seesaw, shuttlecock and rug games, wrestling, and tug-of-war), contests (for pinecake making, Korean costumes, and folk singing), and food and crafts booths. At the festival there were long lines of people at the food and crafts booths. Ten Korean restaurants built open-air cafeterias, mostly selling barbecued beef (*pulgogi* and *kalbi*), kimch'i, and rice. That year all the restaurants were from Queens, whereas the year before they were all from Manhattan. By 4 P.M. most of the restaurants had run out of food.

In 1985, at the fourth annual festival, more than 30,000 Koreans attended from as far away as Massachusetts, Washington, D.C., Philadelphia, Connecticut, and New Jersey. In addition, I saw perhaps one hundred non-Koreans, some by themselves and others with Korean friends. They were of diverse racial or ethnic backgrounds: elderly whites, young Latin Americans, and a few African Americans. Eleven American public officials were introduced, and eight more sent telegrams that were read, including one from Geraldine Ferraro, a former Queens member of the House of Representatives and candidate for U.S. vice president in 1984. The politicians who were present delivered short speeches.

For the Korean audience, the *changsu mudae* (folk song contest for longevity) was the highlight of the day. The elderly Korean contestants seemed especially excited, and many were ready to take part in singing and dancing on stage. Several young people told me that they were impressed with the performances of the elders. Some elderly Americans joined in singing old popular songs; and one old woman danced, to the crowds' delight. In the late afternoon, the entertainers were professional singers, dancers, and comedians, some of them invited from Korea. The final event was a raffle. In 1984 the prizes were one hundred color television sets. (In 1989, the prizes were Hyundai, Excel, and Sonata automobiles, round-trip tickets to Korea, and other expensive items.) At the end of the festival, people seemed reluctant to leave the park. Several times during the festivities there was an announcement about a voter registration drive. During the entire day I served as a voter registration volunteer with members of Korean American Women for Action. We registered more than 150 Korean Americans and ten non-Koreans, which was more than we had expected.

## Korean Locality Organization
## in Queens: Flushing

The first Korean residents settled in Flushing in 1962. By 1990 there were many organizations located in the neighborhood, including several that served citywide Korean interests. In this section, I focus on the Korean American Association of Flushing (KAAF) and its political evolution.

According to Lee Chong Dae, the organization's eighth president, the KAAF was organized by store owners in 1980 as the Korean Merchants Association of Flushing. The group was weak at first and suffered financial problems that the first president resolved by providing needed funds himself. In 1983, the KAAF was represented by President Lee's dance team and a Korean karate team in that year's Flushing town festival, a first step toward sharing Korean culture and establishing political relations with other Flushing residents.

President during the KAAF's third and fourth years, Hong Chong Hak made great contributions to the organization. While continuing to run his real estate agency, he actively tried to resolve conflicts among Korean merchants by taking on the role of mediator. He also worked to promote relations between Koreans and other ethnic groups, including the Flushing Chinese Business Association (see Chen 1992) and the Flushing Merchants Association, a mainly white group. He worked closely as well with Julia Harrison, the New York State assemblywoman for Flushing. (Hong's and Harrison's offices are located in the same building.) Mr. Hong's interest in civic affairs, he told me, came from his experience as a realtor.[3] When he took non-Korean potential buyers or tenants to see houses, they often commented that Koreans were too focused on making money and did not communicate enough with other groups or participate in community affairs. He agreed. He felt that, if Koreans want to live in the United States, they should participate in American society and listen to what others have to say. In addition to the KAAF, Mr. Hong has involved himself in the Korean Association of Greater New York and the Korean

---

3. In addition, Mr. Hong's experience in the U.S. Army might have encouraged him to participate in American society. He volunteered for the army and served for several years. I found that it is not unusual for immigrant men to go into the army, attracted by the benefits and a chance to learn English and experience American culture. Because they come from a country where army service is mandatory, they seem to be used to the idea of enlisting.

*Plate 9.* A scene inside the Korean pavilion, Queens Festival, 1989. Photo author

Chamber of Commerce. He also founded the Queens Korean Culture Society in 1988 to participate in the annual Queens Festival. (See plates 9, 10, and 11; also Chen 1992: 232–45.) Mr. Hong was actively involved in Korean Americans for David Dinkins during the 1989 mayoral election. He said: "In the future, after making coalitions with other Asian groups, as a second step, we should think of aligning ourselves with Hispanics. As far as American politics is concerned, we ought to give first and then think of asking for something later, not the other way around. We cannot demand what we want without making a contribution to the welfare of the local community."

In 1984, when Lee Chong Dae became president, the general assembly voted to change the organizations name to the Korean American Association of Flushing in order to represent a wider cross-section of Koreans than simply merchants alone. The organization had initially formed to promote friendships among business owners, but the focus inevitably

**[167]**

*Plate 10.* Calligraphy demonstration inside the Korean pavilion tent, Queens Festival, 1989. Photo author

*Plate 11.* A picnic with typical Korean dishes, Queens Festival, 1989. Photo author

shifted to encouraging participation in Flushing community affairs. At monthly meetings, members listen to lectures about credit unions, income tax, and real estate and exchange news about goings-on in the local community. Guests from Flushing's African American community have been invited to exchange views, as have representatives of the Boys Club, the Flushing Council on Culture and the Arts, and the local Democratic party club. The KAAF makes campaign contributions to local elected officials and donations for auxiliary patrol cars to the 109th police precinct in Flushing. In recent years, the association has participated in local political meetings and social events, conducted voter registration drives, provided an employment service to job seekers, offered information and referrals to agencies for Korean mentally retarded persons, and participated in cultural and multiethnic festivals. In 1989, the association played a central lobbying role in a protest against the reassignment to the borough of Staten Island of Dr. Roh Young Myun, deputy chief medical examiner for Queens. The association stressed the importance of Dr. Roh's continued work in the heavily Korean-populated borough of Queens. The association pressed elected officials and local community leaders to write letters, which resulted in a victory when Dr. Roh's transfer was rescinded.

One important concern of the association is security for businesses. (For similar concerns among Chinese immigrant business owners, see Chen 1992.) Mr. Lee, the fifth president, told me:

> As an ethnic minority, we were looked down upon. So we must protect our rights. We organized a network for crime prevention, calling it *pansanghoe* or *cho* (sets).[4] Incidents happen once or twice a month. To provide security for businesses, five stores constitute one set, with the leader of each set being a member of the board of directors of our association. So far, twenty-nine sets have been organized. Recently, even tenants in apartments are being organized. Suppose that something happens to a store. It is immediately brought to the attention of the leader of that set. If the solution is beyond his or her control, it is reported to the headquarters of this association, which is in direct contact with the 109th police precinct. There is now a Korean policeman at that station.

In 1984, there was a tenant-landlord dispute in a rental apartment building in Flushing where most tenants were Korean, about forty households. These tenants were opposed to conversion to a cooperative, but the

4. Such networks have been organized by government agencies in Korea to encourage mutual aid among neighbors.

landlord would not compromise. Some tenants asked Mr. Lee to help; however, because they were not members of the KAAF, he did not. But, soon the landlord also appealed to him for help, so Mr. Lee and other members successfully mediated the dispute. They then decided to organize the residents in sets similar to those among merchants.

The August 1984 monthly meeting of the association was held in Mr. Lee's office, his t'aekwŏndo studio in Flushing. He reported on events in the Flushing Korean community and lamented that only fifty-eight Korean Americans were registered to vote compared with several hundred Flushing Chinese. Then he discussed a recent case of conflict between a Korean merchant and a Chinese merchant and its resolution through the mediation of the association. For the voting committee, Cho Do Hyun (who later became the ninth KAAF president) said that each member should get five Koreans to register to vote using the set organization model.

The invited guest, Kim Tal Su, a former elected official in Korea, spoke first about the Korean American Senior Citizens Society (sangnokhoe) in Flushing. He then talked about building pan-Asian identity in Flushing: "It is not sufficient just to organize Koreans to pressure the Americans. Only if we cooperate with the other Asians, first with the Chinese, can we achieve our goals. In America, as in Korea, you must qualify yourself as a voter by placing your name on the register.[5] Otherwise, it is hard for us to stand firmly for our own rights. The more among the 40,000 Koreans in Flushing we register to vote, the faster will we be counted by American politicians. Our center sent out 1,000 letters to educate Koreans about voting, enclosing voter registration forms." Finally, members discussed how they could participate in a fundraising dinner party for the Queens Council on the Arts. Someone mentioned that the main office of this cultural organization was planning to move from Jamaica to Flushing and that the council had an interest in supporting ethnic cultural performances. The meeting began at 8 P.M. and was not over until 11 P.M.

In Flushing, the Korean community cooperates closely with the Chinese community (see Chen 1992). For instance, when Theresa Kim, a Korean, was murdered in 1984, the Flushing Chinese Business Association (FCBA) helped the Korean association deal with the situation. They also made joint efforts to solve disputes between Chinese and Korean business proprietors. As a result of their communication and joint efforts,

5. This is not the case in Korea, where a citizen can vote without registering.

the two organizations officially became sister organizations in 1985 to cooperate in political, economic, and social activities. For example, they discussed how to persuade both Chinese and Korean businesses to make English store signs now that more non-Asians were shopping in them. After the KAAF election for officers in 1986, the FCBA held a party to congratulate the new board of directors. In return, the KAAF invited FCBA leaders to a party at a Korean restaurant in Flushing along with officers from the 109th police precinct and representatives of Queens College, including myself. The two groups also organized a cleanup campaign on Main Street and Roosevelt Avenue in downtown Flushing in 1985.

In 1989, after several years of stalemate and turmoil in the KAAF presidential elections, Pyun Chun Soo, who runs an educational center, was elected as the tenth president. The association has since provided some one hundred job referrals to both Korean and American companies, has organized the first Annual International Health Day in 1989 in collaboration with Flushing Hospital and Medical Center, and has held seminars for Korean undocumented workers. The association also donated two scholarships to Queens College in Flushing in 1990. Mr. Pyun led a drive to change the Flushing Christmas Tree Lighting Committee into the Holiday Decoration Committee to celebrate both that holiday and the Lunar New Year observed by Korean and Chinese residents. The association now works with the Flushing Chinese Business Association, the Flushing Merchants Association, the Flushing Chamber of Commerce, and Community Board 7. Members participated actively in the 1989 city elections by sponsoring fundraising parties for mayoral candidate David Dinkins, city councilwoman Julia Harrison, state assemblyman Morton Hillman, and state senator Leonard Stavisky. Even more significant, with KAAF's active support, the Chinese Parents Association and the Korean Parents Association formed an Asian Parents Council in 1987. In 1989 this group succeeded in electing Chinese and Korean candidates to the board of Community School District 25.

## Korean Locality Organization in Queens: Elmhurst

According to an account in the Korean press (*Korea Times*, 23 December 1984), the Korean owner of an Elmhurst boutique was verbally abused and seriously beaten by the police in October 1984. Apparently a

Latin American customer bought a pair of shoes but returned them the next day and asked for a refund. The store owner, Mr. Cha, wrote a credit slip. The customer demanded cash and after a quarrel called the police. The police accepted the customer's report of what happened. Then Mr. Cha refunded the cash. When he asked for the names of the police officers, they arrested him for being uncooperative. While the police were taking him to the 110th precinct, they beat him. One said, "I really hate you Koreans. You'd better go back to your own country" (my translation from the *Korea Times* article). Mr. Cha was seriously injured; but even while escorting him to the hospital, the police continued to beat him.

This incident was widely publicized in the New York Korean community, and many people came to Mr. Cha's aid. Soon a handbill appeared encouraging Koreans to rally at Queens County Criminal Court:

> Mr. Cha Eui Tai, a Boutique Shop Owner in Jackson Heights, Queens, was subjected to gang-like beating at the hands of the police of 110th precinct on October 18th, '84. Later, he was charged with a misdemeanor for "resisting arrest." The Korean community of New York was seethed in anger over the unwarranted brutality and discrimination against citizens of Asian heritage by the officers involved in the case. Various youth and community organizations have come together to form the Cha Eui Tai Support Committee. On December 5th, Mr. Cha will stand trial for the charge issued against him. The Committee requests people of conscience of all races to fill the courtroom to support human rights and to see that Korean Americans get just treatment in society.

The incident, which made many people aware of the absence of an organized Korean voice in Elmhurst, led to the birth of the Korean American Association of Mid-Queens in February 1985.

Shortly after the Cha incident, a second one took place in March 1985. A cab driver, Mr. Pyo, was seriously beaten by police officers of the same Elmhurst precinct (Korea Times, 27 March 1985). According to the Korean press report, Mr. Pyo came out of a bar after drinking one bottle of beer, drove over the speed limit, and was chased by police. When the police stopped him, he pointed to his taxi medallion. The police then started to hit him, accusing him of being uncooperative. He was beaten unconscious. Before being sent to the hospital, he was beaten again by police at the station. Later he was sent to a Korean surgeon, who gave him eight stitches. He had to stay in the hospital for a month and a half to recover and charged with drunk driving.

Haninhoe and the new Korean American Association of Mid-Queens registered a complaint at the 110th precinct. The captain told them, "In reality, the police officers wanted to arrest him for drunken driving. But, as Mr. Pyo resisted, it was inevitable for police officers to restrain him. I myself regret it" (*Korea Times*, 1 April 1985; my translation).

Two groups of young activists—Korean Americans for Social Concern and Young Koreans United (YKU)—took up both cases. They asked for the cooperation of African American as well as Korean religious leaders. At an April 1985 demonstration in front of the 110th precinct in Elmhurst, some three hundred people gathered for more than an hour and a half. (I was present at the demonstration.) Not only young activists but also many adult church members attended, encouraged by religious leaders. These leaders, including Buddhist priests, spoke out, furious about police violence and racism in America. Three demands were made: indictment of those involved in beating Mr. Cha and Mr. Pyo, a promise that charges against Mr. Pyo would be dropped, and a formal apology from the captain of the 110th precinct. This was the first time that Korean church leaders showed an interest in local issues.

Following the demonstration, Elmhurst Korean association leaders pursued a strategy different from that of the activist groups. Leaders were nervous about demonstrations, thinking, it might fan anti-Korean feelings in the city. Therefore, an umbrella organization, Haninhoe, and the new Korean American Association of Mid-Queens opened a campaign to communicate directly with the New York City Police Department and, in particular, the 110th precinct.

The reaction of those who demonstrated in front of the Elmhurst police station was not typical of Koreans in Queens. My informants showed three different reactions to the incidents. One was a passive position, which argued that it was the fault of the victim, who either was impolite to the police or did not communicate well due to limited English. Mrs. Kwon, a Korean dress designer, stated: "I would examine myself to see whether I behave properly before I criticize Americans. I have lived here without knowing English or American law. Let's try to understand the American law, first of all, and adopt the American way of life, such as observing traffic laws and other proper behaviors." Similarly, Mr. Park, a pharmacist, stated: "Look at the Cha incident. If he were white, he would not be treated that way. It is very important to have a command of English. There is a great difference when one speaks politely or not. Perhaps he hurt the feelings of the police by talking to them impolitely, or not fluently, although he might not have been conscious of this."

The second reaction was to see these incidents in a broader perspective, saying that similar things happen to all Koreans and identifing with the victims on the basis of one's personal experiences. Such persons argued that Korean Americans should not tolerate such treatment. Mr. Kim, a garment factory worker, said that not only Mr. Pyo but all Korean immigrants received bad treatment once they were brought to a police station.

The third perspective called for a more developed political response among Koreans. Mr. Kim, a restaurant owner in Jackson Heights, said: "We Koreans should protest against any police brutality related to racism. More Koreans should attend demonstrations. I do not understand what all these Korean ministers are doing. They should bring out their church members as demonstrators." He told me about a similar incident ten years ago in Chinatown, when all Chinese merchants closed their stores to protest a case of police brutality. Eventually the police department had to apologize publicly, and the officer responsible for the unprovoked violence was suspended.

Chun Sung Jin is the founder of the Elmhurst-centered Korean American Association of Mid-Queens (KAAMQ). He arrived in America with his family at Christmas in 1970 and lived in Elmhurst, where his business is still located, before moving to Bayside in 1976. He is regarded as one of the old-timers in the Elmhurst Korean community. His wife, a nurse, has worked at Elmhurst City Hospital. Few of the old-timers bought homes in Elmhurst; and most who became established, like Mr. Chun, moved to the more desirable school districts in Bayside or Little Neck in Queens or to Long Island. A real estate and insurance broker in Elmhurst, Mr. Chun has a particularly interesting view of change in the Elmhurst community over two decades. As he sees it, Elmhurst is well supplied with Korean churches. While many of the church officers and ministers now live in other neighborhoods, Elmhurst remains an area of first settlement and is a good location for attracting new immigrant church members. According to him, food businesses in Elmhurst are more successful than they are in other neighborhoods. The ratio of food businesses (of all types) to other businesses is 20 percent greater in Elmhurst than elsewhere. Over time many nonfood businesses move to Manhattan. Mr. Chun said of Elmhurst's location, "In terms of transportation, it is very convenient. That's why it constantly attracts many newcomers." As he remembers, immigrants to Elmhurst came in the following order: first Cubans, then Colombians, then Chinese, and finally Koreans. Some Japanese also settled in Flushing in 1970 but later moved to Fort Lee, New Jersey.

In the early 1970s, many Korean nurses arrived to work at Elmhurst

City Hospital and moved into apartment buildings nearby. At that time Korean nurses were welcomed warmly. Before 1972, Koreans in Queens numbered less than 20,000. In 1976, when Mr. Chun became a naturalized U.S. citizen, there were 30,000 to 40,000 Koreans in New York City. By 1985 there were nearly 25,000 Koreans in Elmhurst and Jackson Heights, 40,000 in Flushing and Bayside, and 150,000 in New York City as a whole. I asked Mr. Chun how the KAAMQ came into being. He said:

> I would like to prove that Koreans can be united, that Koreans can make it. People seem to believe that Koreans cannot be united. I was willing to throw myself into it, even sacrificing my business for one year. However, I was very clear that it would be a different organization from the established organizations, such as the Korean Association of Greater New York. That group was very political and tried to win the favor of the Korean government. What was more important, I thought, was that Koreans in Elmhurst and Jackson Heights needed a channel through which they could communicate directly with the various levels of city government, like police officers, and through which city government could talk to Koreans about its concerns. So the main purpose of the organization is to champion the rights of Koreans in this neighborhood. Since we live in a foreign country as a minority and face language and cultural barriers, we need to talk to the majority population and to city government. I am determined. I work as hard as if I carried the cross on my back by myself. However, to be honest with you, it is sometimes difficult to work with Koreans because they are not always logical.

As a result of crime, difficulties with city inspectors, and problems with local police, many Koreans talked about the need to organize the Koreans in Elmhurst and Jackson Heights. The existing organization, Korean Merchants of Elmhurst, was dormant. Mr. Chun recalled: "In particular, we needed to speak up—to police officers or American public officials—for any Korean or for Koreans in general. Now, we had an incident [of police brutality] which happened to a Yellow Cab driver, Mr. Pyo. In my opinion, prevention is more important than cure. People often asked for help— 'Please find a good store for me,' 'I was severely beaten by the police,' 'I am being evicted by a bad landlord.'"

Mr. Chun's civic activities quickly expanded. Through Kim Sung Soo, the executive director of the Korean Produce Retailers Association, he met with members of the Neighborhood Stabilization Program in Woodside about a particular housing problem facing Koreans. One landlord hunted for Korean tenants, because they were said to pay rent faithfully and not complain about bad service. Once they moved in, this landlord rapidly raised their rent. When tenants decided to move, the landlord refused to return their security deposits. So tenants were forced to pay a lot of money, a situation that Mr. Chun brought to the attention of the city.

In May 1985, a month after the April demonstration, the 110th police precinct in Elmhurst invited the vice president of Haninhoe and Mr. Chun to meet with their night detail about police problems with the Korean community. Forty-two police officers listened to the Korean spokesmen, who talked about Korean culture and attitudes toward the police. They told the officers about the community's shock when an elderly businessman was beaten to death with a baseball bat by a robber. Forty white Americans had been present at the scene, but no one did anything.

Over time, the KAAMQ leadership succeeded in establishing face-to-face relationships with city government officials and civic leaders. The association regularly attended meetings of Community Board 4, the 110th Police Precinct Community Council, Your Block Association, the Elmhurst Lions Club, the Elmhurst Rotary Club, and the Elmhurst Chamber of Commerce. With several KAAMQ leaders, I attended a 110th Police Precinct Community Council meeting on 17 April 1985. First, all those present pledged allegiance to the American flag. After announcements by the council president, there was a report on donations to assist police activities. Six council officers were on stage. All were white and elderly, as is usual in Elmhurst civic organizations. It was reported that six hundred council newsletters had been distributed. At the start of the meeting there were thirty-seven people attending, but four or five more came later. Among those present were Mr. Chun; Hong Seungha, vice president of the KAAMQ; and Andy Nam, auditor of the association. I expected that the Koreans would be given a chance to talk about recent incidents of police brutality, but the chairman quickly stated that Koreans had been trying to improve relations with the 110th precinct. That was all. This was a great disappointment to the Koreans as was evident in their side comments as the program continued. Three police officers were invited to talk about the new community patrol system and about drug sales in the precinct.

As a result of the association's active participation in local community affairs, one member, Ms. Pak Daok, was appointed to Community Board 4 in January 1986. Later two more Korean members were added to the board. The board and the association jointly organized a seminar about city government operations for the Korean community in Elmhurst in March 1986. Members of Community Board 4 and representatives from the sanitation, consumer affairs, and police departments attended the meeting, which was chaired by Mrs. Pak and Kim Sung Soo, now president of the Korean Small Business Service Center of New York. About forty people attended, including twenty-five Koreans and a few Chinese. At this meeting, Community Board 4 Chairperson Rose Rothchild said, "This is the first time in which any immigrant community asked for communication with governmental agencies. I am very pleased with this request." Mr. Chun said in both Korean and English that it was the Korean community's desire to be in closer contact with government agencies. He stressed that this was the only way to reduce tension and avoid mistakes. John Rowan, the Community Board 4 district manager, said, "We have difficulty contacting these new immigrants. You are part of this community. We would like to hear from the Chinese community, too." Officers of the Department of Sanitation explained their jobs and the rules and regulations for local commercial strips. This was followed by questions from the Korean merchants. A man who ran a stationery store said, "I have a problem with sanitation. While the Sanitation Department does not fine the white store owner next to me, despite the fact that they have more garbage than me, they charge me with a fine, which I don't understand. I do not have time to go to court to appeal nor money to hire a lawyer. Therefore, I end up with having to pay fines." When dealing with city governmental officials, Korean immigrants often believe that they experience ethnic discrimination.

In New York City, conflict between Korean merchants and African American customers began in Harlem in 1982 and resulted in a six-month picket in 1984–85. Since then, more incidents have occurred in Brooklyn and Queens, usually beginning over an accusation of shoplifting. (For a more detailed discussion on black-Korean tension, see Ong, Park, and Tong 1994.) Korean merchants and leaders all over the city understood that they needed to open communication with the black community. In Queens, Korean-black cooperation began at the 1985 Elmhurst demonstration concerning police brutality against Koreans, where Reverend Herbert Daughtry of the Black United Front was a guest speaker. More lasting local Korean-black ties began in 1987. Each summer since then, a cleanup campaign among black and Latin American children has been organized by a group of African American adults concerned about youth issues in Lefrak City, an apartment complex adjacent to Elmhurst (see

Gregory 1993). This effort has been supported by the KAAMQ, which has contributed cleaning gear and gifts for the children and has hosted dinners in Korean restaurants to celebrate the efforts. Merchants have donated refreshments, free haircuts, and school supplies and pose with cleanup team members during picture-taking sessions. The Korean owner of one local grocery store also offered to hire two cleanup team members when business picked up.

## Citywide Electoral Politics and Korean American Interests

Among Asian Americans, research has consistently found that higher income, educational attainment, and occupational status are strongly correlated with higher rates of political involvement (Nakanishi 1986: 12). Factors associated with low levels of political participation are lack of English fluency and lack of personal involvement in domestic issues and events. Among Korean Americans, most immigrants who are legal residents are not yet citizens, and they come from a nation where political participation has been associated with oppositional politics and the threat of state retaliation.

In New York, Korean interest in local elections began to accelerate after the 1984 presidential election, and immigrants' focus on small business activities served as the channel for their participation in electoral politics. When the mayoral campaign in New York City began in 1985, several candidates invited Korean business leaders to meetings and events, seeking their support. Mayor Edward Koch, for example, invited fifty individuals to his official residence, Gracie Mansion, demonstrating an interest in this immigrant population not evident four years earlier. As the mayoral campaign developed, the Korean community became divided, one section supporting the incumbent, Mayor Koch, the other supporting his Democratic party primary opponent, Carol Bellamy. Koch was endorsed by the umbrella organization and the leading newspaper, the *Korea Times*. Supporters argued that Koch had helped many Korean Americans and that "there is a good chance for him to be reelected, so we'd better support him. Otherwise he is going to do harm to us." Supporters of Bellamy stressed her support for commercial rent control, an issue of crucial importance to Korean small business proprietors and one opposed by Koch.

## A Koch Ethnic Rally

When I arrived at City Hall, there were many people there already, intending either to participate in the rally or simply watch. Signs were in English and other languages. Those in English read "Norwegians love Koch," "Lithuanians for Koch," "Pakistan and American Friendship," "Armenians for E. Koch," "Finns for Koch," "Greek Americans," "Chinese, we support Mayor Koch," "German Americans for Koch," "Filipinos for Koch," "Indians for Koch, Indian Community of N.Y.," and "Hungarians for E. Koch."

The program started with the introduction of Koch's staff and campaign aides. Their message could be summarized like this: Without Koch, the city would be broke; we'd better thank him by reelecting him. Koch himself then said, "In New York City 25 percent are people born in a foreign country. I myself am a Polish Jew." He looked tired from the toll of his heavy campaign schedule. During the rally, there were performances of ethnic dances. Suddenly, some Armenians standing among the spectators shouted: "There are 60,000 Armenians—all of us are for you, Mayor Koch!" Then a former Indian ambassador was introduced—and a Chinese dragon dance performed. Kang Ik Cho, president of Haninhoe, said to me, "We attend this rally in consideration of the rights and interests of Koreans in New York, but we should participate in it more actively." Although each ethnic group was supposed to bring at least thirty attendees, only ten people from the Korean community came. Nevertheless, their sign was large and quite noticeable. All of the Korean attendees were from Haninhoe. Mr. Kang told me, "We should have also brought a Korean dance group." But another Korean commented, "If we want to do that, we need money for it. The dancing groups, such as those of the Indians, Chinese, and others, do not come here for nothing. They are paid. The same is also true of the Indian attendees."

## The Coalition for Commercial Rent Control

Commercial rent control to protect small business proprietors from arbitrary rent increases became the most important issue for the Korean community in the September 1985 mayoral primary election. Carol Bellamy was endorsed by the Korean American Small Business Task Force for Commercial Rent Control, which included twenty-one Korean occupational and local associations. Members of this task force had asked,

[179]

"What has Koch done for us?" Their answer was "Nothing. He is only defending the developers' and landlords' interests. We, as small business proprietors, suffer from uncontrolled commercial rent increases. Let's vote for Bellamy." The task force and the Coalition for Small Business Preservation held several hearings during the campaign to highlight this issue for the benefit of candidates for mayor, borough president, and city council. According to Rim Kwang-woo, co-chair of the task force, "Last year commercial rent went up 500 percent, and as a result more than eight hundred small businesses went bankrupt in New York City." The following excerpts are from the task force's letter to Honorable Jerome O'Donovan of the city council's Committee of economic development:

> There are 32 [Korean] stores in Bedford-Stuyvesant of Brooklyn. Store rents started a couple of years ago to be doubled or tripled. 17 out of 32 merchants are faced with the renewal of leases within two to three years when they will be asked to pay triple rents. . . . all of these seventeen would leave the area at that time. Ironically, these Korean merchants are now threatened to leave the community by the black picketers; there has been a boycott. A laundromat run by a Korean merchant was kicked out after he established the business five years from an empty space. Last year the store was valued at more than $150,000. The landlord was greedy enough to ask him to leave without one penny compensation. Mr. Ahn, age 65, lost the wealth he created, $150,000. He had no other way to turn. His immigrant dream ended up as becoming a proletarian. The city's rent system deprived him of his American dream, wealth, and human dignity.

The task force's aim was to save Korean small businesses from landlords' refusals to renew leases after raising rents by 100 percent or more. These efforts made it even more apparent that small business proprietors were now the major political force in the Korean community.

By 1985, half of the thirty-five city council members supported the rent control bill (Intro. 914); support increased from fourteen to nineteen members during the mayoral campaign. Early in the year, Mayor Koch shifted from his negative attitude on the issue and appointed a committee to study the commercial rent control bill presented by city councilwoman Ruth Messinger. In June 1985 nearly one thousand Korean business proprietors demonstrated for Intro. 914 at City Hall. The Korean coalition's strategy was to lobby members of the city council to support the bill until the primary election in September. After the primary and until inauguration of the new mayor in January, they planned a petition campaign. After January 1986, they planned to make support for the bill an issue in the elections for New York state senators and assembly members in order to bring greater pressure on the city council and the Mayor.

Korean newspapers closely reported the debate on rent control. Carol Bellamy and the city council candidate for Flushing, Julia Harrison, were invited to speak at an August 1985 forum on commercial rent control in Flushing, where their support received enthusiastic response from the Korean community. Bellamy reaffirmed her position and accused Koch of offering tax exemptions to big developers and ignoring small business. Harrison expressed a similar view, saying that commercial rent hikes harmed the general citizenry as well as small businesspeople. Some 120 Koreans, Chinese, and white Americans from Queens attended this forum. According to Kim Sung Soo, who organized the task force and later became vice president of the Coalition for Fair Business Rents, "This problem with commercial rent control can be compared to the fight between David and Goliath. It is necessary to hold the upper limit on rent increases to 10 or to 15 percent. Also, if this new bill doesn't pass, in five or ten years most of the self-employed small businesspeople will be taken over by large chain stores. That's why more than 99 percent of Korean produce retailers support this bill" (*New York Daily News*, 3 September 1985). But a letter from Eva Tan, mayoral advisor for Asian affairs, reaffirmed Koch's opposition: "As you may be aware, Mayor Koch testified in opposition to Intro. No. 914 at hearings before the City Council's Economic Development Committee last year. In his testimony, the mayor stated his intention to veto any commercial rent control measure, be it in the form of binding rent arbitration, or in the form of across-the-board rent ceilings. He did so in the firm belief that such legislation would be detrimental to New York city's economic and fiscal health."

Korean merchants' political activism on this issue was impressive to both Koreans and non-Koreans. Yet their support did little for Bellamy, who lost the September primary to Koch. Then the Korean community was divided. Task force leaders continued to press political officials to support commercial rent control, but the umbrella organization aligned with Koch. A fundraising party for Koch was organized after the primary, and more than $25,000 was raised from Koreans. Koch went on to victory, and no commercial rent relief for small business has been enacted.

This chapter has discussed Korean immigrants' political development, which grew from the concerns of small business owners. In both local and electoral politics, the Korean community has developed new modes of activism. In the Koch/Bellamy election campaign and in voter registration drives, Koreans have concentrated on voting and seeking to influence elected officials. Through the demonstrations against police brutality in Elmhurst and for commercial rent control at City Hall, they displayed militancy and concerted action in defense of their rights. By the mid-1980s, Koreans no longer stood outside the politics of New York City. They had learned how to bargain for their interests with local and city officials. It would be incorrect to say that Korean immigrants have become powerful and unified but be remiss to assert that they are doing nothing more than mimicking the styles, agendas, and strategies of other minority groups. Both the political vehicles and the issues they carry demonstrate the centrality of small business interests in the Korean communities of New York City.

# [9]

# The Comforts of Christianity for Korean Immigrants: Religion and Reproduction of Small Business Acitivty

If you are a Korean in America, then you probably attend a Christian church. Koreans often say: "If three Chinese get together, they will open a restaurant; if three Japanese, they will establish a company. If three Koreans, they will start a church." Today there are close to 2,000 Korean American Christian churches across the United States. Compared to the overall statistic of one church for every 730 Americans, there is one church for every 300 Koreans in the United States (*Korea Times*, 29 April 91). In the mid-1980s, in the New York metropolitan area, there were 350 Korean Protestant churches, almost one-sixth of the 1,800 Protestant churches in New York City. From 1984 to 1986, a new Korean church was founded every six days.[1] As of 1994, there were five hundred to six hundred Korean Protestant churches in the city (*New York Newsday*, 6 September 94).

As I relate religious ideas and practices among Korean immigrants to their ideology of anjŏng, this study links religion to society and economics (see Turner 1991). Immigrants such as dry cleaners, who can afford to close their stores on Sunday in order to go to church, are envied for having "clean businesses." It is no exaggeration to say that, although Koreans spend most of the week at their stores, on Sundays they make time of their own at church.

In Korea, Buddhists substantially outnumber Christians; but Korean

1. Between 1981 and 1984, 80 churches were founded; but from 1984 to 1986, 129 churches were founded, an average of 60 churches per year (*Korea Times*, January 1987).

immigrants in the United States are overwhelmingly Christian. In 1982, Christians in South Korea constituted 25 percent of the population of 39 million; in America, Christians (mostly Protestant) accounted for 65 percent of the Korean population (*Tonga Ilbo*, 10 February 83). As we will see, immigrants' involvement in both small business and Protestant Christianity are part of the creation of a new Korean American culture. My analysis of their relationship is based on research in Queens, specifically through participant observation at the Central Presbyterian Church of Queens from 1985 to 1987, interviews with ministers at other Elmhurst churches, and interviews with many churchgoers.[2] I begin with an ethnographic overview of how immigrants' small business activity relates to their religious ideas and practices. Then I explore symbol and meaning in Christianity among immigrants. Discourse on Korean immigrant Christianity identifies three different categories of churchgoers: those who go for reasons of convenience, born-again Christians, and critical churchgoers. I expand this discourse by further proposing that immigrants' espousal of Christianity should be viewed as a revitalization movement within the context of immigrant construction of a new cultural identity.

Studies of Korean immigrant churches have followed three approaches (Sharon Park, personal communication). Some scholars have focused on the immigrant church and its role in accelerating (I. Kim 1981) or retarding (Choy 1979) immigrants' assimilation into mainstream society. Others have applied the compensatory model, viewing the church as an institution that provides immigrants with social status and prestige that they could not attain in mainstream institutions (Shin and Park 1988; Min 1992). Still other researchers have explored individual religious motives for attending Korean churches (Hurh and Kim 1984). In sum, scholars agree that the church serves as immigrants' main institution for socializing, seeking, status, and meeting physical and spiritual needs (H. Kim 1977c; Hurh and Kim 1980; I. Kim 1985). My approach differs from these studies because I view the Korean immigrant church in a broader historical context and expand the analysis by relating what actually happens in church.

## Christianity in Korean History

Christianity was first introduced at the end of the feudal Chosŭn dynasty (1392–1910), provoking conflict with the established neo-Confucian

2. Among my 109 interviewees, all but 15 regularly attended church or temple.

ideological system. Later, during Japanese rule, some Christian church leaders fought against the colonial cultural policy, which imposed Japan's own state cult of Shintoism on Koreans and banned other religions that showed anticolonial sentiment. Since Korea's liberation in 1945, many religions and sects have emerged so that contemporary Korea is a religiously pluralistic society.

The years between 1945 and 1961 were a period of historical and political turmoil.[3] Church leaders, however, enjoyed social prestige and privilege due to their dominant position in both Korean politics and international relations with Western countries.[4] Interestingly, scholars note a significant correlation between the growth of Christianity in Korea and the increase of state power and authority, both of which rest on anti-Communist and nationalist ideologies (see K. Kim 1988, 1994). The pro-government activities of the Christian community resulted in governmental support for their evangelical movements.[5] Moreover, church leaders have interpreted Korea's economic growth in the context of millenarianism. "They urged that exodus from the economic poverty and from Korea's marginal status in world politics had been already promised by God in his preparation of the Second Advent" (K. Kim 1994: 13).

But rapid economic growth and a sociocultural transformation process controlled by the authoritative government split church leaders into two factions with regard to theological interpretation and the role of religion in society. Some liberal theologians and church activists criticized Park's regime for its illegitimate monopoly of political resources, distortion of social justice, and exploitation of human rights. They were attacked by conservative church leaders, who have been dominant within the Christian community.

Sociologically speaking, during the past forty years, the Christian church in Korea has become a social community as well as a religious one. The church functions as a place where refugees from North Korea and poverty-

3. These events include Korea's partition into North and South (1945), the First Republic (1948–60), the Korean War (1950–53), the April student revolution (1960), the Second Republic (1960–61), and the military coup (1961).

4. This enthusiasm was exemplified by the millenarian cults and prophetic movements that swayed the whole country during the late 1950s and the 1960s, epitomized by the Zion Church of Presbyter Taeson Park, the Revival Church of Presbyter Woonmong Na, and the Unification Church of Reverend Sunmyung Moon.

5. During the 1970s and 1980s, Christians competitively launched church expansion movements, increasing membership and property holdings. At the same time, church leaders organized frequent mass rallies such as the World Pentecostal Campaign of 1973 and Expo '74 in 1974.

stricken citizens of South Korea deal with their anxieties about a war-torn nation. Kwang-ok Kim (1994) notes that the church has become a place where people confirm their individual achievements in the secular field of life. Equally important, as a result of the massive rural-to-urban migration, there are many "hometown churches" in large cities. Bible study groups, visiting service teams, overnight and dawn prayers, mass prayers for national security and prosperity, pilgrimages, sharing meals after Sunday service, public confession, and occasional aid for life crises are some of the major activities of these churches.

## Korean Immigrant Protestant Churches and the Provision of Capital, Labor, and Information

Christianity plays a large role in the life of the Korean American community. Some landlords or apartment sharers provide discounts in rent, or even restrict rentals, to fellow Christians. People who have been refused job interviews have at times complained about employers' preferential treatment of Christians. Some Korean Buddhists convert to Christianity when a family member's marriage proposal is refused by family that is Christian. The sucess of political events and activities such as voter registration drives or efforts at reducing tension with other ethnic groups depends on the cooperation of the Christian churches. Outside the ethnic community as well, Korean Christians engage in civic activities. For example, when white Americans in Elmhurst revived the Christmas tree lighting ceremony in the 1980s, a Korean choir from the local Bansŭk Methodist Church was invited to sing carols. For three consecutive years they praised God through song at this annual event.

The social role of Christianity in the larger American community partially explains why Christianity rather than Buddhism attracts more adherents in the Korean American community. Christian churches play the dual and contradictory role of promoting the American dream and preserving Korean identity. In other words, Christian churches contribute significantly to the construction of a Korean American culture, while Buddhist churches emphasize the preservation of traditional Korean culture.[6] The

6. On 28 May 1985, for example, many Buddhist temples in New York celebrated the 2,529th birthday of Buddha. At the Wŏn'gak Sa, a Korean temple, a lantern parade and the chanting of the Buddhist liturgy were followed by a *Kayagŭm* (Korean zitherlike instrument) concert, a court dance, a Buddhist dance, a *Sal'puri* (a dance of exorcism now considered a Korean classical dance), a *P'ansori* concert (folktales sung to drum accom-

explosive growth of Korean Christianity in New York City, however, cannot be attributed to conversion from Buddhism to Christianity. More frequently, immigrants move from being nonreligious to becoming active Christian believers.

Social interaction among members of Korean churches is very intense. Typically, members go to church early on Sunday morning and spend the entire day there. During the course of the day they participate in a coffee hour, lunch, a service for youth organizations, staff and committee meetings, evening worship, and other events—all in addition to the regular morning service. Businessmen may play golf together before Sunday service. In many churches, a Saturday service and Bible study on either Thursday or Friday are offered as well. Some members attend daily morning worship before work or go to overnight prayers. Still others attend monthly local prayer meetings at a member's residence.

Korean devotion to small business success is ideologically intensified at church. Churches help immigrants with small business activities in several indirect ways. For example, members are often heavily involved in rotating credit clubs (kye). These clubs have regular meetings where each member pays a fixed or a variable amount of dues. In my interviews with eight ministers in Elmhurst, seven admitted that their church members organized kye at their churches and that members joined kye through networks developed at church. Mr. Choi joined *pŏnho-kye*, or number kye, at a garment factory where he works. The wife of the owner of a garment factory organized the rotating credit club with variable dues ($755 for Mr. Choi) and a pot of $20,000. She recruited members through her church, where she is a deaconess, as well as from her husband's employees.

Networks at churches also provide labor pools and business information. Business owners often ask their ministers or church members such as officers to introduce them to potential employees. Through the church, small business owners meet and discuss capital formation, labor issues, and business information. On occasion, joint ventures are formed. In a few cases, ministers themselves own businesses to supplement small church salaries or become business partners with their members.

When a church member first establishes his or her own business, and even later when he or she is well established, ministers visit them at work and they pray together. Ministers sometimes even pray outdoors with

paniment), a folk song concert, and other art forms cultivated by folklorists as examples of Korea's indigenous culture. Performances of this type are rare in Korean Christian church functions.

Korean street peddlers. In New York, I observed daily prayer meetings at garment factories, groceries, nail salons, body shops, the KPA, and the fish store owners' association. As a matter of fact, business owners often attributed improved productivity and harmonious labor relations to prayer meetings at work.

Ministers or their wives may actively search for new business locations for church members or give advice about how to establish and run small businesses. While some ministers' wives seek employment as nurses or garment workers, others become partners in fellow church members' businesses, such as nail salons.[7] Reverend Kim's wife earns her living as a samplemaker. Her husband, who remigrated from South America to Elmhurst, summarized what is happening at his Namsan Korean Community Church:

> Compared with Koreans in South America, I do not have to help Koreans here. When they first arrive in New York, they have already established connections such as schoolmates, relatives, or community organizations. However, they ask for a place to live. They sometimes ask me to get a job for them. Sometimes they do not welcome a minister's visit because they want to save face. They exchange information among themselves at church, especially those of the same occupation. I have seen kye organizing a few times. Still some ask me to lend a big sum of money, something like $2,500, and others ask me to increase their fortune. A few people ask me to find a good man or woman for marriage. Since they are young people, they are also busy with their jobs.

The rosters of church membership also reflect immigrants' small business orientation. Reverend Lee, minister of a typical immigrant church in Elmhurst called Queens Methodist Church, stated:

> I started my service here four years ago when around thirty elderly ladies couldn't follow the oldest Korean church in Elmhurst, New York Methodist Church, to Long Island. So my church played the role of branch church to the New York Methodist Church. Now every Sunday about eighty-five people attend my service, counting only adults. Of them there are twenty elderly ladies, and the rest are either in their thirties or forties. Most of them work, including housewives. More than half of them have their own small businesses; less than 5 percent are professionals; workers are about

7. Such employment is rare in Korea. In America, however, it is partly due to the insufficient salaries of church ministers who serve small immigrant churches as well as the pervasive influence of immigrant ideology centering on small businesses.

10 percent. The average length of American residence is about five or six years. Sixty percent of my church members live in Elmhurst. In my opinion, Korean churches are made up of personal connections in terms of school, hometown, and workplace.

At church, ministers' sermons often carry indirect messages concerning small business activity. On 1 December 1985, Reverend Han of Los Angeles was specially invited to preach a Thanksgiving Day sermon to the Korean Central Presbyterian Church of Queens. In his sermon, he remarked:

> Deaconess Kang used to run a big garment factory in Los Angeles. She used to hire more than one hundred workers, who worked to such an extent that her business became successful. But all of a sudden, because of the recession, she had to lay off half of her workers. To make matters worse, she lost everything to the IRS. Then she came to my church out of despair, crying all the time. Later on she became born again. There are two different kinds of thanks: One is "therefore thanks"; the latter is "in spite of thanks." When Mrs. Kang came to my church crying, she felt "therefore thanks"; when she was born again, she felt "in spite of thanks." Anyone can express "therefore thanks," thanking God for the good he has done for them, but it is not easy to give "in spite of thanks," which is more important. Gradually Mrs. Kang realized that, although she went bankrupt, she could still receive God. She may be a failure in laymen's terms but is not seen that way by God. As in everything, there is God's intention. Be thankful for everything.

In a few cases, the Korean church itself becomes a kind of small business with detailed lists of donations and other contributions made by church members, who have their names printed in the Sunday worship programs.

## Being Christian

While it is true that some Koreans attend church primarily for social reasons and without serious commitment to faith, others are deeply religious. Mr. Cho, who cannot face daily life without enlisting God's grace, constantly reads the Bible at the Elmhurst Korean Senior Center. Some youth who are very devout may go to theological seminary and enter the ministry. Mr. Pyun is a medical technician who has lived in the United States for more than eighteen years. Five years ago he studied at a Bible college, paying tuition for two years in order to be a Sunday school teacher. Mr. Lee owns a garment factory and takes courses to complete a three-year program at a theological seminary. But Korean immigrant churches are both loose and inclusive. As I have mentioned, there are at least three different ways to be a Korean Christian in the United States: to be a convenient churchgoer, to be born again, and to be critical Christian.

### Convenient Korean Churchgoers

The most popular category is composed of immigrants who go to church pragmatically. This stems from their understanding of the church as a kind of cultural institution. They are searching for life experiences rather than a set of beliefs. They go to church basically to see fellow Koreans and speak Korean without necessarily appreciating that the church is a religious institution. For example, Mr. Kim, a garment factory worker whom I met regularly at the Korean Central Presbyterian Church of Queens, does not even admit to being Christian.

As students of Korean immigration have pointed out, immigrants throughout the United States tend to be quite religious; and the Christian church serves important social functions in immigrant communities (see Dearman 1982; H. Kim 1977b; I. Kim 1985; Hurh and Kim 1980). Among Koreans, convenient Christians attend church largely for social functions. Services provided to members may include "Korean and English language classes, information and training in ways to cope with American society, and a milieu in which to interact with other Koreans. Counseling, fellowship, mutual aid, economic, and countless minor services are also supplied by the churches. . . . Korean churches are centers where the attempt to preserve language, social bonds, and customs central to Korean identity is very visible" (Dearman 1982: 180).

### Born-Again Korean Christians

The born-again Christian is very religious and often fundamentalist. For Korean immigrants, to be "born again" (*kŏdŭpnam*) ties the immigrant Christian experience to the tradition of Korean religion.

When a friend showed me a bruise resulting from her minister's "sacred blow" (*anch'al*) and when I saw parents who were too happy in their Christianity to cry over their daughter's murder by a youth gang, I was at first puzzled. These actions could not be explained simply by references to the sociological functions of convenient Christianity in the immigrant community. I needed to understand how immigrants came to attribute these actions to God's will. For immigrants, kodupnam means that one is liberated from secular concern about prestige, wealth, status, scholarship, beauty, appearance, honor, or saving face. With the recognition that they are now truly Christian, born-again Koreans come to view the horizons of life as greatly expanded. Being born again—with the religious behavioral forms that accompany it—characterizes the centrality of Christinaity to Korean immigrants in America, but it differs from the beliefs of most other Americans.

For those in the Korean immigrant community, there are three different ways to become born again as a Christian: being born again without a witnessing experience; being born again by seeing, hearing, or silently communicating with God in solitude; and being born again through an ecstatic experience in which one collapses, speaks in tongues (*pangon*), or translates when others speak in tongues.[8] I was astounded at what happened during one Central Presbyterian Church revival meeting I attended. While singing together, suddenly everybody raised their hands as if they were going to receive a divine inspiration called *sŏngyŏng* (the Holy Ghost). Then the presiding minister placed his hands on one man's head, an act called *ansu*, and offered a prayer. The man fell down as if his feet had been pulled out from under him. Later I heard that other people who couldn't fall down felt uncomfortable because they might have been suspected of lacking faith in God.

At another revival meeting, members first acknowledged the grace received from God throughout the year and the revitalizing power. This was followed by *tongsong kido*, or prayer in unison. After vigorous "amens," the entire congregation shouted. Some even cried. A person near me kept praying, "Oh, Jesus. Please hold me tightly. Please guide me to the right way to live, I beg you." A congregant, Mr. Nam, a bakery owner, told me how he came to speak in tongues: "As I prayed and prayed, I had a cramp in my tongue. Surprisingly enough, as I kept on saying, 'Thank you, God,' strange talk came out from my mouth, automatically. My tongue became

8. In Korea the born-again phenomenon can easily be observed at evangelical or fundamentalist churches, but one rarely comes across it in Presbyterian or Methodist churches. In the United States it can be found at most Korean churches except for Methodist ones. I witnessed the phenomenon at a Presbyterian church, although it was not formally acknowledged there.

rigid, and I became too feverish to be normal. Then my pastor told me to speak freely. My wife followed me, talking irrepressibly. My pangŏn lasted around fifty minutes." According to him, those who can translate when someone speaks uncontrollably have gone deeper spiritually than those who merely speak in tongues. Italian, Greek, Spanish, and some unknown languages are said to emerge in the pangŏn experience among Korean American Christians.

Although Mr. Ha had not sought pangŏn, it emerged after one month of all-night prayer. He interpreted his experience by saying that, when one is born again, the horizons of life are expanded: "If you experience pangŏn without a religious perspective, it is like dumb-talking or like playing. But it is clear that with pangŏn nothing remains impossible. One opens oneself and gives oneself to Jesus Christ. Similarly, pangŏn is the way God confirms what he has said through the voices of human beings. Sometimes we get a response from God through the one who offers prayer, and sometimes through somebody else." Similarly, Mr. Park explained: "I was very negative about immigrant life. As I started to lead a religious life, however, I could overcome many problems with finance, human relations, and a future career. I was guided directly by God. I owe this to my brother's friend. We used to be a Buddhist family. I have now persuaded even my parents to go to church. How nice it is!"

These born-again individuals have reinterpreted their decision to migrate to America, the land of Christianity. As Mrs. Lee told me they have come to see it as enabling them to meet the Messiah. This interpretation both glorifies her immigration and rationalizes downward mobility from her occupation as a teacher in Korea to a garment factory worker in Queens. Mr. Pyun, a medical technician, is the founder of his church. He feels that Christian belief provides for more than liberation of the individual. His concern is the spiritual liberation of an ethnic minority, the Koreans in America.

Reverend Ahn's sermon on Thanksgiving drew a parallel between Korean immigrants' espousal of Christianity and early episodes in American history:

American prosperity is only possible because of the Americans' deep belief in God, as we see in the observance of Thanksgiving. Although Americans have a short history compared to the five thousand years of Korean history, they first came to Jamestown in Virginia. Around 1620 many took the *Mayflower* and came to Plymouth like the recent Korean

immigrants. As most of them were Calvinist, these Protestants were looking for religious freedom beyond the reach of Episcopalianism and Ca-
tholicism. Those Protestants led a very religious life based on the Bible.
Even on a dollar we can read "In God We Trust." In a totally foreign land
they kept their composure, thanks only to their strong belief in God. It is
neither white American Protestants nor American Indians who own this
land. It belongs only to God. So let's adopt the way Protestants adapted
themselves to this new land—with a strong belief in God.

His sermon implied that Korean immigrants were brought here on a
special mission: to save the increasingly atheistic Americans.

It is not easy for every Korean immigrant to become established, to
fulfill the anjŏng dream of success. Sinsuk described to me how difficult it
was to deal with immigration problems, particularly with undocumented
status. Yet thanks to being born again, her eyes gleamed with hope. Before
pangŏn, she suffered because her mother could not come to the United
States. She used to cry a lot. Her father stayed illegally in America and
eventually divorced his wife to remarry in order to obtain a green card.
With his green card he could invite his children in Korea to come to
America, but not his ex-wife.

At the beginning of a revival meeting Mr. Ha, who had spoken in
tongues, told Sinsuk how to prepare for pangŏn. "Step one, atone for sins;
step two, admit that you have received Jesus Christ; step three, make clear
that you will follow him; step four, look for grace." After twenty minutes in
which she repeated the words "Please pardon me," he let her say a prayer
for grace. "If one is sure that one has received grace, then one looks for
the Holy Ghost, and then one also can believe that one has received divine
inspiration." Sinsuk followed his directions. In just two or three minutes
pangŏn came upon her, even before Reverend Ahn laid his hands on her
head.

In Mr. Nam's testimony, it is evident that he is liberated from the habit
of evaluating people according to their educational level, a habit that for
Koreans derives from the Confucian emphasis on scholarship. He feels
free to engage in hard manual work in the context of a religious commitment (see Weber 1930: 151): "All problems are coming from people's
arrogance or pride, which come from being a Ph.D. or thinking they are
somebody. If one denies oneself completely, and thereby suppresses pride
or arrogance or any secular desire, and as one has more self control, I
think one is near to deep belief. I used to be hot-tempered and looked
down upon those without education. When I became born again, I could

get rid of those bad habits. Following what is written in the Bible, I decided to work hard, live a fair and just life, and always be thankful to others for what I am and what I have."

### Critical Korean Christians

Many studies have shown that the majority of Korean American churches belong to denominations with conservative theologies or are nondenominational (Dearman 1982). Shim has concluded that the response of Korean churches to the social challenges of the present is meager and inadequate: "Their primary concern today is institutional survival" (Shim 1977: 57). It is not clear, however, whether this claim is particularly true of Korean immigrant churches or applies as well to other churches in America.

Korean Christians belonging to my third category hold critical views of this situation and often show interest in new and emerging progressive theologies. Some individuals in my first and second categories may also join critical Korean Christians in questioning the social complacency of Korean churches. Not all born-again Christians feel sanguine about their churches. Some feel ambivalent about where the Korean churches are headed. They feel manipulated and swindled, particularly members of alienated groups such as women, the working class, undocumented workers, and the elderly. In their comments, criticism is broad and relates to churches' selfishness, exclusiveness, and lack of social concern, particularly in areas of community affairs, interethnic relations, and the well-being of second generation Korean Americans. Many resent churches' focus on materialism, related to *kipok* (to make a good fortune) and *sinang* (belief). Rev. Kim said cynically: "It is our goal to rescue many human beings from sin, like those of our countrymen who are just crazy about running their greengrocery or seafood stores. They are interested in making the church bigger and more prosperous without paying attention to Christianity at all. Yet I see everyone, including religious priests and those with religious posts, fighting over who is getting power. How bad it is! Don't worry about how much you can contribute to the church but think of how much remains as your own share after donating to the church." In other words, criticisms of the church also are related to criticisms of aspects of the immigrant ideology of small business establishment.

A dozen elderly individuals exchanged their views casually while playing cards one day in Elmhurst:

Person 1: Besides problems with youth or juvenile delinquency, the way Koreans go to church without deep thought is a problem. For example, while they are very familiar with Christmas, they do not remember their parents' day of death or birth.

Person 2: You are right there. Once you are Korean, you have to have concern for Korean roots. How come people go to church in order to cure disease and to receive fortune rather than to live a life as a good human being or to love your neighbors? There is no paradise, you know.

Person 3: However, one has to hold religion just as one holds on to a center in the mind, like holding the mind with a stick.

Jenny, a Korean-born but U.S.-raised woman (a member of the knee-high generation of Korean Americans) was critical of Korean churches:

I was fundamentalist until I became a college sophomore, going to church regularly and actively involved in church activities in a rather naive way. I went to church because I was sometimes honored. As I studied sociology, I became critical of such institutionalized religion. I went through a radical transformation. I realized that human beings are more important than anything else in society. God is a symbolic being, invented by human beings in order to express their thanks. I am not what I used to be. Now, to be honest with you, it is not my habit to go to church. In addition, I want to give a true education to other little Korean American children. True belief depends on the way one thinks, and it might vary given one's condition, such as childhood. Now I want to live a life as a decent human being, caring about human honesty, justice, and human communication. . . . As I see people at the Korean churches, although it is Western religion, they care only about status competition because they still have Confucian logic. If not that, then church becomes small business oriented. There is preaching but no application or practice. I see only clannish behavior or regionalism. Of course, many Koreans get together and comfort one another. They are hypocritical. There I see a *kyeju* (kye organizer), a so-called Christian who ran away after collecting money. I see a patriarchal church. Women often do only kitchen work and are not allowed to participate in decision making. Nevertheless, I see potential at the Korean churches.

Steve, another member of the knee-high generation, said: "I am not a Christian. I am rather sensitive to harm done to the Korean community by the churches. Whatever resources there are, such as money, seem to be drained. And yet they are busy only with building their sacred churches."

A second-generation Korean American, Alex, shared the same opinion: "Presently Korean ministers are engrossed in money making. They are often busy with building their own sacred church; they try to compete [with] each other by drawing a larger congregation or taking away another congregation, which is against God's will."

James, another knee-high generation Korean American, is a certified public accountant who is well known in the community. Because his wife attended church for many years, he once made an effort to attend himself. He was asked immediately to give a seminar on income tax, financial management, and other subjects. He gladly consented. Then a few days later he was given the title of deacon. This made him disgusted with the church, and he soon stopped attending.

To summarize, in addition to religious faith, Korean Americans become Christians for help in adapting to American life, for the companionship of fellow Koreans, for positions of prestige in the church hierarchy, and to realize their dream of small business establishment. They are well aware of all these motivations and can cite them to explain church attendance. Mr. Lee, a shrimp wholesaler, is explicit about why his fellow Koreans go to church: "They go to church for friendship and, secondly, for self-promotion. Otherwise why would people contribute so much, even borrowing up to $100,000 from others? For instance, a gas station owner wants to be known as Deacon Kim."

## Interpretation

Korean Christians appear to perceive God as a generous spirit who is sympathetic toward the incompleteness of human beings.[9] God is always understanding of human desire rather than a strict judge of behavior. In this context, the image of God is similar to that of Buddhist deities (K. Kim 1994: 25). Thus, immigrants at church services participate vigorously in the ritual communication with God by responding in the form of sighing, murmuring, or uttering incomprehensible languages as they become possessed by spirituality.

Youngsook K. Harvey argues that the traditional Korean religious focus on shamanistic possession has characteristics that proved advantageous to

9. Elsewhere I have addressed the relationship between Korean American Christianity and other religious traditions of Korea and Weber's thesis of worldly asceticism (Park 1989).

Christian missionaries. "Stylistically, it predisposed the Koreans to Pentecostal, fundamentalist Protestant Christianity, and the Christian concept of the Holy Ghost was compatible with the shamanistic concept of spirit possession." Harvey sees the deaconesses in Korean Christian churches as the functional equivalent of shamans (1979: 205–34; 1987: 149–70).

The born-again phenomenon among Korean immigrants also exhibits parallels the worldly asceticism of the early Protestant experience as analyzed by sociologist Max Weber in *The Protestant Ethic and the Spirit of Capitalism* (1930). According to him, these Protestants rejected an empty search for worldly pleasure, and the direct experience of God's grace provided guidance for concrete action in the mundane world.[10] Worldly-ascetic, born-again Korean Christians feel similarly lifted from the social considerations of family background, educational level, wealth, and status. When immigrant small business owners become Protestant, they find that "their hard work and sincere efforts in making money are justified in religious terms" (Weber 1930: 171). Korean immigrants' small business activities allow them to develop a new outlook on religion; and their overwhelming religious conversion develops from how they as a racial minority understand, analyze, and create strategies for existing in their new environment. Koreans come voluntarily to the United States with aspirations for better economic well-being. By adopting the religious language that they believe their American hosts use, Koreans dream that they will have success. They also believe it is their mission to revitalize Christianity, even among other Americans. The Korean Christian religious movement can be interpreted as part of the immigrants' struggle for survival, part of the process that middle-class Koreans undergo as they become small business proprietors and a racial minority in the United States.

10. Regarding this issue in Korean Won Buddhism, see Cozin (1987).

# PART III

# Reassessing the Korean American Dream

# [10]

# Conclusion

Koreans in America have constructed an immigrant ideology of anjŏng (establishment, security, or stability). At its core is chagigage katki (establishing one's own business). These notions affect social practices in all the realms of their lives: kinship obligations, gender roles, concepts of ethnicity, political organization, and religious practice. A Korean myself, I am reminded by their efforts of two Korean folktales, each involving a rabbit and turtle.

In one story, a dragon king in the depths of the ocean is struck with a rare disease. He is advised to eat the liver of a rabbit. Because it is not possible to send one of his fish subjects onto land, the king summons a turtle who thrives both in water and on the land. After much effort, the turtle finds a rabbit and lures her to the sea with stories about the beautiful ocean world. The turtle carries her on his back to a sea castle chamber to await an audience with the king. When the king demands her liver, she is speechless with horror but quickly gathers her wits and declares that she has left her liver at home. She adds that her liver has special healing properties and is sought by everyone, so she hides it in a secret place. The king then orders the turtle to return the rabbit to land to obtain the liver. Upon reaching land, the rabbit hops away into the mountains, never to be seen again.

The other story is similar to Aesop's well-known fable. Here, the rabbit is overconfident in a race with a turtle. At the beginning of the race, the rabbit is far ahead and ridicules the turtle. Eventually, however, the rabbit takes a nap, while the slow turtle perseveres and wins the race.

The first story is about shrewdness. Despite difficulties, if you are able to gather you wits instead of panicking, you will be able to overcome trouble quickly. Similarly, Korean immigrants face hardships in the United States; but if they apply their own resources, they will succeed. The second story is about perseverance. It implies that, no matter how capable you are, if you are overconfident, you are liable to lose the race to a less capable but harder-working opponent.

In the first story, rabbit wins. In the second, rabbit loses. These two stories tell us a great deal about Korean immigrants and their current predicament. Immigrants see their lives as embodied in the dilemmas presented in these stories. Some people have been rewarded, while others find that shrewdness no longer works and ponder the longer-term victory of the persevering turtle. Although all immigrants are not confident about quick success, all continue to emphasize the anjŏng ideology and its accompanying social practices. But as many undertake the often slow and lengthy journey toward establishment, they discover that their immigrant ideology hinders personal fulfillment and enjoyment of life in America. They are not meeting success as rabbits and are unsure if they really want to be turtles.

Today, the Korean immigrant dream is not working for everyone, and its differential success is leading to class polarization. As we have seen, small business establishment is the critical factor determining status within the Korean immigrant community. Small business success produces a drastically different class structure than that found in Korea. The ideology of establishing one's own business persists despite the increasingly incomplete realization of this dream. Underneath the continuing quest, however, we can find increasing antagonism among different class segments and growing acknowledgment of such conflict.

Clearly, not all Korean immigrants succeed in realizing their dream of owning a business. Mr. Pu became a factory worker after failing in a small business. He has been in America since 1973. He first worked for Korean Air Lines and was sent to their branch office in New York. After three and half years, he decided not to return to Korea. Instead, he bought a laundromat in New Jersey from another Korean with savings and loans from a relative and a friend. It cost about $27,000. The business was in a poor neighborhood, and with insufficient operating funds it failed in one year. Next he sublet a vegetable stand in Greenpoint, Brooklyn, through someone his wife knew. He was inexperienced, business was competitive, and in a year he failed again. Then he became a partner in a candy store in midtown Manhattan, again through a contact of his wife. His partner needed more capital, sales were low, and the business ran a deficit. After one year, Mr. Pu sold out to his partner. He then got a job as general manager in a retail clothing store. Although he had problems with customers, he put up with the job for two years. At last, through a friend from his previous workplace, he got a job in a white American-owned factory that produces soap and toothpaste. Most workers are American-born except for three Korean and two Filipino immigrants. Mr. Pu makes $500 a week.

The overall failure rate of small businesses is high. In 1995, Sung Soo Kim reported that, "every month, 50 families are closing their stores and returning to Korea. . . . Over the last four years, more than 1,600 Korean-owned stores folded, leaving about 3,500 produce and grocery stores still operating" (*New York Daily News*, 21 May 1995). Mr. Juch of the Korean-American Grocers Association estimated in 1993 that of his 3,000 members one-third were considering quitting the grocery business, while another third would take another job if they could get one (*New York Times*, 29 November 1993). In addition, the number of Korean immigrants who come to the United States has declined. In the past decade, immigration from South Korea has plummeted by two-thirds, from a high of 35,849 in 1987 to 10,799 in 1994. No other major immigrant-sending country has shown such a dramatic drop (*New York Daily News*, 21 May 1995).

## Reassessing the Korean American Dream

After Koreans come to America, most experience downward mobility in both objective terms and their self-evaluations. As some greengrocers lament, "we deal only with rotten tomatoes." This does not mean that they are ashamed to be greengrocers. By embracing the slogan "all trades are equal," they find some solace. As they live in the United States longer, however, they realize that even in America there is little prestige for small business proprietors, and they recall the higher status they enjoyed in Korea. Therefore, the longer they live in America, the more that many Korean immigrants reassess and even question their American dream. According to one immigrant, "to a great extent, America is only seen as good by Koreans in Korea. I no longer see it this way." Contrary to their expectations, they find that America is not paradise. It is not "full of gold," even if they work hard. It is also a racist society. Nevertheless, their perception of America is very different from that of other minorities, such as African Americans and Latin Americans, who have organized to engage in struggles after their civil rights.

We need to distinguish the objective face of mobility as studied by scholars from its subjective dimension as experienced by new immigrants themselves (see Conk 1978: 66). Some Koreans do realize their American dream in terms of upward mobility. If we look at the Korean grocery worker who moves up to owner and then proprietor of several groceries, this mobility is apparent. But when we realize that this grocer is a former Korean college professor, then mobility is more difficult to assess. Moreover, upward mobility for Korean immigrants into the ranks of small business ownership does not always translate into success. "Korean small businesses are confronted with so many problems: more than 85 percent of business owners themselves work up to 10 hours [a day]; more than 70 percent of businesses are relying on family labor; more than 73 percent lack operating funds; 54 percent of them feel overcompetition among the same kind of business; 57 percent also express problems with labor relations; 94 percent barely maintain the present store, without much profit" (*Korean American Small Business Service Center Newsletter* 1987).

Bonacich is appropriately cautious in applying the term *success* to Korean small businesses: "If we mean by 'success' making millions of dollars, or even hundreds of thousands, Korean enterprise could not be deemed successful except in rare instances. . . . If, on the other hand, we mean by 'success' survival and modest growth to the point where many people can make a decent living by American standards, we must conclude that Korean immigrant enterprise is largely successful" (1980: 178). When Koreans say "anjŏng," their image of the process of establishment is far from simply emulating the material "life-styles of the rich and famous." For them, it first means settling down—a sense of comfort now that they have solved basic problems of survival. Further steps along the anjŏng course solidify and widen this sense.

A full analysis of immigrant ideology tells us much about the lives of Korean Americans in all their contradictory aspects. Today, we see small rebellions against the Korean American dream. First, although married women's labor contributes greatly to the realization of the immigrant dream, women have also come to challenge the traditional roles of men. In other words, the circumstances that help women to gain and raise their voices also lead them to question their relationship to men. Second, we see increasing generational conflict. When children of the immigrant generation declare that they are not going to listen to their parents, the parents feel betrayed. They did not expect to be challenged about their basic assumptions concerning the Korean American dream, least of all by their children. Third, immigrants unexpectedly encounter ethnic and racial conflict because of their involvement in small business activities in city neighborhoods. African American/Korean tension vividly shows us one cost of immigrant entrepreneurship. Finally, the Korean American dream reaches its limits when immigrants learn about the reality of racism directed at them and find they must leave their stores and participate in the American political process. In these and other ways, Korean immigrants are reexamining anjŏng, and their faith in the American dream. This reassessment speaks to the critical role of ideology in understanding culture and change.

## Ideology and Culture

Based on my study of middle-class Korean immigrants who have begun their American lives in menial jobs in small business, we can identify certain theoretical points regarding ideology. As Gramsci has stated, all people are philosophers "in so far as . . . in their practical activity . . . there is implicitly contained a conception of the world" (1971: 344). According to their emphasis on anjŏng, Korean immigrants share a conception of U.S. society based on the conviction that "I will be rewarded in proportion to how hard I work."

But anjŏng for Korean Americans is not just a way of looking at the world. Their immigrant ideology also becomes a material force for reorganizing their social and cultural practices. I suggest that human consciousness plays a far more important role in the process of ideological formation than functioning as a mere reflex of structural reality. I view ideology as a process in which systems of ideas (will, attitudes, world views, consciousness, philosophy, beliefs, values, and knowledge) work as rationales for individuals to deal with real-life situations. A new ideology is constructed strategically as a conscious, mobilizing force. In this way, it is not new material conditions per se, but the actors' critical analyses of the changing material conditions that produce a new ideology. People are not passive bearers of ideology but "active appropriators who reproduce existing structures only through struggle, contestation and a partial penetration of structures" (Willis 1977: 175).

Korean immigrants have constructed and elaborated the ideology of anjŏng in order to realize their American dream. They develop a detailed scenario for how the ideology of can be materialized. In this quest, each Korean immigrant succeeds in convincing him or herself that involvement in small business activities is the path to the American dream. In short, immigrant ideology plays an active role as a conscious, mobilizing force. Furthermore, this new ideology contributes to the overall transformation of immigrant life. Anjŏng channels immigrant cultural processes in family and kinship organization, gender roles, ethnicity, politics, and religion. It reformulates both thinking and practice. In summary, the anjŏng ideology causes immigrants to organize their lives in a way entirely different from their previous existence in Korea.

Small business activities today are a symbol, perhaps the *key* symbol, of Korean American identity and success. But today, some Korean immigrants are considering the warning from the overconfident rabbit in the race with the turtle. They find it necessary to reassess the Korean American dream. As they experience life in America, Korean Americans create new identities, new cultural forms, and new ideologies. Ultimately, through these acts of creation, they reshape American dreams.

# Glossary

| | |
|---|---|
| *anch'al* | sacred blow |
| *anjŏng* | establishment or stability |
| *ansu chipsa* | hand-laying deacon |
| | |
| *chaebŏl* | conglomerates or business groups |
| *chagigage katki* | establishing one's own business |
| *chagŭn chip* | little house; secondary sons' line of descent |
| *changno* | elder |
| *changsu mudae* | folk song contest for longevity |
| *chesa* | sacrificial rite for deceased ancestors |
| *chip* | house, household, family |
| *chipsa* | deacon |
| *cho* | set |
| *chŏng* | deep affection |
| *chongson* | the eldest son of one's son and heir |
| *chŏnse* | paying a large refundable deposit on occupancy but without monthly rent |
| *chungsanch'ŭng* | middle-propertied stratum |
| *chwadae* | stoop line |
| *ch'anmo* | cook |
| *ch'ilsun* | a seventieth birthday |
| *ch'inmokhoe* | a social gathering |
| *ch'inmok kye* | friendship kye |
| *ch'injok* | kin |
| *ch'inch'ŏk* | relatives |
| *ch'injŏng* | the wife's natal family |
| *ch'ŏgajok* | kin who immigrat to America through a wife's connection |
| *ch'on* | the basic unit of genealogical distance |

[207]

## Glossary

| | |
|---|---|
| *ch'onggak* | bachelor |
| *ch'usŏk* | the mid-autumn festival |
| | |
| *han* | unresolved longing |
| *Haninhoe* | Korean Association of Greater New York |
| *Hanint'ongsin* | Korean communication |
| *hanŭli munŏjida* | the sky is going to collapse. |
| *hoegap* | a sixtieth birthday |
| *hohye* | reciprocity |
| | |
| *ibuk saram* | those who migrate from North Korea to South Korea |
| *ilchŏmose* | a generation and a half |
| *ingwa ŭngbo* | causality |
| *injong* | race |
| *insam* | ginseng |
| *isan kajok* | divided family |
| | |
| *kalbi* | Korean beef spare ribs |
| *kayagŭm* | Korean zitherlike instrument |
| *kibok* | to make a good fortune |
| *kiil* | in memory of a relative on the anniversary of the day of his or her death |
| *kimch'i* | fermented peppery vegetable |
| *kkaekkŭthan* | clean |
| *kŏdŭp nam* | born again |
| *komo* | father's sister |
| *kwŏnsa* | exhorter |
| *kujŏng* | lunar New Year's Day |
| *kukche kyŏrhon* | international marriage |
| *kumŏng kage* | a small shop |
| *kŭn chip* | big house; major line of descent |
| *kut* | shaman ritual |
| *kye* | Korean rotating credit society |
| *kyechu* | kye organizer |
| | |
| *migukpyŏng* | American fever |
| *minjok* | ethnicity or nation |
| *munjung* | lineage |
| | |
| *nakch'al kye* | bidding kye |
| *namjon yŏbi* | men are honored, but women are abased |
| *namyŏn (ramen)* | noodle |
| *noryŏkŭi taekka* | reward for one's work or effort |
| *nui (or nuna)* | sister |
| *nunch'iboda* | studying one's face |

| | |
|---|---|
| *ŏbŏi nal* | parents' day |
| *oesamch'on* | wife's mother's brother |
| *ŏnni* | older sister |
| *ŏrini nal* | children's day |
| *ŏrŭn* | adult |
| | |
| *paegil* | baby's first hundred days |
| *palbara samchŏlli* | sew three thousand *li* (a unit of length, equivalent to 400 meters or one quarter of a mile) |
| *panch'an* | side dishes |
| *pangŏn* | speaking in tongues |
| *pansanghoe* | a neighborhood association |
| *pigongsik imin* | informal immigrants |
| *pŏnho-kye* | sequence kye |
| *poram* | just reward |
| *ppaek* | social connections |
| *pulgogi* | roast meat |
| *pundan* | Korea's partition into North and South |
| *punga* | setting up a branch family |
| *Pusan* | city in Korea |
| *p'ansori* | folktales sung to drum accompaniment |
| *P'yŏngyang* | city in Korea |
| | |
| *salp'uri* | dance of exorcism, a Korean classical dance |
| *samch'on* | relative within three degrees of relationship; uncle |
| *sangin pŏnyŏng-hoe* | merchant associations |
| *Sangnokhoe* | Senior Citizens Society |
| *sarangbang* | a drawing room |
| *Seoul [sŏul]* | capital of South Korea |
| *sidaek* | husband's family |
| *sikmo* | houseworker |
| *sinse* | one's circumstances |
| *sŏngyŏng* | Holy Ghost |
| *sŏnbae* | a senior |
| | |
| *tangnae* | kin within eight degrees of relationship |
| *tol* | baby's one-year birthday |
| *tongyanggye* | people from the Asian continent |
| *tut'ŏun kwangye* | deep or thick relation |
| *t'aekwŏndo* | Korean martial arts |
| *t'aryŏng* | a rhythmic pattern of drum |
| *t'ongsŏng kido* | prayer in unison |
| *ttosuni* | very tough and bright girl |

| | |
|---|---|
| *waenom* | a derogatory term for the Japanese |
| *walgadak* | slang for a wild girl |
| | |
| *yangban* | the two classes of nobility, civil and military |
| *yangi* | Western barbarians |
| *yŏja yuhaksaeng* | female student studying abroad |
| *yŏkimin* | return migration |
| *yŏnt'an* | charcoal briquettes |
| *yŏsŏnghoe* | women's organization |
| *yubokch'in* | one's near relatives, for whose death one wears mourning |
| *yumo* | nanny |

# Appendix

The following tables present informants' data on household form and division of labor to show how Korean immigrants organize domestic life.

**Household form (N = 94)**

| Household form | Number | Percent |
| --- | --- | --- |
| Persons separated from their families (or with roommates) | 17 | 18 |
| Husband and wife | 13 | 14 |
| Husband, wife, and children | 36 | 38 |
| Families of brother or sister | 8 | 9 |
| Parents and daughter's family | 10 | 11 |
| Parents and son's family | 7 | 7 |
| Parents and married children | 1 | 1 |
| Family and kin roommate | 1 | 1 |
| Family and non-kin roommate | 1 | 1 |

**Plans for Future Household Members
(N = 21)**

| Sponsor | Number |
| --- | --- |
| Wife or children of future member | 8 |
| Brother's or sister's family | 7 |
| Parents | 3 |
| Children's wives or grandchildren | 2 |
| Parents-in-law | 1 |

**Plans for Future Household Members**
**(N = 23)**

| Relationship of future member to sponsor | Number |
|---|---|
| Wife or mother's side | 6 |
| Husband or father's side | 17 |

**(N = 22)**

| Gender of Sponsored Kin | Number |
|---|---|
| Female (including children) | 15 |
| Male (including children) | 7 |

**Who cooks (N = 90)**

| Household members | Number of households | Percent |
|---|---|---|
| Mother | 33.5 | 37 |
| Grandmother | 12 | 13 |
| Other women | 14 | 16 |
| Daughter | 2 | 2 |
| Mother's or father's sister | 2 | 2 |
| Mother's or father's brother | 3 | 3 |
| Father | 3.5 | 4 |
| Equally | 17 | 19 |
| Roommates | 3 | 3 |

**Division of Labor**

| Household members | Dishwashing | Cleaning kitchen | Cleaning bathroom | Taking out garbage | Ironing |
|---|---|---|---|---|---|
| Mother | 24 | 32.5 | 29.5 | 19.5 | 14 |
| Grandmother | 10 | 9 | 7 | 3 | 3 |
| Other women | 9 | 14 | 12 | 1 | 3 |
| Daughter | 5 | 4 | 2 | 0.5 | 1.5 |
| Mother's or father's sister | 1 | 2 | 1 | 2 | 0 |
| Mother's or father's brother | 2 | 2 | 2 | 1 | 0 |
| Father | 6.5 | 4.5 | 3.5 | 16.5 | 4 |
| Son | 1.5 | 0 | 0 | 5 | 0 |
| Grandfather | 0 | 0 | 0 | 1 | 0 |
| Equally | 32 | 23 | 31 | 37.5 | 9 |
| Cleaning person | 0 | 0 | 1 | 0 | 0 |

**Division of Labor**

| Household members | Vacuuming | Making bed | Laundry |
|---|---|---|---|
| Mother | 12.5 | 24 | 21.5 |
| Grandmother | 4.5 | 6 | 9.5 |
| Other women | 5 | 5 | 11 |
| Daughter | 4 | 1 | 4.5 |
| Mother's or father's sister | 3 | 1 | 1 |
| Father | 15.5 | 5 | 5 |
| Son | 5.5 | 0 | 2 |
| Grandchildren | 3 | 0 | 2.5 |
| Equally | 11 | 49 | 32 |

**Work Employment of Children outside Household
(Families with children, N = 61)**

| Children's employment | Number | Percent |
|---|---|---|
| Full-time work | 19 | 31.1 |
| Helping family business | 7 | 11.5 |
| Part-time work | 2 | 3.3 |
| Summer work | 2 | 3.3 |
| No work | 11 | 18.0 |
| Too young to work | 20 | 32.8 |

**Child-Care Arrangement**

| Childcare providers | Dress, feed, bathe, and put to bed | Supervise/ discipline | Oversee homework | Give allowance (or spending money) |
|---|---|---|---|---|
| Children (voluntary) | 17 | 5 | 7 | |
| Mother | 7.5 | 7 | 6 | 14 |
| Father | | 2 | 1 | 3 |
| Mother and father | 1 | 4 | 2 | 6 |
| Other kin | 4.5 | 5 | 1 | 0 |
| Total | 30 | 23 | 18 | 23 |

**Day Care**

| Day care providers | Number |
|---|---|
| Mother | 13 |
| Sibling | 1.5 |
| Kin baby-sitter | 15.5 |
| Non-kin baby-sitter | 1 |
| Day-care center | 0 |

# References

Abelmann, Nancy, and John Lie. 1995. *Blue Dreams: Korean Americans and the Los Angeles Riots*. Cambridge: Harvard University Press.

Ahn, Byung Chul. 1986. "The Impact of Resources and Values on Men's Changing Roles in the Family." Ph.D. diss., Cornell University.

Amsden, Alice. 1989. *Asia's Next Giant: South Korea and Late Industrialization*. New York: Cambridge University Press.

Ardener, Shirley. 1964. "The Comparative Study of Rotating Credit Associations." *Journal of the Royal Anthropological Institute* 94: 201–9.

Barringer, Herbert, and Sung-Nam Cho. 1989. *Koreans in the United States: A Fact Book*. Honolulu: East-West Center.

Barth, Fredrik. 1969. *Ethnic Groups and Boundaries*. Boston: Little, Brown and Company.

Bascom, William R. 1952. "The Esusu: A Credit Institution of the Yoruba." *Journal of the Royal Anthropological Institute* 82: 63–69.

Bonacich, Edna. 1979. "The Present, Past, and Future of Split Labor Market Theory." *Research in Race and Ethnic Relations* 1: 16–64.

———. 1988. "The Social Costs of Immigrant Entrepreneurship." *Amerasia Journal* 14: 119–28.

———. 1993. "The Other Side of Ethnic Entrepreneurship: A Dialogue with Waldinger, Aldrich, Ward, and Associates." Department of Sociology, University of California, Riverside.

———. 1994. "Asians in the Los Angeles Garment Industry." In *The New Asian Immigration in Los Angeles and Global Restructuring*, ed. Paul Ong, Edna Bonacich, and Lucy Cheng, 137–63. Philadelphia: Temple Uinversity Press.

Bonacich, Edna, Ivan Light, and Charles C. Wong. 1976. "Small Business among Koreans in Los Angeles." In *Counterpoint: Perspectives on Asian America*, ed. Emma Gee, 436–49. Los Angeles: Asian American Studies Center, University of California.

Bonacich, Edna, and John Modell. 1980. *The Economic Basis of Ethnic Solidarity*. Berkeley: University of California Press.

Bonnett, Aubrey W. 1981. *Institutional Adaptation of West Indian Immigrants to*

References

*America: An Analysis of Rotating Credit Associations*. Washington, D.C.: University Press of America.

Bottomore, Tom, ed. 1983. *A Dictionary of Marxist Thought*. Cambridge: Harvard University Press.

Bourdieu, Pierre. 1984. *Distinction: A Social Critique of the Judgment of Taste*. Cambridge: Harvard University Press.

Bourdieu, Pierre, and Jean-Claude Passeron. 1970. *Reproduction in Education, Society and Culture*. London: Sage.

Bouvier, Leon F., and Robert Gardner. 1986. *Immigration to the U.S.: The Unfinished Story*. Washington, D.C.: Population Reference Bureau.

Chai, Alice Yun. 1981. "Korean Women in Hawaii, 1903–1945." In *Women in New Worlds*, ed. Hilah F. Thomas and Rosemary Skinner Keller, 328–44. Nashville, Tenn.: Abington.

Chan, Sucheng. 1991. *Asian Americans: An Interpretive History*. Boston: Twayne.

Chang, Edward Tea. 1990. "New Urban Crisis: Korean-Black Conflicts in Los Angeles." Ph.D. diss., University of California, Berkeley.

Chemical Bank Report. 1983. *Koreans in New York: The New Pioneers in American Enterprise*. New York: Chemical Bank.

Chen, Hsiang-shui. 1992. *Chinatown No More: Changing Patterns of Chinese Organization in Queens, New York*. Ithaca: Cornell University Press.

Cho, Hye-jong. 1988. *Han'gukui Yosongkwa Namsong* [Men and women in Korea]. Seoul: Munhakkwa Chisong.

Cho, Un, and Hagen Koo. 1983. *Capital Accumulation, Women's Work and Informal Economies in Korea*. Women in International Development Working Paper 21. East Lansing: Michigan State University.

Ch'oe [Choi], Jai-seuk. 1964. "Traditional Values in Korean Family." *Journal of Asiatic Studies* 2: 43–47.

——. 1966. *Tongjok Chiptanui Chojikkwa Kinumg* [The function and organization of lineages]. *Minjok Munhwa Yon'gu* 2: 75–146.

Choi, Chungmoo. 1992. "Korean Women in a Culture of Inequality." In *Korea Briefing, 1992*, ed. D. Clark, 97–116. Boulder, Col.: Westview.

Choy, Bong-Youn. 1979. *Koreans in America*. Chicago: Nelson-Hall.

Chu, Judy. 1988. "Social and Economic Profile of Asian Pacific American Women: Los Angeles County." In *Reflections on Shattered Windows: Promises and Prospects for Asian American Studies*, ed. Gary Y. Okihiro, Shirley Hune, Arthur A. Hansen, and John M. Liu, 193–205. Pullman: Washington State University.

Chun, Kyung-soo. 1984. *Reciprocity and Korean Society: An Ethnography of Hasami*. Seoul: Seoul National University Press.

Conk, Margo. 1978. "Social Mobility in Historical Perspective." *Marxist Perspectives* 6, no. 3: 52–69.

Cozin, Mark. 1987. "Won Buddhism: The Origin and Growth of a New Korean Religion." In *Religion and Ritual in Korean Society*, ed. Laurel Kendall and Griffin Dix, 171–84. Korea Research Monograph 12. Berkeley: Institute of East Asian Studies, University of California.

Danta, Ruby. 1989. "Conversion and Denominational Mobility: A Study of Latin American Protestants in Queens, New York." M.A. thesis, Queens College, City University of New York.

Dearman, Marion. 1982. "Structure and Function of Religion in the Los Angeles

Korean Community: Some Aspects." In *Koreans in Los Angeles*, ed. Eui-young Yu, Earl H. Phillips and Eun Sik Yang, 165–84. Los Angeles: Koryo Research Institute, Center for Korean American and Korean Studies, California State University.

Deuchler, Martina. 1977. "The Tradition: Women during the Yi Dynasty." In *Virtues in Conflict: Tradition and the Korean Woman Today*, ed. Sandra Mattielli, 1–47. Seoul: Korea Branch of the Royal Asiatic Society.

Deyo, Fred, ed. 1987. *The Political Economy of the New Asian Industrialism*. Ithaca: Cornell University Press.

Eckert, Carter, Ki-baik Lee, Young Ick Lew, Michael Robinson, and Edward Wagner. 1990. *Korea Old and New: A History*. Cambridge: Korea Institute, Harvard University.

Economic Planning Board, Republic of Korea [EPB]. 1989. *Yearbook of Korean Statistics*.

Evans, Peter. 1979. *Dependent Development: The Alliance of Multinational, State, and Local Capital in Brazil*. Princeton: Princeton University Press.

Fenton, Edward. 1975. *Immigrants and the Union, A Case Study: Italians and American Labor, 1870–1920*. New York: Arno,

Fitzpatrick, Joseph. 1971. *Puerto Rican Americans*. Englewood Cliffs, N.J.: Prentice-Hall.

Foner, Nancy. 1975. "Women, Work, and Migration: Jamaicans in London." *Urban Anthropology* 4: 229–249.

——. 1987. "Introduction: New Immigrants and Changing Patterns in New York City." In *New Immigrants in New York*, ed. Nancy Foner, 1–34. New York: Columbia University Press.

Gardner, Robert W., Bryant Robey, and Peter C. Smith. 1985. *Asian Americans: Growth, Change, and Diversity*. Washington, D.C: Population Reference Bureau.

Geertz, Clifford. 1962. "The Rotating Credit Association: A 'Middle Rung' in Development." *Economic Development and Cultural Change* 10 (April): 241–63.

Glenn, Evelyn Nakano. 1986. *Issei, Nisei, War Bride: Three Generations of Japanese American Women in Domestic Service*. Philadelphia: Temple University Press.

Godelier, Maurice. 1975. "Modes of Production, Kinship, and Demographic Structures." In *Marxist Analyses and Social Anthropology*, ed. Maurice Bloch, 3–28. London: Malaby.

Gramsci, Antonio. 1971. *Selections from the Prison Notebooks*, edited and translated by Quintin Hoare and Geoffrey Nowell Smith. New York: International.

Grasmuck, Sherri, and Patricia Pessar. 1991. *Between Two Islands: Dominican International Migration*. Berkeley: University of California Press.

Gregory, Steven. 1992. "The Changing Significance of Race and Class in an African American Community." *American Ethnologist* 19: 255–74.

——. 1993. "Race, Rubbish, and Resistance: Empowering Difference in Community Politics." *Cultural Anthropology* 8: 24–48.

Harvey, Youngsook Kim. 1979. *Six Korean Women: The Socialization of Shamans*. American Ethnological Society Monograph 65. St. Paul, Minn: West.

——. 1987. "The Korean Shaman and Deaconess: Sisters in Different Guises." In *Religion and Ritual in Korean Society*, ed. Laurel Kendall and Griffin Dix, 149–70. Korea Research Monograph 12. Berkeley: Institute of East Asian Studies, University of California.

References

Hing, Bill Ong. 1993. *Making and Remaking Asian America through Immigration Policy, 1850–1990*. Stanford: Stanford University Press.

Hong, Lawrence. 1982. "The Korean Family in Los Angeles." In *Koreans in Los Angeles*, ed. Eui-Young Yu, Earl H. Phillips, and Eun Sik Yang, 99–132. Los Angeles: Koryo Research Institute, Center for Korean American and Korean Studies, California State University.

Hoyt, Edwin T. 1974. *Asians in the West*. New York: Nelson.

Humm, Maggie. 1990. *The Dictionary of Feminist Theory*. Columbus: Ohio State University Press.

Hurh, Won Moo, and Kwang Chung Kim. 1979. *Assimilation Patterns of Immigrants in the United States: A Case Study of Korean Immigrants in the Chicago Area*. Washington, D.C.: University Press of America.

——. 1980. *Korean Immigrants in America: A Structural Analysis of Ethnic Confinement and Adhesive Adaptation*. Macomb: Department of Sociology and Anthropology, Western Illinois University.

——. 1984. *Korean Immigrants in America*. London: Associated University Press.

Ishi, Tomoji. 1988. "International Linkage and National Class Conflict: The Migration of Korean Nurses to the United States." *Amerasia Journal* 14: 23–50.

Janelli, Roger, and Dawnhee Yim Janelli. 1978. "Lineage Organization and Social Differentiation in Korea." *Man* 13: 272–89.

——. 1982. *Ancestor Worship and Korean Society*. Stanford: Stanford University Press.

——. 1988–89. "Interest Rates and Rationality: Rotating Credit Associations among Seoul Women." *Journal of Korean Studies* 6: 165–91.

Jones, Leroy, and Sakong Il. 1980. *Government, Business, and Entrepreneurship in Economic Development: The Korean Case*. Cambridge: Harvard University Press.

Keely, Charles B. 1980. "Immigration Policy and the New Immigrants." In *Sourcebook on the New Immigration*, ed. R. Bryce-Laporte, 15–25. New Brunswick, N.J.: Transaction.

Kendall, Laurel. 1983. "Introduction." In *Korean Women: View from the Inner Room*, ed. Laurel Kendall and Mark Peterson, 5–21. Cushing, Maine: East Rock Press.

——. 1985. "Ritual Silks and Kowtow Money: The Bride As Daughter-In-Law in Korean Wedding Rituals." *Ethnology* 10: 253–67.

Kendall, Laurel, and Griffin Dix, ed. 1987. *Religion and Ritual in Korean Society*. Korea Research Monograph 12. Berkeley: Institute of East Asian Studies, University of California.

Kendall, Laurel, and Mark Peterson, ed. 1983. *Korean Women: View from the Inner Room*. Cushing, Maine: East Rock Press.

Khandelwal, Madhulika. 1991. "Indians in New York City: Patterns of Growth and Diversification." Ph.D. diss., Carnegie-Mellon University.

Kiefer, C.W., S. Kim, K. Choi, L. Kim, B. L. Kim, S. Shon, and T. Kim. 1985. "Adjustment Problems of Korean American Elderly." *Gerontologist* 25: 477–82.

Kim, Bok-Lim. 1977. "Asian Wives of U.S. Servicemen: Women in Shadows." *Amerasia Journal* 4: 91–115.

Kim, Hyung-chan. 1977. *The Korean Diaspora*. Santa Barbara, Calif.: American Bibliographical Center-Clio Press.

Kim, Illsoo. 1981. *New Urban Immigrants: The Korean Community in New York*. Princeton: Princeton University Press.

——. 1985. "Organizational Patterns of Korean-American Methodist Churches: Denominationalism and Personal Community." In *Rethinking Methodist History: A Bicentennial Historical Consultation*, ed. Russell E. Richey and Kenneth E. Row, 228–37. Nashville, Tenn.: Kingswood.

——. 1987. "The Koreans: Small Business in an Urban Frontier." In *New Immigrants in New York*, ed. Nancy Foner, 219–42. New York: Columbia University Press.

Kim, Kwang-ok. 1988. "Religion: Experience or Belief System? A Korean Case." In *Society and Culture in the Pacific Region*, ed. Sang Bok Han and Kwang-ok Kim, 237–61. Seoul: Seoul National University Press.

——. 1994. "Ritual Forms and Religious Experiences: Protestant Christians in Contemporary Korean Political Context." Unpublished manuscript. Department of Anthropology, Seoul National University.

Kim, Seong-kyung. 1990. "Capitalism, Patriarchy, and Autonomy: Women Factory Workers in the Korean Economic Miracle." Ph.D. diss., City University of New York.

Kim, Sil Dong. 1979. "Interracially Married Korean Immigrants: A Study in Marginality." Ph.D. diss., University of Washington, Seattle.

Kim, Sung Soo. 1986. "The Patterns of Korean Enterprises." In *The Korean Community in America*, ed. Miguksogui Haninsahoe, 66–79. Seoul: Korean Association of New York.

Kim, Sung Soo. 1988. Speech at an awards ceremony. July 6. U.S. Department of Agriculture. Photocopy.

Kim, Tu-hon. [1949] 1969. *Han'guk Kajok Chedo Yon'gu* [The Study of the Korean family system]. Seoul: Ulyu-Munhwasa.

Kim, Unsil. 1993. "The Making of the Modern Female Gender: The Politics of Gender in Reproductive Practices in Korea." Ph.D. diss., University of California, San Francisco and Berkeley.

Kim, Warren Y. 1971. *Koreans in the United States*. Seoul: Po Chin Chai.

Kingston, Maxine Hong. 1975. *The Woman Warrior*. New York: Vintage.

Kitano, Harry, and Lynn Kyung Chai. 1982. "Korean Interracial Marriage." *Marriage and Family Review* 5: 75–89.

Koh, James Y., and William G. Bell. 1987. "Korean Elders in the United States: International Relations and Living Arrangements." *Gerontologist* 27: 66–71.

Koo, Hagen. 1982. "A Preliminary Approach to Contemporary Korean Class Structure." In *Society in Transition*, ed. Yunshik Chang, 45–66. Seoul: Seoul National University Press.

——. 1987. "The Emerging Class Order and Social Conflict in South Korea." *Pacific Focus* 2: 95–112.

*Korean American Small Business Service Center Newsletter*. 1987. New York: Korean American Small Business Service Center of New York.

Korean Association of New York. 1985. *History of the Korean Association of New York* [Haninhoe Yoksa]. Seoul: Onul.

*Korean Business Directory* [Hanin Yŏpsorok]. 1990. New York: Korea News.

*Korean Directory of Greater New York* [Haninrok]. 1990. New York: *Daehan*.

Korean National Bureau of Statistics. 1980a. *Annual Report on the Economically Active Population Survey*. Seoul: Economic Planning Board, Korean Government.

——. 1980b. *Social Indicators in Korea*. Seoul: Economic Planning Board, Korean Government.

——. 1984. *Korean Statistical Yearbook*, vol. 31. Seoul: Economic Planning Board, Korean Government.

Kupka, August. 1949. *History of Flushing, N.Y.* Reprinted by the Queens Historical Society, 1983.

Lamphere, Louise. 1986. "From Working Daughters to Working Mothers: Production and Reproduction in an Industrial Community." *American Ethnologist* 13: 118–30.

——. 1987. *From Working Daughters to Working Mothers*. Ithaca: Cornell University Press.

Larrain, Jorge. 1979. *The Concept of Ideology*. London: Hutchinson.

——. 1983. *Marxism and Ideology*. Atlantic Highlands, N.J.: Humanities Press.

Lee, Ki-baik. [1961] 1984. *A New History of Korea*, trans. Edward Wagner with Edward Schultz. Cambridge: Harvard University Press.

Lee, Kwang-Kyu [Yi Kwang-gyu]. 1975. *Kinship System in Korea*. 2 vols. New Haven, Conn.: Human Relations Area Files.

——. 1977. *Han'guk Kajokui Sajok Yon'gu* [Historical studies of the Korean family]. Seoul: *Ilchisa*.

——. 1984. "Family and Religion in Traditional and Contemporary Korea." In *Religion and the Family in East Asia*, ed. George A. Devos and Takao Sofue, 185–200. Berkeley: University of California Press.

——. 1991. *Chaemi Han'gukin*. [Koreans in the United States]. Seoul: Ilchokak.

Lee, Tong-won [Yi tong-won]. 1981. *"Toshi Kajoke Kwanhan Yon'gu—Kyolhone Taehan T'aedo Pikyo: 1958–1980"* [The study of the urban family: Comparison of attitudes on marriage, 1958–1980]. *Han'guk Munhwa Yon'guwon Nonch'ong* 39: 197–227.

Lenin, Vladmir I. 1960. *Selected Works*. Moscow: Foreign Languages Publishing House.

Levine, Daniel B., Kenneth Hill, and Robert Warren, ed. 1985. *Immigration Statistics: A Story of Neglect*. Washington, D.C.: National Academy Press.

Light, Ivan. 1972. *Ethnic Enterprise in America*. Berkeley: University of California Press.

——. 1984. "Immigrant and Ethnic Enterprise in North America." *Ethnic and Racial Studies* 7: 195–216.

Light, Ivan, and Edna Bonacich. 1988. *Immigrant Entrepreneurs: Koreans in Los Angeles, 1965–1982*. Berkeley: University of California.

Lim, Hyun-chin. 1982. *Dependent Development in Korea, 1963–1979*. Seoul: Seoul National University Press.

Mannheim, Karl. 1936. *Ideology and Utopia*. London: Routledge and Kegan Paul.

Mar, Don. 1991. "Another Look at the Enclave Economy Thesis: Chinese Immigrants in the Ethnic Labor Market." *Amerasia Journal* 17: 5–21.

Marshall, Adriana. 1987. "New Immigrants in New York's Economy." In *New Immigrants in New York*, ed. Nancy Foner, 79–102. New York: Columbia University Press.

Marx, Karl. [1859] 1971. *A Contribution to the Critique of Political Economy*. London: Lawrence and Wishhart.

Marx, Karl, and Frederick Engels. [1845–6] 1970. *The German Ideology*. London: Lawrence and Wishhart.

Mason, Edward, M. J. Kim, D. Perkins, K. S. Kim, and D. Cole. 1980. *The Economic and Social Modernization of the Republic of Korea*. Cambridge: Harvard University Press.

Mattielli, Sandra, ed. 1973. *Virtues in Conflict: Tradition and the Korean Women*. Seoul: Korea Branch of the Royal Asiatic Society.

Mauss, Marcel. [1925] 1967. *The Gift: Form and Functions of Exchange in Archaic Societies*. New York: Norton.

McLellan, David. 1986. *Ideology*. Minneapolis: University of Minnesota Press.

Medick, Hans, and David Warren Sabean, ed. 1984. *Interest and Emotion*. Cambridge: Cambridge University Press.

Min, Pyong Gap. 1984. "A Structural Analysis of Korean Business in the United States." *Ethnic Groups* 6: 1–25.

——. 1988a. *Ethnic Business Enterprise: Korean Small Business in Atlanta*. New York: Center for Migration Studies.

——. 1988b. "Korean Immigrant Families." In *Ethnic Families in America*, ed. Charles Mindel, Robert Habenstein, and Roosevelt Wright, 199–229. New York: Elsevier.

——. 1990. "The Social Costs of Immigrant Entrepreneurship: A Response to Edna Bonacich." *Amerasia Journal* 15: 187–94.

——. 1992. "The Structure and Social Functions of Korean Immigrant Churches in the United States." International Migration Review 26:1370–1394.

——, ed. 1995. Asian Americans: Contemporary Trends and Issues. Thousand Oaks, London, and New Delhi: Sage.

Min, Pyong Gap, and Charles Jaret. 1985. "Ethnic Business Success: The Case of Korean Small Business in Atlanta." *Sociology and SocialResearch* 69: 412–35.

Moon, Hyung June. 1976. "The Korean Immigrants in America: The Quest for Identity in the Formative Years, 1903–1918." Ph.D. diss., University of Nevada, Reno.

Morgen, Sandra, and Ann Bookman. 1988. "Rethinking Women and Politics: An Introductory Essay." In *Women and the Politics of Empowerment*, ed. Ann Bookman and Sandra Morgen, 3–32. Philadelphia: Temple University Press.

Nakanishi, Don. 1986. "Asian American Politics: An Agenda for Research." *Amerasia Journal* 12: 1–28.

*New York Times*, New York City Planning Department, and New York City Economic Development Administration. 1973. *New York Market Analysis*. New York: New York Times Company.

Ong, Paul, ed. 1994. *The State of Asian Pacific America: Economic Diversity, Issues and Policies*. Los Angeles: LEAP Asian Pacific American Public Policy Institute and UCLA Asian American Studies Center.

Ong, Paul, Edna Bonacich, and Lucie Cheng, ed. 1994. *The New Asian Immigration in Los Angeles and Global Restructuring*. Philadelphia: Temple University Press.

Ong, Paul, Kyeyoung Park, and Yasmin Tong. 1994. "The Korean-Black Conflict and the State." In *The New Asian Immigration in Los Angeles and Global Restructuring*, ed. Paul Ong, Edna Bonacich, and L. Cheng, 264–94. Philadelphia: Temple University Press.

Ortner, Sherry B. [1993] 1979. "On Key Symbols." In *Reader in Comparative Religion: An Anthropological Approach*, ed. William A. Lessa and Evon Z. Vogt, 92–98. New York: HarperCollins.

Ortner, Sherry B. and Harriet Whitehead, ed. 1981. *Sexual Meanings: The Cultural Construction of Gender and Sexuality*. Cambridge: Cambridge University Press.

Park, J. K., J. S. Le, and T. H. Kim. 1984. *A Study of Leisure Facilities and Programs for the Korean Elderly*. Survey Report 7. Seoul: Korean Institute on Gerontology.

Park, Jong Sam. 1975. "A Three Generation Study: Traditional Korean Value Systems and Psychosocial Adjustment of Korean Immigrants in Los Angeles." D.S.W. diss., University of Southern California.

Park, Kyeyoung. 1989. "'Born Again': What Does It Mean to Korean-Americans In New York City?" *Journal of Ritual Studies* 3: 287–301.

Patterson, Wayne. 1988. *The Korean Frontier in America: Immigration to Hawaii, 1896–1910*. Honolulu: University of Hawaii Press.

Pessar, Patricia. 1987. "The Dominicans: Women in the Household and the Garment Industry." In *New Immigrants in New York*, ed. Nancy Foner, 103–30. New York: Columbia University Press.

Portes, Alejandro, and Robert L. Bach. 1985. *Latin Journey*. Berkeley: University of California Press.

Portes, Alejandro, and John Walton. 1981. *Labor, Class and the International System*. New York: Academic Press.

Ryu, Sook Ryul. 1996. "Poem by a Yellow Woman." Seoul, Korea. Photocopy.

Safa, Helen. 1987. "Work and Women's Liberation: A Case Study of Garment Workers." In *Cities of the United States*, ed. Leith Mullings, 243–68. New York: Columbia University Press.

Sanders, Jimmy, and Victor Nee. 1987. "Limits of Ethnic Solidarity in the Ethnic Enclave Economy." *American Sociological Review* 54: 809–20.

Sanjek, Roger. 1982. "The Organization of Households in Adabraka: Toward a Wider Comparative Perspective." *Comparative Study of Society and History* 24: 57–103.

———. 1994. "The Enduring Inequalities of Race." In *Race*, ed. Steven Gregory and Roger Sanjek, 1–17. New Brunswick, N.J.: Rutgers University Press.

———. n.d. *The Future of Us All: Race, Immigration and Neighborhood Politics in New York City*. Unpublished Book Manuscript.

Sassen-Koob, Saskia. 1981. "Notes Towards a Conceptualization of Immigrant Labor." *Social Problems* 29: 65–85.

Shim, Steve S. 1977. *Korean Immigrant Churches Today in Southern California*. San Francisco: R and E Associates.

Shin, Eui Hang, and H. Park. 1988. "An Analysis of Causes of Schisms in Ethnic Churches: The Case of Korean American Churches." *Sociological Analysis* 49: 234–48.

Smith, Anthony. 1973. *The Concept of Social Change*. London: Routledge and Kegan Paul.

Sorensen, Clark. 1984. "Farm Labor and Farm Cycle in Traditional Korea and Japan." *Journal of Anthropological Research* 40: 306–23.

———. 1988. *Over the Mountains Are Mountains: Korean Peasant Households and Their Adaptations to Rapid Industrialization*. Seattle: University of Washington Press.

Tachiki, Amy, Eddie Wong, Franklin Odo, with Buck Wong, ed. 1971. *Roots: An Asian American Reader*. Los Angeles: Asian American Studies Center, UCLA.

Tauber, Gilbert, and Samuel Kaplan. 1966. *The New York City Handbook*. New York: Doubleday.

Therbon, Goran. [1980] 1982. *The Power of Ideology and the Ideology of Power*. London: New Left Books.

Troll, Lillian, Sheila Miller, and Robert Atchley. 1979. *Families in Later Life*. Belmont, Calif.: Wadsworth.

Turner, Bryan. 1983. *Religion and Social Theory*. London: Sage.

U.S. Bureau of the Census. 1983. *1980 Census of Population*. Vol. 1: *Characteristics of Population*. Washington D.C. : U.S. Government Printing Office.

——. 1984. *1980 Census of Population*. Vol. 1: *Characteristics of Population*. Washington, D.C.: U.S. Government Printing Office.

U.S. Immigration and Naturalization Service. 1952–1995. *Annual Reports*. Washington. D.C.: U.S.Government Printing Office.

Vincent, Joan. 1974. "The Structuring of Ethnicity." *Human Organization* 33: 375–79.

Waldinger, Roger. 1986. *Through the Eye of the Needle: Immigrants and Enterprise in New York's Garment Trades*. New York: New York University.

Weber, Max. 1930. *The Protestant Ethic and the Spirit of Capitalism*, translated by Talcott Parsons. New York: Scribner's.

Williams, Raymond. 1977. *Marxism and Literature*. Oxford: Oxford University Press.

Willis, Paul. 1977. Learning to Labor: How Working Class Kids Get Working Class Jobs. New York: Columbia University Press.

Wolf, Eric. 1982. *Europe and the People Without History*. Berkeley: University of California Press.

Wright, Erik Olin. 1980. "Varieties of Marxist Conceptions of Class Structure." *Politics and Society* 3: 323–70.

——. 1985. *Classes*. London: Verso.

Yanagisako, Sylvia. 1979. "Family and Household: The Analysis of Domestic Groups." *Annual Review of Anthropology* 8: 161–205.

Yi, Eunhee Kim. 1993. "From Gentry to the Middle Class: The Transformation of Family, Community, and Gender in Korea." Ph.D. diss., University of Chicago.

Yi, Jeong-duk. 1993. "Social Order and Contest in Meanings and Power: Black Boycotts against Korean Shopkeepers in Poor New York City Neighborhoods." Ph.D. diss., City University of New York.

Yoo, Ok-Za. 1985. "Korean Women in the Home and Workplace: Their Status Since 1945." *Korea and World Affairs* (Winter): 820–72.

Yoon, Hyungsook. 1989. "Kinship, Gender and Personhood in a Korean Village." Ph.D. diss., Michigan State University.

Young, Philip K. Y. 1983. "Family Labor, Sacrifice and Competition: Korean Greengrocers in New York City." *Amerasia Journal* 10: 53–71.

Yu, Eui-Young. 1986. "Population Characteristics of Koreans in America and Their Settlement Patterns." In *The Korean Community in America*, Korean Association of New York, ed. 13–25.

——. 1990. *Korean Community Profile: Life and Consumer Patterns*. Los Angeles: Korea Times.

Yu, Eui-Young, Earl H. Phillips, and Eun Sik Yang, editors. 1982. *Koreans in Los Angeles*. Los Angeles: Koryo Research Institute, Center for Korean American and Korean Studies, California State University

Yuan, Xiaoxia. 1986. "A Profile of Business in Elmhurst Corona, Queens." M.A. thesis, Queens College, City University of New York.

# Index

Ahn, Byung Chul, 88

*anjŏng* (establishment, security, or stability), 3–4, 67, 72, 77–78, 113, 155, 183, 193, 201–206
couples with children, 81
established families and the Korean elderly, 89–93
families with co-resident adult relatives, 86–89
five stages of establishment, 75, 76, 77–78
married couples, 80–81
single life, 78–80
*See also* Korean American dream; and family life; small businesses

American fever. *See* immigration history and process

Barth, Fredrik, 140
Bell, William G., 90
Black/Korean relations, 1, 41, 143–146, 150, 153, 169, 173, 177–178
Bonacich, Edna, 7, 12, 14, 15, 38, 41, 42, 43, 45, 46, 47, 56, 59, 61, 132, 204
Bourdieu, Pierre, 32

Chen, Hsiang-shui, 166, 167, 169, 170
*chip* (Korean household unit), 72–73, 80, 93, 95–96, 102
*See also* anjŏng: five stages of establishment
Cho, Hye-jong, 114

*ch'ŏgajok* (kin who immigrates through wife's connections), 98, 104
Choi, Chungmoo, 114, 115
church. *See* religion
class structure. *See* small businesses
community organizations of, 156–161

Dearman, Marion, 190
downward mobility, 27–29, 43, 52, 128, 203
dry cleaning stores, 46–47, 52–53, 146

education, 17, 29, 31–32, 76, 83, 85–87
ethnic economy and ethnic labor market, 45–46, 65–67
interethnic relations, 65
working conditions, 47, 66. *See also* race and ethnicity: workers
ethnic enclave economy, 60. *See also* non-ethnic enclave economy

family life
child care arrangements, 77, 81–84, 87
elderly, 77, 84, 87, 89–93, 103, 106, 110–111
family structure in Korea, 72–73, 93
filial piety, 90, 95
housework and domestic chores, 78–81, 87–89, 113, 121, 124, 128–130, 133
housing conditions, 74
immigration impact on, 22, 34
one-point-five and second generation. *See* knee-high generation

*The Anthropology of Contemporary Issues*

A SERIES EDITED BY

ROGER SANJEK

*Underground Harmonies: Music and Politics in the Subways of New York*
by Susie J. Tanenbaum

*City of Green Benches: Growing Old in a New Downtown*
by Maria D. Vesperi

*Strawberry Fields: Politics, Class, and Work in California Agriculture*
by Miriam J. Wells

*Renunciation and Reformation: A Study of Conversion in an American Sect*
by Harriet Whitehead

*Upscaling Downtown: Stalled Gentrification in Washington, D. C.*
by Brett Williams

*Women's Work and Chicano Families: Cannery Workers of the Santa Clara Valley*
by Patricia Zavella